ESS, JULY 4, 1776.

e thirteen united States of

y for one people to dissolve the political bands which have connected them with another, and to
of Nature's God entitle them, a decent respect to the opinions of mankind requires that they
truths to be self-evident, that all men are created equal, that they are endowed by their Creator
s.——That to secure these rights, Governments are instituted among Men, deriving their just
tive of these ends, it is the Right of the People to alter or to abolish it, and to institute new
s to them shall seem most likely to effect their Safety and Happiness. Prudence, indeed,
; and accordingly all experience hath shewn, that mankind are more disposed to suffer, while
. But when a long train of abuses and usurpations, pursuing invariably the same Object
off such Government, and to provide new Guards for their future security.—— Such has
alter their former Systems of Government. The history of the present King of Great
t of an absolute Tyranny over these States. To prove this, let Facts be submitted to a cand
for the public good.—— He has forbidden his Governors to pass Laws of immediate
and when so suspended, he has utterly neglected to attend to them——— He has refused to
the right of Representation in the Legislature, a right inestimable to them and formidable
and distant from the depository of their public Records, for the sole purpose of fatiguing them int
sing with manly firmness his invasions on the rights of the people.——— He has refused for
hable of Annihilation, have returned to the People at large for their exercise; the State remain
——— He has endeavoured to prevent the population of these States; for that purpose obstruc
r, and raising the conditions of new Appropriations of Lands.——— He has obstructed the
He has made Judges dependent on his Will alone, for the tenure of their offices, and the amoun
icers of Officers to harass our people, and eat out their substance.—— He has kept among
to render the Military independent of and superior to the Civil power.——— He has combined
s; giving his Assent to their Acts of pretended Legislation:—— For Quartering large bodies of
rders which they should commit on the Inhabitants of these States:—— For cutting off
For depriving us in many cases, of the benefits of Trial by Jury.—— For transporting us beyon
bouring Province, establishing therein an Arbitrary government, and enlarging its Bounda
these Colonies:—— For taking away our Charters, abolishing our most valuable Laws, a
and declaring themselves invested with power to legislate for us in all cases whatsoever.—
s.—— He has plundered our seas, ravaged our coasts, burnt our towns, and destroyed the lives
works of death, desolation and tyranny, already begun with circumstances of Cruelty & Perfidy
—— He has constrained our fellow Citizens taken captive on the high Seas to bear Arms agains
s.—— He has excited domestic insurrections amongst us, and has endeavoured to bring on the

Franklin, Jefferson, & Madison:
ON RELIGION AND THE STATE

First Edition
Published by CIAC Press
(Center for Indigenous Arts & Cultures Press)

CENTER FOR INDIGENOUS ARTS & CULTURES
A division of Southwest Learning Centers, Inc.
A non-profit, educational organization, est. 1972
P. O. Box 8627
Santa Fe, NM 87504-8627
Phone: 505-473-5375
Fax: 505-424-1025
Email: Indianbooks@comcast.net
Website: www.Indianartbooks.com

Designed by Angie Yan Schaaf

Printed in China by C & C Offset Printing Co., Ltd.

Schaaf, Gregory
Franklin, Jefferson & Madison: On Religion and the State
p.   cm.
Includes illustrations, bibliographical references, biographical data & index.

1. United States History, Colonial, Revolutionary, Early National
2. Constitution, United States
3. Bill of Rights, United States
4. Church & State
5. Religion, European & American
6. Biography, American
7. Law, Constitutional
I. Schaaf, Gregory. II. Center for Indigenous Arts & Cultures. III. Title.

ISBN 0-9666948-9-9

To: Michael & Maureen,
Our dear friends who share
our love of history and cultures.

VOLUME ONE

U.S. CONSTITUTION & BILL OF RIGHTS SERIES

Franklin, Jefferson, & Madison:
ON RELIGION AND THE STATE

Gregory Schaaf, Ph.D.

CIAC PRESS

CIAC Press
Santa Fe, New Mexico

First Edition

Dedicated to my mother and father,
Luella and Curtis Schaaf,
who taught me the power of prayer
and to respect the rights of others.

Special Thanks to:

United States National Archives

Library of Congress

Aurora Foundation

Southwest Learning Centers, Inc.

Contents

Acknowledgments

Although the efforts of many people made this book possible, Jeffrey Bronfman deserves special recognition. In conversations that began more than a decade ago, the necessity of writing this book became evident to us both. Through Jeffrey's generous commitment to the fulfillment of this service, the research representing the foundation of this study was funded.

Throughout the several years of dedicated work that finally led to this publication, the project was guided by Jeffrey Bronfman's vision, understanding and sense of the elemental importance that our First Freedom — as enshrined within our Bill of Rights — be honored through this kind of historical study. In a very real sense, this work is a collaborative effort representing our mutual offering back to this great country.

My wife, Angie Yan Schaaf, worked side-by-side with me in the National Archives and Library of Congress. She helped process hundreds of original letters and manuscripts. Each document was copied, scanned, and word-processed. Printed documents were converted through an optical character reader. She followed the manuscript through eight successive drafts, designing and typesetting the final layout of the book.

Proofreading the manuscript was a joint effort assumed by several volunteers. Our dear friend Seth Roffman, the Director of Southwest Learning Centers, Inc. made the largest number of corrections. Kris Ota, a professional proofreader with experience at various major New York publishers, was amazing in her ability to connect divergent points and cull out redundancies in the manuscripts. She must have a photographic memory. David Lenderts, Tai & Satara Bixby, Marion Seymour and Veet Deha also proofread chapters at various stages of completion. We got the whole family involved in reading chapters: our mother Luella Schaaf, sisters Kim & Charlotte Schaaf, brothers-in-law Tom Arney & Grant Kalivoda, nephew Tony Chiboucas and niece Lori Brown, aunt Martha and uncle Bill Quint, our cousins Billy and Pam Quint, Cindy and Brian Kelly were part of the united clan effort.

We give high praise to scores of librarians and archivists. The staff at the National Archives and Library of Congress was commendable. The many teams of compilers of materials from across the country are helping to revolutionize historical research.

Introduction

"THE ROOTS OF RELIGIOUS FREEDOM AND CIVIL LIBERTIES IN AMERICA"

Searching the roots of religious freedom and civil liberties in America can be an experience comparable to the pursuit of happiness. My personal search began over a quarter of a century ago, in 1976, during the Bicentennial of the Declaration of Independence. As a young graduate student at the University of California, I discovered in the attic of an 83-year-old grandmother a collection of original, previously unpublished letters written by George Washington, Thomas Jefferson, John Hancock, and George Morgan, Indian agent for the Continental Congress. News articles describing the discovery were published in the *New York Times, Los Angeles Times, London Times,* as well as news wire services around the world. *National Geographic Magazine* reported the story as the "rare document discovery of the Bicentennial." A feature article in *People Magazine* introduced an expanded story to a broad general audience.[1]

The opportunity to rewrite the first chapter of U.S. history became the topic of my doctoral dissertation and my first book, *Wampum Belts & Peace Trees.*[2] I was invited to deliver a speech at the United Nations and to testify before a committee of the United States Senate on the origins of the U.S. Constitution.[3] As a university professor of history and ethnic studies, I enjoyed teaching students to love the study of history, to respect different cultures, and to pursue a better understanding of the U.S. Constitution and Bill of Rights. I then retired to Santa Fe, New Mexico, where I continue to serve as Director of the Center for Indigenous Arts and Cultures. Together with my wife, Angie, we established a non-profit publishing company, CIAC Press, and commenced work on two main topics of books: "The American Indian Art Series" and the "U.S. Constitution & Bill of Rights Series."[4]

This book represents the first volume of the "U.S. Constitution & Bill of Rights Series." Future volumes will focus on the development of ideas related to the Constitution, Bill of Rights, and amendments. What were the origins of the ideas that became the cornerstones of the American legal system and the seminal concepts for our social, political and religious principles? Freedom of the press, right of assembly, right to a fair trial, protections against illegal search, and other critical issues are among a growing list of topics to be addressed in the series.

Volume One - *Franklin, Jefferson & Madison: On Religion and the State* — profiles the lives of three individuals who played important roles in the formation and establishment of the United States of America. The focus centers on their ideas related to religion and the state. An extensive search was undertaken of original documents in the National Archives, Library of Congress, and other repositories of historic records. Each reference to religion and the state were culled out and organized chronologically. Research trips to Washington, D.C.

and other locations yielded a gold mine of letters sent, letters received, biographical notes, transcripts of Congress and the Constitutional Convention, speeches for public assemblies, genealogical records, last wills and testaments. Each document was copied, filed, and analyzed.[5]

Key phrases addressing religion and the state were then searched on the Internet using a powerful search engine, www.google.com. In less than a second, all matches appeared on our computer screen. The results were simply amazing. Connections were made tracing the development and dissemination of powerful ideas exchanged between individuals over time. We came to the conclusion that our generation has inherited the most powerful tool ever devised to search history. Much credit must be given to hundreds of historians and archivists who have united with professional webmasters to put historical documents online. Furthermore, teams of editors have worked methodically to organize and publish the papers of Benjamin Franklin, Thomas Jefferson, and James Madison, as well as other historic figures. Their collective work and recent computer advancements made this book possible.[6]

The unique contribution of this book offers a fresh look at ideas that set precedence for interpreting the U.S. Constitution and Bill of Rights. By following the ideological origins related to religion and the state, it is hoped that we may better understand provisions such as the First Amendment protection of the "free exercise of religion." Other important issues that were debated involved whether or not the U.S. government should establish an official religion. Should U.S. federal tax dollars be allocated to select religious groups? Should U.S. federal officials become involved in the manner in which religious groups exercised their religious freedom? The answers to these questions were generally a resounding NO!

Franklin, Jefferson, and Madison wrote passionately about their views on religion and the state. Their religious and political ideas were complex and changed over time. Searches of their family histories revealed their religious roots. Many of their early family members suffered from religious persecution in Europe. Their families came to America with hopes of finding religious freedom and civil rights. Stories of the personal experiences of their parents, grandparents, and preceding generations influenced their worldviews. When their deep desires for freedom and liberty were oppressed by British colonialism, the task of defending their rights resulted in the American Revolution. They risked their own lives in establishing the United States, as many of their brothers and sisters in arms died defending the country. If they did not succeed in winning the Revolutionary War, they contemplated the gruesome thought that they might be hung for treason. Their shared experience inspired each of them to value principles surrounding the right of "life, liberty and the pursuit of happiness."[7] They took it personally because their lives were on the line.

Chapter One presents the life of Benjamin Franklin (1706-1790) in a new light by revealing his private feelings about religion. His religious sentiments changed many times throughout his life. His ancestors were mostly dissenters from the Church of England. They secretly read the scriptures when it was against the law to possess a Bible. Benjamin Franklin later lobbied against the establishment of one, sole official church in America. He advocated religious diversity and exercised different religious viewpoints. For example, when he began to gaze at the heavens through a telescope as a young man, he imagined that there must be a multitude of planets similar to Earth. He pondered the possibility that life forms and even people might inhabit some planets. He speculated that each solar system was created by divine beings and one Supreme Being governed the universe. Franklin also developed a system of self-improvement through moral and religious teachings that he tried to practice faithfully. In later life, he became close friends and published the sermons of Reverend George Whitefield, the charismatic evangelist who set fire to a religious revival movement known as the "Great Awakening." In the sunset of his life, Dr. Franklin recommended the benefits of public prayer to the delegates of the Constitutional Convention. This chapter revises the general view that Franklin was simply a deist in the Age of the Enlightenment who conceived God to be the architect of the cosmic clock of divine providence.[8]

Chapter Two traces the life of Thomas Jefferson (1743-1826), author of the Declaration of Independence and the second President of the United States. Family lore related his descendence from Welsh kings and Scottish and English aristocrats, giving him a firsthand reason for taking a stand against a ruling class in America. He believed in popular sovereignty, as he revealed in a letter to George Washington, "It is an axiom in my mind that our liberty can never be safe but in the hands of the people themselves."[9] The Virginia planter was a student of philosophy, law, and political theories of Locke, Rousseau, Montesquieu, and Voltaire. In 1776, he not only penned the Declaration of Independence, but also contributed to the Virginia Constitution the phrase, "All men are equally entitled to the free exercise of religion . . . ."[10] He worked for years and eventually witnessed the passage of "A Bill for Establishing Religious Freedom." For Jefferson, "Freedom of Religion" was a "divine right." He stood strongly against the establishment of a state religion, advocating a clear separation between Church and State. He joined his colleagues Franklin and Madison in protesting against federal tax dollars going to favored churches. Jefferson placed religion outside of the "jurisdiction" or legal authority of the State. Civil government officials clearly were being instructed to assume a "hands-off" policy regarding matters of religion.

Jefferson personally advised young people to read the Bible and to recognize "divine inspiration." He believed that faith in God could have a powerful effect on a person. He felt God was watching over us. Furthermore, if one strongly believed they were acting with God's approval, the realization could be truly inspiring. He recognized that "Jesus embraced with charity and philanthropy our neighbors, our countrymen, and the whole family of mankind."[11] Jefferson also promoted tolerance for all religions. He believed in uniting humanity, "gathering all into one family under the bonds of love, charity, peace, common wants and common aids."[12]

Chapter Three follows the life of James Madison (1751-1836), framer of the U.S. Constitution and the third President of the United States. He was a fifth generation American of English ancestry. Like Jefferson, he was raised in Virginia and attended the Episcopal Church, an American branch of the Anglican Protestants. He graduated from a Presbyterian college, the parent institution of Princeton University, and studied under President John Witherspoon who was noted for his orations on moralistic toleration. At the age of twenty-three, Madison took a strong stand for separation of Church and State. He spoke out in defense of religious and civil liberties. He believed that "All men are equally entitled to enjoy the free exercise of religion." Madison got tough with government officials who crossed the line and tried to limit a citizen's religious freedom: "The Rulers who are guilty of such an encroachment, exceed the commission from which they derive their authority, and are *Tyrants*."[13] American citizens, Madison argued, not only had a right to the free exercise of religion, they also had a patriotic duty to protest against anyone who tried to take away this fundamental right. He pointed out the lessons of the American Revolution that taught people to defend their freedoms with all their might. Madison took a bold step in defending all religions, not only those of the Christian faith. He was against Christianity being established as the "State Religion." If the government could create a religious tax, they could also force citizens to "conform" to any religion of their choosing. This would be wrong, Madison argued. Acceptance of all religions was the key to true religious freedom. There could be no exceptions.[14]

Exploring the lives and understanding the worldviews of America's founders can be a meaningful experience. Researching and writing this first volume of "The U.S. Constitution & Bill of Rights Series" has been a joy. We hope that you as well will find joy in reading these books. We encourage you to see that your local libraries, schools, and places of worship secure copies for the benefit of present and future generations. Furthermore, we seek to spread the international distribution of these books so individuals around the world may better understand the roots of liberty, freedom, and justice for all.

Chapter One

"BENJAMIN FRANKLIN ON RELIGION & THE STATE"

Benjamin Franklin is honored as the elder American statesman, diplomat, Indian treaty negotiator, philosopher, scientist, humorist, and more. However, his profession as a publisher and his efforts to record his autobiography made him more famous because he assumed control of his own press. His publication of *Poor Richard's Almanack* proved to be one of the best selling books in American history. The power of Franklin's pen gave him a direct means of communication with a broad sector of the American public. His influence helped give American people the self-confidence needed to create the United States of America.

Dr. Franklin's religious views changed and matured throughout his life. Although widely associated with deism and Unitarianism, his roots were Protestant from Old England. To better understand Franklin's personal beliefs, one must dig deeply into the documentary evidence and ponder when he is being serious and when he has his tongue in his cheek.

THE ROOTS OF BENJAMIN FRANKLIN

Dr. Franklin's family history begins in the church register at 13th Century Ecton Parish in Northamptonshire, province of Canterbury and diocese of Peterbourgh, in the Midland circuit. This region in central England was known for well-bred horses, cattle, and sheep, delicious cheese and butter, as well as hand-dyed wool and finely woven fabrics. Many Iron-Age settlements were attracted to these fertile lands that were fought over in ancient history. At the time of Roman occupation, two roads were built into the Coritani territory. While the Saxons reigned, the region was within the kingdom of Mercia.[1]

During one of his missions to England, Franklin visited his old family homestead. He wrote in his *Autobiography* about his family history:

> I learned that the family had lived in the same village — Ecton, in Northamptonshire — for three hundred years . . . When I searched the register at Ecton, I found an account of their birth, marriages, and burials from the year 1555 . . . I perceived that I was the youngest son of the youngest son for five generations back. My grandfather Thomas, who was born in 1598, lived at Ecton till he grew too old . . . My grandfather had four sons that grew up, viz., Thomas, John, Benjamin, and Josiah [his father].[2]

Dr. Franklin was named after his Uncle Benjamin, who eventually moved to Boston and lived with the family for many years.

Uncle Benjamin influenced his young nephew in matters of religion and politics:

> [Uncle] Benjamin was bred a silk-dyer, serving an apprenticeship at
> London. He was an ingenious man . . . He was very pious, a great attender
> of sermons of the best preachers, which he took down in his shorthand,
> and had with him many volumes of them.[3]

Dr. Franklin acquired many of his uncle's manuscripts on religion. He also secured a set of pamphlets that introduced him to religious issues from the generations of his grandfather and father.

The Franklin family was deeply involved in the Protestant Reformation and the split of the Anglicans away from the Catholic Church:

> This obscure family of ours was early in the Reformation, and continued
> Protestants through the reign of Queen Mary [1553-58], when they
> were sometimes in danger of trouble on account of their zeal against pop-
> ery. They had got an English Bible, and to conceal and secure it, it was
> fastened open with tapes under and within the cover of a joint-stool.
> When my great-great-grandfather read it to his family, he turned up the
> joint-stool upon his knees, turning over the leaves then under the tapes.
> One of the children stood at the door to give notice if he saw the appar-
> itor coming, who was an officer of the spiritual court. In that case the
> stool was turned down again upon its feet, when the Bible remained con-
> cealed under it as before. This anecdote I had from my Uncle Benjamin.[4]

The image of Franklin's own ancestors having to hide their family Bible and read it secretly made him realize the risks of asserting religious freedom. Officers of the Court formerly searched out and punished people when possession of a Bible was a crime. This later influenced Dr. Franklin's opinion regarding the importance of separating Church and State.

His father and uncle risked their lives and freedom by holding secret religious meetings that did not conform to the official state religion:

> The family continued all of the church of England till about the end of
> Charles II's reign [1675-85], when some of the ministers that had been
> outed for nonconformity holding conventicles in Northamptonshire,
> Benjamin and Josiah adhered to them, and so continued all their lives. The
> rest of the family remained with the Episcopal Church.[5]

Thus, in 1683, before Dr. Franklin was born, his father, an earlier wife and their children made a bold decision to leave their homeland. They embarked on a dangerous escape, traveling by ship from England to Boston, Massachusetts in search of religious freedom and a new life in America.

Dr. Franklin's father, Josiah Franklin (1653-1745), was married four times. He was 30-years-old when he arrived in Boston, a seaport of some 5,000 people mostly of the Puritan religion. There he established himself with his second wife, Anne Franklin. His training as a dyer of textiles did not land him a job, so he learned the art of candle and soap making. Several years later, his wife died while giving birth to their seventh child. The young widower soon married Abiah Folger of Nantucket who would bear him ten more children. Benjamin was their eighth child and the youngest son.

BENJAMIN FRANKLIN'S CHILDHOOD

When Benjamin Franklin was born on January 17, 1706, Boston had grown to 7,000 inhabitants. The total population of the American colonies then was approximately 275,000. The British and their Indian allies were at war against the French and their Indian allies, a battle for control of America called "Queen Anne's War" or the "Second French and Indian War." Ben was only two at the time of the war's most violent episode, the attack of Deerfield, Massachusetts, where fifty-six were killed and a hundred residents taken captive and driven on a forced march through heavy snows to Canada.[6]

Rev. Ebenezer Pemberton at the Old South Church in Boston baptized young Benjamin. The Congregational Church was established on a democratic basis in 1669 by religious dissenters who protested against the requirement of religious conversion for membership. They believed in the "Gospel of justice, inclusiveness, and reconciliation." Their church was to become a rallying point and meeting place for Samuel Adams and the Sons of Liberty. Here was where the Boston Tea Party would be planned. They also would be the only Congregational Church in Boston to remain Trinitarian during the Unitarian movement, meaning that they believed in the "Father, Son, and Holy Ghost."[7]

In 1714, Josiah and Abiah Franklin enrolled eight-year-old Benjamin in grammar school. They had great hopes that their son would become a minister. While young Ben excelled in reading and writing, he failed arithmetic. Josiah was so upset, he removed his son from school after less than two years of formal education. From this point forward, Ben was largely self-educated, except for his mother and father's teachings. He recalled:

> My original habits of frugality continuing, and my father having, among his instructions to me when a boy, frequently repeated a proverb of Solomon, 'Seest thou a man diligent in his calling, he shall stand before kings, he shall not stand before mean men.'[8]

Young Ben returned as his father's assistant in the candle and soap business. However, Benjamin was not ready to resign himself to a humble trade. His imagination, creativity, and sense of adventure abounded. At the age of ten, Ben taught himself to swim and became an avid swimmer. One day he came up with a brainstorm to swim faster. His idea led to his first invention — swimming fins — the first in a long line of unique innovations.

The following year, 1718, Ben became an apprentice in the printing shop of his big brother, James Franklin. At the age of 12, Ben set type, organized pamphlets, and sold publications as a street vendor. He began avidly reading different authors and developed a technique to improve his own writing. He collected quotes on slips of paper and organized the slips in a preferred sequence. He wrote an introduction to each quote, cited the quote, analyzed the meaning, and then wrote a transitional phrase to lead into the next quote. Some historians came to pass down this approach to their students, a technique still practiced today as a method for historical investigation.[9]

FRANKLIN'S EARLY PHILOSOPHY & RELIGION

During Benjamin's early years, his ideas regarding religion began developing. He was raised in the Episcopal Old South Church, an Anglican parish that traced its roots to the Church of England. King Henry VIII founded the Church of England when the Pope refused to recognize the king's divorce. Young Franklin began to explore religious writings by dissenters of the established Church.

As Ben matured, he embraced a philosophy based on the benefits of good works. Virtue led to rewards in life and the afterlife. To perform good works for one's fellow man was to him a service to God. Crime would not go unpunished, so the best thing one could do in life was to perform good works. These fundamental ideas inspired Franklin throughout years of public service. He thought carefully about what he could do for the greater good of society.

Franklin developed strong opinions regarding morality. He considered what was and was not proper behavior in society. While morality was an important theme in Sunday sermons, Franklin questioned whether some ministers were more concerned with their parochial interests rather than with the larger community. He disdained religious quibbling over minute details of dogma. He witnessed how people fought over conflicting religious interpretations and polemic arguments. He considered this divisive at times when their community and all the colonies needed to be united.

Benjamin received religious education as a child. As he grew into puberty, he began reading diverse religious texts and observed the minute issues of doctrine that were the focus of religious debates in Boston and abroad:

> My parents had early given me religious impressions, and brought me through my childhood piously in the Dissenting way. But I was scarce fifteen, when, after doubting by turns of several points, as I found them disputed in the different books I read, I began to doubt of Revelation itself. Some books against Deism fell into my hands; they were said to be the substance of sermons preached at Boyle's Lectures. It happened that they wrought an effect on me quite contrary to what was intended by them; for the arguments of the Deists, which were quoted to be refuted, appeared to me much stronger than the refutations; in short, I soon became a thorough Deist.[10]

Deism is a belief in God as the source of finite existence, a philosophy of the Age of Reason. Deists question the supernatural dimension of religion. This religious movement became established in the 17th and 18th century in England and the American colonies. Franklin began to explore deism at the age of fifteen.

Beginning in 1721, a time when he became a vegetarian for a while, he felt strongly enough about his intellectual yearnings to contribute to the public dialogue. He started writing anonymous articles for the *New England Courant*. His big brother, James, was not so discreet and was jailed twice for writing political satires on the Puritan leadership. The Franklin boys learned the value of "freedom of the press" the hard way. Ben was only fifteen when he had to assume responsibilities to edit the paper, set the type and roll the presses. He also worked to increase the paper's distribution. At times of mounting political pressure against the newspaper, Ben stood up to defend the publication and refused to surrender.

FRANKLIN'S LETTERS TO THE EDITOR SIGNED "SILENCE DOGWOOD"

At the age of sixteen, Benjamin decided to take a more clever approach to poke fun at old Puritanical thinking in colonial Boston. In 1722, he began writing a series of letters to the editor. To make his points stronger, he wrote the letters under the persona and pen name of Mrs. Silence Dogwood, a supposed middle-aged widow who "looked at the world with a humorous and satiric eye." Mrs. Dogwood's letters on love and courtship captured public interest. Her commentary on important community issues, such as public education, got people thinking. No one knew that Benjamin was the real author. Mrs. Dogwood's ninth letter questioned who were the greater threats to society — the openly profane or religious pretenders:

> Corruptio optimi est pessima
>
> To the author of the New England Courant.
>
> SIR,
>
> It has been for some Time a Question with me, Whether a Commonwealth suffers more by hypocritical Pretenders to Religion, or by the openly Profane? But some late Thoughts of this Nature, have inclined me to think, that the Hypocrite is the most dangerous Person of the Two, especially if he sustains a Post in the Government, and we consider his Conduct as it regards the Publick.[11]

Franklin abhorred hypocrisy. He was critical of government officials, especially those who used religion to seek their political gains.

Franklin dubbed corrupt politicians "State Hypocrites." Under the guise of Mrs. Silence Dogwood, Franklin sharpened his pencil:

> The first Artifice of a State Hypocrite is, by a few savoury Expressions which cost him Nothing, to betray the best Men in his Country into an Opinion of his Goodness; and if the Country wherein he lives is noted for the Purity of Religion, he the more easily gains his End, and consequently may more justly be [exposed] and detested. A notoriously profane Person in a private Capacity, ruins himself, and perhaps forwards the Destruction of a few of his Equals; but a publick Hypocrite every day deceives his betters, and makes them the Ignorant Trumpeters of his supposed Godliness: They take him for a Saint, and pass him for one, without considering that they are (as it were) the Instruments of publick Mischief out of Conscience, and ruin their Country for God's sake.[12]

Religious pretenders were the greater threat to society, Mrs. Dogwood asserted.

Such pretenders were hypocrites because they were using religion as a means to achieve their political ends. This resulted in a group of blind followers espousing false causes in the name of God.

Franklin, through Mrs. Dogwood, sought to expose these religious pretenders:

> This Political Description of a Hypocrite, may (for ought I know) be taken for a new Doctrine by some of your Readers; but let them consider, that a little Religion, and a little Honesty, goes a great way in Courts. 'Tis not inconsistent with Charity to distrust a Religious Man in Power, tho' he may be a good Man; he has many Temptations "to propagate publick Destruction for Personal Advantages and Security:" And if his Natural Temper be covetous, and his Actions often contradict his pious Discourse, we may with great Reason conclude, that he has some other Design in his Religion besides barely getting to Heaven.[13]

Franklin's plain logic shined through when he claimed, "a little Religion, and a little Honesty, goes a great way in the Courts." He poked fun at the Pennsylvania judicial system, implying that too much religion and too little honesty existed in the courts.

> But the most dangerous Hypocrite in a Common-Wealth, is one who leaves the Gospel for the sake of the Law: A Man compounded of Law and Gospel, is able to cheat a whole Country with his Religion, and then destroy them under Colour of Law: And here the Clergy are in great Danger of being [deceived], and the People of being [deceived] by the Clergy, until the Monster arrives to such Power and Wealth, that he is out of the reach of both, and can oppress the People without their own blind Assistance.[14]

Franklin painted a frightening picture of what happens when Church and State are not clearly separated, claiming that the result is the destruction of society under the pretense of the law. Furthermore, he contended that politicians who justify their actions by invoking God's will are potentially dangerous.

Franklin put forth the idea that when politicians and religious leaders form an unholy alliance, the result may be oppression against the people:

> And it is a sad Observation, that when the People too late see their Error, yet the Clergy still persist in their [praise] on the Hypocrite; and when he happens to die for the Good of his Country, without leaving behind him the Memory of one good Action, he shall be sure to have his Funeral Sermon [stuffed] with Pious Expressions which he dropt at such a Time, and at such a Place, and on such an Occasion; than which nothing can be more prejudicial to the Interest of Religion, nor indeed to the Memory of the Person [deceased]. The Reason of this Blindness in the Clergy is, because they are honourably supported (as they ought to be) by their People, and see nor feel nothing of the Oppression which is obvious and burdensome to every one else.[15]

His point was that the clergy should be more concerned with the needs of the people than the needs of politicians. Tangled relationships between Church and

State resulted in oppression unfelt by either the clergy or the politicians. The people were left to suffer.

Franklin asserted that exposing the clergy and politicians who were working in collusion was an act of love for God and country:

> But this Subject raises in me an Indignation not to be born; and if we have had, or are like to have any Instances of this Nature in New England, we cannot better manifest our Love to Religion and the Country, than by setting the Deceivers in a true Light, and undeceiving the Deceived, however such Discoveries may be represented by the ignorant or designing Enemies of our Peace and Safety.[16]

Franklin employed the persona of Mrs. Dogwood to make the point that people should wake up and see the light. The public needed to be on their guard against ambitious politicians and self-serving clergymen. Church and State demanded separation.

To drive home his point, Franklin brought forth evidence from an English political analyst:

> I shall conclude with a Paragraph or two from an ingenious Political Writer in the *London Journal,* the better to convince your Readers, that Publick Destruction may be easily [carried] on by hypocritical Pretenders to Religion.
>
> A raging Passion for immoderate Gain had made Men universally and intensely hard-hearted: They were every where devouring one another. And yet the Directors and their Accomplices, who were the acting Instruments of all this outrageous Madness and Mischief, set up for wonderful pious Persons, while they were defying Almighty God, and plundering Men; and they set apart a Fund of Subscriptions for charitable Uses; that is, they [mercilessly] made a whole People Beggars, and charitably supported a few necessitous and worthless FAVOURITES.[17]

Public money should not go to religious groups, Franklin asserted. The result would lead to a conspiracy between Church and State. This would in turn lead to plundering the people in defiance of "Almighty God." The fleecing of the people's pockets under the auspices of public charity would be an act of hypocrisy. Franklin sounded the alarm over politicians who sought support from the clergy to get elected, then awarded favorite churches public tax money.

The only public defense against an unholy alliance between Church and State was public exposure of the offense. This was Franklin's purpose in writing Dogwood Letter #9.

> I doubt not, but if the Villainy had gone on with Success, they would have had their Names handed down to Posterity with Encomiums; as the Names of other publick Robbers have been! We have Historians and ODE MAKERS now living, very proper for such a Task. It is certain, that most People did, at one Time, believe the Directors to be great and worthy Persons. And an honest Country Clergyman told me last Summer, upon the Road, that Sir John was an excellent publick-spirited Person, for that

he had beautified his Chancel.[18]

Citing the name Sir John made readers wonder which Sir John was Mrs. Dogwood indicting. Use of the term "Sir" narrowed the choices down to members of the British aristocracy. Franklin used sarcasm to criticize the use of public money to beautify the "Chancel," a private area in the Church reserved for high-church officials.

Franklin was critical of the special status claimed by aristocratic politicians and leaders of the official state religion. His Mrs. Dogwood called for the general public to judge their leaders based on sound evidence:

> Upon the whole we must not judge of one another by their best Actions; since the worst Men do some Good, and all Men make fine Professions: But we must judge of Men by the whole of their Conduct, and the Effects of it. Thorough Honesty requires great and long Proof, since many a Man, long thought honest, has at length proved a Knave. And it is from judging without Proof, or false Proof, that Mankind continue Unhappy.
>
> I am, SIR,
> Your humble Servant,
> SILENCE DOGWOOD.[19]

Franklin concluded with a call for reason. How should we, the people, judge our religious and political leaders? One must look at the whole of their public service record.

Finally, after writing 15 or 16 letters under his pseudonym, Benjamin confessed that he was the author. His big brother scolded him harshly. However, others were amazed that a teenager could pull off such a ruse. People also recognized that young Ben had a special talent as a writer.

EARLY BATTLES, LOVE, AND A QUEST FOR PERSONAL INDEPENDENCE

While the Franklins were associated with South Church in Boston, they came to be at odds with Rev. Cotton Mather, the Puritan leader of North Church. Rev. Mather was a formidable opponent, a Harvard University graduate who was involved in the infamous Salem witch trials of 1692. He was the author of *Memorable Providences Relating to Witchcraft and Possessions* (1689) and a book on satanic possession, entitled *Wonders of the Invisible World* (1693, new ed. 1956).

In 1723, after a public debate with Rev. Mather over smallpox inoculation, Ben's older brother, James Franklin, was thrown into jail. Young Ben did his best to publish several issues of the newspaper on his own. When James was released, he took his frustration out on Ben, physically beating up his younger brother several times. Finally, Benjamin could take no more. At the age of 17, he ran away from home.

In September of 1723, Ben Franklin and his friend, John Collins, took a boat to New York. After failing to find work, they walked across the colony of New Jersey, taking a boat the final leg of the journey to Pennsylvania. On October 6th, worn out and nearly penniless, their future unknown, they arrived in Philadelphia, a seaport of then less than 10,000 people. They had only enough money to buy a little bread. Walking down the cobblestone streets, Ben was eating a fresh-baked bun when he first laid eyes on Deborah Read, the young girl who one day would become his bride. She was standing in the doorway of her family's home. She was well dressed, clean, and well groomed. Franklin had been on the road for weeks and must have looked like a vagabond. The two were brought together when Ben got a job in her neighborhood at Keimer's printing office. He later rented a room in her family home.

Ben found Philadelphia a very different community compared with Boston, a center of Puritan religious orthodoxy. Philadelphia, founded by William Penn as a colony based on religious tolerance, was a place of ethnic and religious diversity. English, Irish, Scots, and Germans, as well as Christian dissenters, Jews, and people from around the world were attracted to the "City of Brotherly Love."

Franklin worked as a printer's assistant while looking for greater opportunities. He met Governor William Keith, who encouraged him to develop his skills as a printer in England. In 1724, Benjamin decided to follow the Governor's advice after receiving promises of official letters of recommendation. As he prepared to depart, Deborah Read reportedly hinted at marriage, but Benjamin was too young to take that step. He and friend James Ralph embarked on a ship and sailed for London, with promises that the Governor's letters of recommendation would be forthcoming. While on board, they met and made friends with an English merchant named Mr. Denham.

FRANKLIN'S FIRST EUROPEAN ADVENTURE AND EARLY WRITINGS ON RELIGION

At the age of 18, sailing across the Atlantic Ocean was an adventure for Benjamin. There were pirates on the high seas and strong storms could threaten their crossing. Fortunately, the seas were calm, and they arrived safely on December 24, 1724 in London, where King George I reigned.

Benjamin found work as a printer at Palmer House, a London print shop. He helped out his friend, James Ralph, until he found work as a schoolteacher. The two later had a falling out after Franklin expressed a romantic interest in James' girlfriend. When not working, Franklin explored the streets of London and did a little girl watching. He also witnessed the extremes of a class society, from ornate palaces and royal residences to bawdy brothels and pubs. He observed how his fellow workers partied away their money, often showing up drunk at work. Franklin espoused the benefits of sober life. He tried, unsuccessfully, to inspire his fellow workers to join him in drinking water instead of beer, wine, and hard liquor. He set an example for the virtues of hard work, carrying two heavy trays of lead type at a time to double his productivity.

Governor Keith's promised letters of recommendation never arrived.

Franklin was disappointed. He accepted the fact that he was on his own. He pursued his own writing, while working hard at developing his skills as a printer. While at Palmer's, he worked on the second edition of William Wollaston's (1659-1724), *The Religion of Nature Delineated.*[20] The principal theme was that "truth is the foundation of morality." Wollaston asked the questions: "Is there such a thing as natural religion; and if there is, what is it?" Wollaston espoused "the pursuit of happiness by the practice of truth and reason."[21]

In 1725, Benjamin Franklin was inspired by Wollaston to write his own metaphysical piece. He privately printed his pamphlet, "A Dissertation on Liberty and Necessity, Pleasure and Pain":

> I. There is said to be a First Mover, who is called God, Maker of the Universe.
>
> II. He is said to be all wise, all good, and all-powerful.
>
> Those two propositions being [allowed] and asserted by people of almost every Sect and Opinion; I have here [supposed] them granted, and laid them down as the Foundation of my argument; what follows then, being a Chain of Consequences truly drawn from them, will stand or fall as they are true or false.[22]

At the age of 19, Franklin sought to explain his personal feelings about God. His attempt reveals insights into the depths of his thoughts. He was quite young to be pondering perhaps the most profound questions regarding the existence and the nature of God.

He recognized God as the Creator of the Universe, the Supreme Being imbued with infinite wisdom, goodness, and power:

> III. If He is all-good, whatsoever He doth must be good.
>
> IV. If He is all-wise, whatsoever he doth must be wise.
>
> The Truth of these propositions, with relation to the two first, I think may be justly called evident; since, either that infinite goodness will act what is ill, or infinite wisdom what is not wise, is too glaring a Contradiction not to be [perceived] by any Man of common Sense, and [denied] as soon as understood.
>
> V. If He is all-powerful, there can be nothing existing or acting in the Universe against or without his Consent; and what he consents to must be good, because He is good; therefore Evil doth not exist.[23]

Thus, the acceptance of God was for Franklin a matter of "common sense." However, how was humanity to deal with the existence of evil in the world? Did evil exist? Or, was evil in the minds of Man?

Franklin rejected the distinction between the "permissive will" of God and "perceptive will":

> Unde Malum? [Why is there evil?] . . . There is nothing in the Universe but what God either does, or permits to be done.

This, as He is Almighty, is certainly true: But what need of this Distinction between doing and permitting? . . . We will reason thus: If God permits an Action to be done, it is because he lacks either Power or Inclination to hinder it; in saying he lacks Power, we deny Him to be Almighty; and if we say He lacks Inclination or Will, it must be either because He is not Good, or the Action is not evil. The former is inconsistent with his before-given Attribute of Goodness, therefore the latter must be true.[24]

Franklin thus challenges the existence of evil in the world. This required a huge leap of faith. People were so conditioned to accept the existence of evil, that young Franklin's postulations inevitably would evoke strong reactions for and against his thesis.

Franklin advanced an old Augustinian philosophy called "aesthetic theodi-cy," a term coined in 1710 by Leibnitz as a "justification of the divine providence by the attempt to reconcile the existence of evil with the goodness and sovereignty of God." The term was derived from the Greek word for "justice."[25]

Franklin expressed a philosophy that addressed the "being, perfections, and government of God and the immortality of the soul."

It will be said, perhaps, that God permits evil Actions to be done, for wise Ends and Purposes. But this objection destroys itself; for whatever an infi-nitely good God has wise ends in [allowing] to be, must be good, is there-by made good, and cannot be otherwise.[26]

Thus, Franklin envisioned a world based on "goodness," rather than a world based on "evil." Acceptance of this philosophy fundamentally changes one's worldview.

Franklin took his philosophy of goodness to the extreme. He postulated that all creatures on earth act according to God's will. Therefore, all actions were inherently good, because God's will is "Almighty."

VI. If a Creature is made by God, it must depend upon God, and receive all its Power from Him; with which Power the Creature can do nothing contrary to the Will of God, because God is Almighty; what is not contrary to His Will, must be agreeable to it; what is agreeable to it, must be good, because He is Good; therefore a Creature can do nothing but what is good.

I would not be understood by this to encourage or defend Theft; tis only for the sake of argument, and will certainly have no ill Effect. The Order and Course of Things will not be affected by Reasoning of this Kind; and 'tis just and necessary, and as much according to Truth, for [Person B] to dislike and punish the Thief who steals his Horse, as it is for [person A] to steal the horse.[27]

He countered potential critics who might question how criminals, under Franklin's philosophy, could be punished. He postulated that while a horse thief might be inherently "good," it was also "good" to punish the horse thief for his crime.

VII. If the Creature is thus limited in his Actions, being able to do only such things as God would have him to do, and not being able to refuse doing what God would have done; then he can have no such thing as Liberty, Free-will, or Power to do or refrain an Action.

> As Man is a Part of this great Machine, the Universe, his regular Acting is requisite to the regular moving of the whole . . . Is it not necessary then, that our Actions should be [overruled] and governed by an all-wise Providence? — How exact and regular is every Thing in the natural world! How wisely in every Part [contrived]! We cannot here find the least Defect! All the heavenly Bodies, the Stars and Planets, are regulated with the Utmost Wisdom! And can we suppose less Care to be taken in the Order of the moral than the natural System? It is as if an ingenious Artificer, having [framed] a curious Machine or Clock, and put its many intricate Wheels and Powers in such a dependence on one another, that the whole might move in the most exact Order and Regularity, had nevertheless [placed] in it several other Wheels endued with an independent Self-Motion, but ignorant of the general Interest of the Clock [maker]; and these would every now and then be moving wrong, disordering the true Movement, and making continual Work for the Mender; which might be better prevented, by depriving them of that Power of Self-Motion, and placing them in a Dependence on the regular Part of the Clock.[28]

Franklin employed the symbol of human will as one of the gears in the great metaphorical clock of the universe. Here we see him emerging as a figure of the Age of Enlightenment. His treatise went on to address issues of pleasure and pain.

In 1725, Benjamin Franklin experienced both pleasure and pain. While his treatise on religion attracted praise among certain circles in London society, his employer was not pleased. He disagreed with Franklin's thesis. The two conflicted to a point where Franklin was compelled to work for a larger printer, John Watts. Franklin occupied his free time attending the theater, reading voraciously, and hanging out at coffee houses engaging in dialogue on topics of the day.

Tragedy befell tragedy in Franklin's life. News arrived from America that his beloved Deborah Read was married to another man. Benjamin was heart-struck. He regretted that he had written her only one letter from London. It was a mistake that he admitted.

THE SELF-IMPROVEMENT PLAN

On July 23, 1726, Benjamin Franklin set sail for America with merchant Thomas Denham, who loaned him the money for his passage and promised him a job in Philadelphia. Benjamin accepted that his hopes and dreams for his London adventure had been thwarted for lack of promised funding and letters of recommendation from Governor Keith. On October 11th, Franklin arrived safely back in Philadelphia. He learned that Deborah Read had married a man named John Rogers, a poor potter. Deborah's life had been thrust into poverty.

Franklin found employment with merchant Thomas Denham, working as a bookkeeper and shopkeeper in a store that imported clothes and hardware. He was promoted to salesman at Denham's shop of international goods which specialized in importing English goods to the American colonies. The opportunity to learn about international trade proved a valuable experience. Mr. Denham was kind to Benjamin and became a virtual father figure. Unfortunately, both Benjamin and Mr. Denham became gravely ill in 1727. Benjamin recovered from his bout with pleurisy, a severe lung infection. Mr. Denham never recovered, but remembered Benjamin in his will, forgiving all debts.

After Mr. Denham's death, Franklin mournfully returned to his former employer, Mr. Keimer. Benjamin trained new workers and eventually managed the printing shop. He supervised the printing of the first printed money in the colonies. He contributed to the design of the bills and built a special copper press to print currency.

Benjamin worked hard while contemplating his personal character. At the age of twenty, he considered what he might do to become a more "moral person." He reflected in his *Autobiography*:

> I grew [convinced] that truth, sincerity and integrity in dealings between man and man were of the utmost importance to the felicity of life; and I [formed] written resolutions, which still remain in my journal book, to practice them ever while . . . [29]

Franklin sought a path of self-improvement by embarking on a course toward "moral perfection." He created a list of four resolutions to follow:

1. "Frugality" - He determined to save money and pay his bills.

2. "Honesty" - He became honest to the letter and sincere "in every word and action."

3. "Industry" - He promised himself to be industrious "to whatever bussiness I take in hand."

4. "Goodness" - He vowed "to speak ill of no man whatever, not even in a manner of truth" and to "speak all the good I know of every body."[30]

Here we find the roots of Franklin's self-improvement plan. He explained in his *Autobiography* that he wanted to be a more moral person.

From out of his initial four resolutions, Franklin developed a more rigorous self-improvement plan based on thirteen virtues of moral perfection:

1. TEMPERANCE. Eat not to dullness; drink not to elevation.

2. SILENCE. Speak not but what may benefit others or yourself; avoid trifling conversation.

3. ORDER. Let all your things have their places; let each part of your business have its time.

4. RESOLUTION. Resolve to perform what you ought; perform without fail what you resolve.

5. FRUGALITY. Make no expense but to do good to others or yourself; i.e.,

waste nothing.

6. INDUSTRY. Lose no time; be always [employed] in something useful; cut off all unnecessary actions.

7. SINCERITY. Use no hurtful deceit; think innocently and justly, and, if you speak, speak accordingly.

8. JUSTICE. Wrong none by doing injuries, or omitting the benefits that are your duty.

9. MODERATION. Avoid extremes; forbear resenting injuries so much as you think they deserve.

10. CLEANLINESS. Tolerate no uncleanliness in body, cloaths, or habitation.

11. TRANQUILITY. Be not disturbed at trifles, or at accidents common or unavoidable.

12. CHASTITY. Rarely use venery but for health or offspring, never to dullness, weakness, or the injury of your own or another's peace or reputation.

13. HUMILITY. Imitate Jesus and Socrates.[31]

He practiced one virtue for a week and then moved on to the next. After thirteen weeks, he repeated the process, returning to the first virtue. Franklin kept notes of his moral progress in his "little virtue book." He continued to evaluate his success for some time, and for many years kept his little book with him.

Little did Franklin realize that his private plan for the improvement of his moral virtue represented the historical roots of the field of "self-improvement." He stood ahead of his time in utilizing a "holistic approach" to the "self" which recognized a connection between "body, mind, and spirit." Ben Franklin perhaps would be amazed to visit a contemporary bookstore or library and see how the field of "self-improvement" has grown.

FRIENDS, FAMILY, & BUSINESS IN PHILADELPHIA

After a period of introspection, Franklin developed a sense of self-confidence and a desire to interact with other people. He sought a positive, productive environment in which ideas could be discussed and debated freely. Out of his desire to explore and to dialogue on topics of his day, Franklin founded an intellectual society called Junto or "Leathern Apron Club." "Junto" derives from a Latin word meaning "to join." The feminine term "junta" refers to a faction joined together in a revolution. This society of young men met on Friday evenings for "self-improvement study, mutual aid, and conviviality." Seeds of the American Revolution were sown in Franklin's group, which later evolved into the American Philosophical Society.[32]

One debate related to this period of Franklin's life — a mystery that has never been resolved — involves the illegitimate birth of his son, William Franklin. The baby was conceived sometime between 1727 and 1730. The identity of William's mother is unknown. Some erroneously speculated she might even have been Benjamin's former sweetheart, Deborah Read Rogers (1708 - 1774), but this was not correct. She had married John Rogers while Franklin was living in London. However, she soon learned that her husband "practiced polygamy," so she "renounced his name." Rogers' scandalous behavior multiplied when he stole a slave and disappeared from Philadelphia in the night. Notices were published in the newspaper:

> John Rogers late of the City of Philadelphia Potter, having absconded some time in December last, and took with him a like[l]y young Negroe Lad about 18 Years of Age, named Limos, he is of a yellowish [Complexion], and Malagascow Negroe, he had on an Ozenbrig Shirt and Frock, a Frize Jacket and Breeches without lining with Brass Buttons. These are to forewarn all Persons from Buying the above said Negroe, he belonging to Solomon Goard of Philadelphia, and whoever will take up said Negroe and secure him and give Notice thereof to Andrew Bradford in Philadelphia, or William Parks in Maryland, shall have Three Pounds and Reasonable Charges.[33]

Reports later surfaced that John Rogers died of unknown causes.

In 1728, Benjamin Franklin and Deborah Read began dating again. Ben apologized for writing Deborah only one letter while in Europe. Their relationship grew and matured over the coming months.

At the time, Franklin was working for Mr. Keimer. Their major project was printing currency. In late February 1728, Franklin and Keimer moved the press to Burlington, New Jersey, where they printed paper money for the colony of New Jersey. They also printed a tract entitled, "A Looking Glass for the Modern Deists or Libertines, Called Freethinkers" (Philadelphia: S. Keimer, 1728). On May 13 or 14, they returned to Philadelphia.

When Mr. Keimer did not reward Franklin for making the business successful, he and his friend, Hugh Meredith established their own print shop, renting the space on June 1, 1728 at 139 Market Street. Between July and October, they helped print part of William Sewall's *History of the Quakers*. They built a reputation as the most hard-working and highly skilled printers in Philadelphia. One local businessman remarked, "For the industry of that Franklin is superior to anything I ever saw of the kind; I see him still at work when I go home from the club, and he is at work again before his neighbors are out of bed." Their printing business flourished over the next decade.[34]

"ARTICLES OF BELIEF AND ACTS OF RELIGION"

While printing by day, Benjamin Franklin worked on his writings by night. He penned a response to "objectionable conduct of freethinkers among his acquaintance." On November 20, 1728, he published his text, "Articles of Belief and Acts of Religion." In the age of the telescope, Franklin pondered the heavens.

Considering that our sun is a star, he imagined many solar systems like ours existed throughout the universe. Each solar system, he concluded, must have been created by a deity. Thus, perhaps there were many deities with one Supreme Being at the head. In comparison with the universe, he realized, earth was a very small planet. At the age of twenty-two, Franklin wrote:

> First Principles
>   I believe there is one most perfect Being, Author and Father of the Gods themselves.
>   For I believe that Man is not the most perfect Being but One, rather that as there are many Degrees of Beings his Inferiors, so there are many Degrees of Beings superior to him.
>   Also, when I stretch my Imagination thro' and beyond our System of Planets, beyond the visible [fixed] Stars themselves, into that Space that is every Way infinite, and conceive it [filled] with Suns like ours, each with a Chorus of Worlds for ever moving round him, then this little Ball on which we move, seems, even in my narrow Imagination, to be almost Nothing, and my self less than nothing, and of no sort of Consequence.[35]

Franklin began his religious treatise by recognizing one Supreme Being. He then proposed that the Supreme Being is the father of other gods. Perhaps he was referring to the Greek and Roman gods of classic literature. The phrase "other Gods" led to Franklin's association with "polytheism," belief in multiple gods. Seeking to explain what people were seeing through telescopes, he imagined the existence of inhabited planets similar to Earth in other parts of the galaxy.

Franklin reconciled humanity's desire for religion with Natural Law:

> But since there is in all Men something like a natural Principle which [inclines] them to DEVOTION or the Worship of some unseen Power;
>   And since Men are endued with Reason superior to all other Animals that we are in our World acquainted with;
>   Therefore I think it seems required of me, and my Duty, as a Man, to pay Divine Regards to SOMETHING.
>   I CONCEIVE then, that the INFINITE has created many Beings or Gods, vastly superior to Man, who can better conceive his Perfections than we, and return him a more rational and glorious Praise. As among Men, the Praise of the Ignorant or of Children, is not regarded by [God] the ingenious Painter or Architect, who is rather [honored] and [pleased] with the Approbation of Wise men and Artists.[36]

Franklin boldly conveyed his own theology, a blend of Christianity, the religions of ancient Italy and Greece, as well as Natural Law and other Enlightenment philosophies. Perhaps he went too far in his enthusiasm to attempt to blend these diverse teachings into something of his own thinking at the time.

Franklin speculated on divine creation and divine beings:

> It may be that these created Gods, are immortal, or it may be that after many Ages, they are changed, and Others supply their Places.

> Howbeit, I conceive that each of these is exceeding wise, and good, and very powerful; and that Each has made for himself, one glorious Sun, attended with a beautiful and admirable System of Planets.
>
> It is that particular wise and good God, who is the Author and Owner of our System, that I propose for the Object of my Praise and Adoration.
>
> For I conceive that he has in himself some of those Passions he has planted in us, and that, since he has given us Reason whereby we are capable of observing his Wisdom in the Creation, he is not above caring for us, being [pleased] with our Praise, and offended when we slight Him, or neglect his Glory.[37]

Franklin here reinforced his idea that there were many planets around many suns in many solar systems around the universe. He speculated that there might be a spiritual deity associated with each of these solar systems. All of these deities, according to Franklin's theory, were descended from the Supreme Being, the Creator of the universe. His speculations on pantheism may have been only fleeting, as he did not dwell on his theory in later life.

His was not an angry God. To Franklin, God was his friend:

> I conceive for many Reasons that he is a good Being, and as I should be happy to have so wise, good and powerful a Being my Friend, let me consider in what Manner I shall make myself most acceptable to him.
>
> Next to the Praise due, to his Wisdom, I believe he is pleased and delights in the Happiness of those he has created; and since without Virtue Man can have no Happiness in this World, I firmly believe he delights to see me Virtuous, because he is [pleased] when he sees me Happy.[38]

Virtue was the path to happiness, Franklin postulated. Some of these ideas he drew from a "Paper of Good and Evil" delivered at their weekly meetings of Junto.

As a young intellectual, Franklin sought to express his religious feelings and his love for God:

> And since he has created many Things which seem purely [designed] for the Delight of Man, I believe he is not offended when he sees his Children solace themselves in any manner of pleasant Exercises and innocent Delights, and I think no Pleasure innocent that is to Man hurtful.
>
> I love him [God] therefore for his Goodness and I adore him for his Wisdom.
>
> Let me then not fail to praise my God continually, for it is his Due, and it is all I can return for his many Favours and great Goodness to me; and let me resolve to be virtuous, that I may be happy, that I may please Him, who is delighted to see me happy. Amen.[39]

Franklin deemed it important to praise God. He believed that God might answer one's prayers and bring goodness into one's life. But it was also Man's duty to be virtuous. Such a spiritual path would lead to happiness and please God.

Franklin offered a reasoned approach to the practice of religion through prayer:

> 1. Adoration. 2. Petition. 3. Thanks.
> [Prelude]
>   Being mindful that before I address the DEITY, my Soul ought to be calm and Serene, free from Passion and Perturbation, or otherwise elevated with Rational Joy and Pleasure, I ought to use a Countenance that expresses a filial Respect, [mixed] with a kind of Smiling, that signifies inward Joy, and Satisfaction, and Admiration.

>   O wise God,
>   My good Father,
>   Thou beholdest the Sincerity of my Heart,
>   And of my Devotion;
>   Grant me a Continuance of thy Favour![40]

Franklin believed in the grace of God. He addressed God through his prayers. He believed that one could communicate directly with God without an intermediary. Thus, he found God in nature, as well as in his daily life:

God was good, Franklin proclaimed. God was our Creator. God was our Father. People need not feel guilty for experiencing pleasure, as some preachers had claimed. On the contrary, he believed that God was pleased when people were happy and joyous. Franklin defined six points regarding the nature of God:

> (1) Powerful Goodness, &c. O Creator, O Father, I believe that thou art Good, and that thou art [pleased] with the Pleasure of thy Children. Praised be thy Name [forever].
> (2) By thy Power hast thou made the glorious Sun, with his attending Worlds; from the Energy of thy mighty Will they first received their prodigious Motion, and by thy Wisdom hast thou prescribed the wondrous Laws by which they move. Praised be thy Name forever.
> (3) By thy Wisdom hast thou formed all Things, Thou hast created Man, bestowing Life and Reason, and placed him in Dignity superior to thy other earthly Creatures. Praised be thy Name [forever].
> (4) Thy Wisdom, thy Power, and thy GOODNESS are every where clearly seen; in the Air and in the Water, in the Heavens and on the Earth; Thou providest for the various winged Fowl, and the innumerable Inhabitants of the Water; Thou givest Cold and Heat, Rain and Sunshine in their Season, and to the Fruits of the Earth Increase. Praised be thy Name [forever].
> (5) I believe thou hast given Life to thy Creatures that they might Live, and art not delighted with violent Death and bloody Sacrifices. Praised be thy Name [forever].
> (6) Thou abhorrest in thy Creatures Treachery and Deceit, Malice, Revenge, Intemperance and every other hurtful Vice; but Thou art a Lover of Justice and Sincerity, of Friendship, Benevolence and every Virtue. Thou art my Friend, my Father, and my Benefactor. Praised be thy Name, O God, [forever]. Amen.[41]

Franklin proceeded to quote some of the writings that influenced his thinking.

He cited William Ray, *Wisdom of God in the Creation* (1691); Sir Richard Blackmore, *Creation* (1712), the Archbishop of Cambray's *Demonstration of the Being of a God* (1705). Franklin also recommended that one should "spend some Minutes in a serious Silence, contemplating on those Subjects." He found benefit in singing *Hymn to the Creator* by John Milton (1608-1674). One might conclude that Franklin created his own theology and outlined his personal approach to religious services. Franklin described his treatise, "a little Liturgy or Form of Prayer for my own private Use."

In 1729, Benjamin Franklin continued his courtship of Deborah Read, although he confessed a short-lived interest in a daughter of a Mrs. Godfrey. Most Friday evenings he reserved for meetings of Junto, his philosophical discussion group of young intellectuals. His friendship with his business partner, Hugh Meredith, however, grew strained due to Meredith's drinking habits. Franklin soon bought out Meredith to become the sole owner and publisher of the *Pennsylvania Gazette,* a newspaper founded by Mr. Keimer.

Franklin anonymously published various pamphlets. His best seller was entitled, "Nature and Necessity of a Paper Currency." He became an advocate for better conditions in colonial jails, a prelude to his many writings on public improvements. He published notices about deists Thomas Woolston and Anthony Collins. In July of 1729, he published three essays on primitive Christianity from a London journal. In September, he printed selections from Xenophon on the Socratic method.

On October 14, Franklin's friend and patron, Andrew Hamilton, was elected Speaker of the House. Franklin became Pennsylvania's official printer. He soon was in charge of printing paper currency for Pennsylvania and other American colonies. This gave Franklin a new sense of security.

Around this time, William Franklin, Benjamin's illegitimate son, was born in Philadelphia. The details surrounding the birth of this child were hushed up. However, Benjamin wanted to raise his son and be his father on a daily basis.

On September 1, 1730, Benjamin Franklin married his early sweetheart, Deborah Read. A common law union had to suffice because they could not determine whether Deborah's former husband, John Rogers, was dead or alive. Deborah was a religious woman. While Benjamin continued in the Presbyterian Church, she remained a member of the Anglican Christ Church. She performed an act of Christian charity when she opened her arms to baby William, who was welcomed immediately into their household. She raised him as her own child. A month after they were married, Benjamin wrote an essay, "Rules and Maxims for promoting Matrimonial Happiness" (October 8, 1730). His system must have been successful to some degree, since he and Deborah Read Franklin were married for forty-three years.

"ON THE PROVIDENCE OF GOD IN THE GOVERNMENT OF THE WORLD"

Toward the end of 1730, Benjamin Franklin delivered before the Junto philosophical club a major essay on religion entitled, "On the Providence of God in the Government of the World." Franklin began by explaining his views on God:

> 1. That he [God] must be a Being of great Wisdom, appears in his admirable Order and Disposition of Things, whether we consider the heavenly Bodies, the Stars and Planets, and their wonderful regular Motions, or this Earth compounded of such an Excellent mixture of all the Elements; or the admirable Structure of Animal Bodies of such infinite Variety, and yet every one adapted to its Nature, and the Way of Life it is to be placed in, whether on Earth, in the Air or in the Waters, and so exactly that the highest and most exquisite human Reason, cannot find a fault and say this would have been better so or in another Manner, which whoever considers attentively and thoroughly will be [astonished] and [swallowed] up in Admiration.[42]

Franklin observed from his study of astronomy that the Universe functioned in perfect harmony. He concluded that motions of heavenly bodies were too perfect to happen by chance. This was evidence of the divine hand of God.

Through the study of nature, Franklin observed the great diversity found in so many species of life on Earth. The gift of life, Franklin concluded, came from God:

> 2. That the Deity is a Being of great Goodness, appears in his giving Life to so many Creatures, each of which acknowledge it a Benefit by their Unwillingness to leave it; in his providing plentiful Sustenance for them all, and making those Things that are most useful, most common and easy to be had; such as Water necessary for almost every Creature's Drink; Air without which few could subsist, the inexpressible Benefits of Light and Sunshine to almost all Animals in general; and to Men the most useful Vegetables, such as Corn, the most useful of Metals as Iron, and the most useful Animals, as Horses, Oxen and Sheep, he has made easiest to raise, or procure in Quantity or Numbers: each of which particulars if considered seriously and carefully would fill us with the highest Love and Affection.[43]

Water, air, light, vegetable, mineral, and animal life, all came from God's divine creation. Contemplating the immensity of Creation inspired Franklin to feel love and affection for God.

The power of God was infinite. Looking at the laws of motion and the physics of the Universe provided further evidence of the presence of God. The invisible force of gravity was considered one of God's powers:

> 3. That he is a Being of infinite Power appears, in his being able to form and compound such Vast Masses of Matter as this Earth and the Sun and innumerable Planets and Stars, and give them such prodigious Motion,

and yet so to govern them in their greatest Velocity as that they shall not [fly] off out of their appointed Bounds nor dash one against another, to their mutual Destruction; but 'tis easy to conceive his Power, when we are [convinced] of his infinite Knowledge and Wisdom; for if weak and foolish Creatures as we are, by knowing the Nature of a few Things can produce such wonderful Effects; such as for instance by knowing the Nature only of Nitre and Sea Salt [mixed] we can make a Water which will dissolve the hardest Iron and by adding one Ingredient more, can make another Water which will dissolve Gold and render the most Solid Bodies fluid — and by knowing the Nature of Salt Peter, Sulphur and Charcoal those mean Ingredients [mixed] we can shake the Air in the most terrible Manner, destroy Ships Houses and Men at a Distance and in an Instant, overthrow Cities, rend Rocks into a Thousand Pieces, and level the highest Mountains. What Power must he possess who not only knows the Nature of every Thing in the Universe, but can make Things of new Natures with the greatest Ease and at his Pleasure![44]

Franklin found God in the study of chemistry. Creation was still in process, he discovered, when observing that two or more substances could be combined to create new compounds. He considered the power of gunpowder which could be used for good or for destruction.

Franklin expressed his opinion that God was actively involved in our present life. He considered but dismissed predestination. He also did not believe that God left life on Earth to chance. He postulated that God "sometimes interferes by his particular Providence." In essence, Franklin believed that God was still fine-tuning Creation, as he explained in his concluding supposition:

That the Deity [God] sometimes interferes by his particular Providence, and sets aside the Events which would otherwise have been [produced] in the Course of Nature, or by the Free Agency of Men; and this is perfectly agreeable with what we can know of his Attributes and Perfections: But as some may doubt whether 'tis possible there should be such a Thing as free Agency in Creatures; I shall just offer one Short Argument on that Account and proceed to [show] how the Duties of Religion necessary follow the Belief of a Providence.[45]

After accepting God's will, one may embrace the duties of religion. This may be considered a necessity for the benefit of society.

Franklin then pondered the question of freedom. Here we find the American roots of liberation theology. Franklin emerges from out of the oppression of Colonial America as a voice affirming that God could help people be free:

You acknowledge that God is infinitely Powerful, Wise and Good, and also a free Agent; and you will not deny that he has communicated to us part of his Wisdom, Power and Goodness; i.e. he has made us in some Degree Wise, potent and good; and is it then impossible for him to communicate any Part of his Freedom, and make us also in some Degree Free? Is not even his infinite Power sufficient for this? I should be glad to hear what Reason any Man can give for thinking in that Manner; 'tis sufficient for me to [show] tis not impossible, and no Man I think can [show] tis improbable . . . [46]

God created humanity. People were intended to be free. Therefore, God would help humanity achieve freedom through His "divine providence," the care God exercised over the Universe.

Franklin then took a bold step in proclaiming that God could deliver freedom to a righteous nation against a cruel tyrant.

> There is a righteous Nation grievously [oppressed] by a cruel Tyrant, they earnestly [entreat] God to deliver them; If you say he cannot, you deny his infinite Power, which you at first [acknowledged]; if you say he will not, you must directly deny his infinite Goodness. You are then of necessity [obliged] to allow, that 'tis highly reasonable to believe a Providence because tis highly absurd to believe otherwise.[47]

His readers could only speculate if the "righteous nation" was America and the "cruel tyrant" was England's King George II. Such an explicit statement could have been judged as act of sedition and landed young Mr. Franklin in jail.

However, Benjamin reassured his readers that the path to freedom was protected by God's divine providence, the "foundation of all true Religion." He recommended praying directly to God:

> Now if tis unreasonable to suppose it out of the Power of the Deity to help and favour us particularly or that we are out of his Hearing or Notice or that Good Actions do not procure more of his Favour than ill Ones. Then I conclude, that believing a Providence we have the Foundation of all true Religion; for we should love and revere that Deity for his Goodness and thank him for his Benefits; we should adore him for his Wisdom, fear him for his Power, and pray to him for his Favour and Protection; and this Religion will be a Powerful Regulator of our Actions, give us Peace and Tranquility within our own Minds, and render us Benevolent, Useful and Beneficial to others.[48]

Love God. Thank God for His goodness and blessings. Recognize God's power and pray for His favor and protection. These are the basic tenets of Benjamin Franklin's religion in 1730, when he was twenty-four years old. He characterized religion as a "powerful regulator of our actions." Religion could give us peace of mind and promote moral character of good to society.

Perhaps Franklin composed his own religious creed in response to his dissatisfaction with the Presbyterian preachers he was listening to on Sundays. He found their sermons dry and lacking in the moral teachings for which he yearned. He considered their orations self-serving, promoting loyalty to their church instead of good citizenship within the larger society. However, he continued to contribute to the church, even though he began to reserve his Sundays for private devotion.

IN THE SERVICE OF FAMILY, SOCIETY, & GOD

In 1731, Benjamin raised the money to start the first circulating library. Members of the Junto philosophical club brought their books to share at the room they rented for their Friday night meetings. From this humble beginning, a public subscription library grew. Over fifty people originally contributed 40 shillings, with a promise of an annual donation to buy new books that they could share in common. Franklin himself was the library's most frequent patron. He devoted an hour or two each day, hoping to catch up on the formal education he missed as a child.

Benjamin praised his wife, Deborah, for helping their family succeed in their daily pursuits. He lauded her industry and frugality, "She assisted me cheerfully in my business, folding and stitching pamphlets, tending shop, purchasing old linen rags for the papermakers, etc., etc."[49] Her only extravagance was to buy her husband a silver spoon and a china bowl. Her explanation was that she thought he deserved such luxuries. Benjamin credited Deborah for their family's progress, quoting an English proverb that says, "He that would thrive, must ask his wife."

Franklin explained his strong religious feelings during this time in his life:

> "I never doubted, for instance, the existence of the Deity [God]; that he made the world, and [governed] it by his Providence; that the most acceptable service of God was the doing good to man; that our souls are immortal; and that all crime will be punished, and virtue rewarded, either here or hereafter. These I [deemed] the essentials of every religion; and, being to be found in all the religions we had in our country. . ."[50]

Thus, Franklin embraced the basic tenets of religious citizens in Pennsylvania.

> "I respected [every religion], [though] with different degrees of respect, as I found them more or less [mixed] with other articles, which, without any tendency to inspire, promote, or confirm morality, [served] principally to divide us, and make us unfriendly to one another. This respect to all, with an opinion that the worst had some good effects, [induced] me to avoid all discourse that might tend to lessen the good opinion another might have of his own religion; and as our province [increased] in people, and new places of worship were continually wanted, and generally erected by voluntary contributions, my mite for such purpose, whatever might be the sect, was never refused."[51]

Franklin supported freedom of religion and diversity, accepting all religious groups. However, he disliked the religious politics that divided religious groups into political factions. He promoted friendly relations between different religious congregations and continued to contribute money to religious groups that requested donations.

FREEMASONRY: A FRATERNITY TO "MAKE GOOD MEN BETTER"

In the late autumn of 1730, Franklin wrote articles on Freemasons in the *Pennsylvania Gazette*. At first he was critical but soon changed his mind. He was attracted by their overall philosophy. While encouraging their members to practice the religious faith of their choosing, they were encouraged on a path of self-improvement and helping others. Their purpose was, and continues to be, "to make a difference for good in the world." They seek to make "good men better." Members are encouraged "to become better men, better husbands, better fathers, and better citizens." This philosophy complemented Franklin's plan for self-improvement.

On February 1, 1731, one month after his twenty-fifth birthday, Benjamin Franklin joined the Freemasons. His fellow members of Philadelphia's St. John's Lodge included William Button, William Allen, Christopher Thompson, Thomas Hart, Samuel Nicholas, John Emerson, Thomas Hart, Thomas Boude, and William Pringle.[52]

Franklin learned that the Freemasons were a secret fraternity with roots back to the Middle Ages and ancient Egypt. Their important symbols included the pyramids and the eye of God, later seen on U.S. one dollar bills. In America, some Masonic groups also incorporated symbols and cultural traditions of American Indians.

Over the next thirty years, Franklin wrote their by-laws, published their writings, and rose to the position of Provincial Grand Master of Philadelphia. Other Americans who became members of Masonic groups included: Ethan Allen, Edmund Burke, John Claypoole, William Daws, John Hancock, John Paul Jones, Robert Livingston, Paul Revere, Colonel Benjamin Tupper and George Washington. American Indians who were Masons included the Iroquois leader, Tah-ge-jute and the Delaware leader Killbuck. Franklin later joined at least eight Masons in signing the Declaration of Independence and nine Masons in signing the U.S. Constitution. Today, the Freemasons are the oldest and largest fraternal organization in the world, with more than two million members in North America alone. They are dedicated to the "Brotherhood of Man under the Fatherhood of God."[53]

"DOCTRINE TO BE PREACHED"

In 1731, Benjamin Franklin wrote an essay entitled, "Doctrine to be Preached." Here he articulated his current religious sentiments:

> That there is one God Father of the Universe.
> That he is infinitely good, Powerful and wise.
> That he is omnipresent.
> That he ought to be worshipped, by Adoration Prayer and Thanksgiving both in [public] and private.

That he loves such of his Creatures as love and do good to others: and will reward them either in this World or hereafter.

That Men's Minds do not die with their Bodies, but are made more happy or miserable after this Life according to their Actions. That Virtuous Men ought to league together to strengthen the Interest of Virtue, in the World: and so strengthen themselves in Virtue.

That Knowledge and Learning is to be cultivated, and Ignorance dissipated.

That none but the Virtuous are wise.

That Man's Perfection is in Virtue.[54]

Franklin's religious beliefs at this point in his life expressed fundamental principles accepted by much of the general public. He envisioned the good influence of a global movement to inspire people toward greater virtues in life.

"COMPASSION AND REGARD FOR THE SICK"

Franklin sought to "practice what he preached" in writing an essay on promoting public support for medical care. In response to an outbreak of smallpox in the spring of 1731, he recounted how Jesus demonstrated model behavior in helping people who were sick or impaired:

The great Author of our Faith, whose Life should be the constant Object of our Imitation, as far as it is not inimitable, always [showed] the greatest Compassion and Regard for the SICK. . .[55]

Benjamin pointed out that Jesus helped even the "meanest of the People." He recalled the "beautiful parable" of the "Samaritan" who helped the traveler wounded by thieves. Franklin concluded:

This Branch of Charity seems essential to the true Spirit of Christianity; and it should be extended to all in general, whether deserving or undeserving, as far as our Power reaches.[56]

Franklin then encouraged his readers to contribute to the care of the sick, rich and poor, irrespective of their character. His call for public support was heard and acted upon through the eventual establishment of general hospitals dedicated to serving the medical needs of indigent patients.

Franklin's concern over public health became even more personal when his wife, Deborah, gave birth on October 20, 1732. They named their baby boy, Francis Folger Franklin. The child was baptized at Deborah's Anglican Christ Church.

THE PENNSYLVANIA GAZETTE, POOR RICHARD'S ALMANAC & SWEET SUCCESS

Benjamin worked hard to support his wife and family. His publication of the *Pennsylvania Gazette* was successful, although his first attempt at a German

language newspaper, *Philadelphische Zeitung,* failed. As an official colonial printer, he received jobs printing new laws and government publications. In 1732, he
supplemented his income by printing five outside jobs, including William
Bowman's *Traditions of the Clergy,* David Evan's *The Minister of Christ,* and
Conrad Beissel's German hymn book *Vorspiel der Neuen-Welt.*[57]

On August 14, 1732, Franklin wrote on the earlier contributions of William
Penn, the former governor of Pennsylvania, "above all his religious care in securing to all its inhabitants that natural Right, Liberty of Conscience, and Freedom
from Spiritual Tyranny." Franklin reported that William Penn's memory "must
ever remain dear to all those who set a just Value on the ample Privileges and
Liberties granted by him, and at this Time fully enjoyed by all the Inhabitants of
this flourishing Colony."[58]

Toward the end of the year, Franklin composed and published his first edition
of *Poor Richard,* a farmer's almanac providing a calendar of useful information
on daily times of sunrise and sunset, the cycles of the moon, recommendations
for planting and harvesting, as well as entertaining quotes on topics of interest
to the common man. The book was an overnight bestseller and was reprinted
three times in the first month. Franklin wrote the narrative of the almanac under
a pen name, Richard Saunders, and adopted the persona of a poor and honest
Pennsylvania farmer. He thanked his readers in each edition and offered sayings
of wit and wisdom, including:

> Early to bed and early to rise,
> makes a man healthy wealthy and wise.

> Little Strokes,
> Fell great Oaks.

> Haste makes Waste.

> Religion is like a Cheddar Cheese,
> 'tis made of the milk of one & twenty Parishes.

> He does not possess Wealth, it possesses him.

> Fish & Visitors stink in 3 days.

> God works wonders now & then;
> Behold! A Lawyer, an honest Man!

> God helps them that help themselves.

> A good Example is the best sermon.

> Without justice, courage is weak.

> A Man without a Wife is but half a Man.

> Take this remark from - Richard - poor and lame,
> Whatever's begun in anger ends in shame.[59]

Franklin sold 10,000 copies of his *Poor Richard's Almanack* a year, a bestseller second only to the Bible. He continued his almanac for twenty-five years, 1732-58. Contemporary versions are still popular and in print.

Franklin adopted a rigorous daily schedule that began with the introspective question: "What good shall I do this day?" He studied five languages: German, French, Italian, Spanish, Latin, as well as English. He began publishing pamphlets in foreign languages, while his *Pennsylvania Gazette* gained a reputation as "the best newspaper in America."

FRANKLIN & THE PRESBYTERIANS

In 1734, Franklin became a member of the Presbyterian Church, but he found the sermons of Rev. Jedediah Andrews uninspiring. However, a new assistant minister, Samuel Hemphill from the University of Glasgow in Scotland, captured Benjamin's attention with his sermons on practical morals. However, in less than a year, Rev. Hemphill stood accused of heresy. He encouraged "free-thinking," a concept considered unorthodox and dangerous by Rev. Andrews and Church elders. They accused Reverend Hemphill of preaching "heterodox sermons," then a punishable offense. The Church council ordered him to stop, but he spoke out on the grounds of religious freedom. He was charged with "erroneous teaching" and his case sent to trial. Franklin became a strong supporter of Rev. Hemphill and championed his cause. Benjamin described Hemphill as "a young Presbyterian preacher . . . with a good voice, and apparently extempore, most excellent discourses, which drew together considerable numbers of different persuasions." Hemphill's sermons, Franklin continued, had "little of the dogmatical kind, but inculcated strongly the practice of virtue, or what in the religious style are called good works." What attracted Franklin, as a fellow freethinker, was considered dangerous by Orthodox Church leaders. Franklin explained, "I became his zealous partisan, and contributed all I could to raise a party in his favor, and we combated for him a while with some hopes of success." Franklin defended Hemphill, stating that a "virtuous heretic shall be saved before a wicked Christian."

In April 1735, Franklin published in the *Pennsylvania Gazette* an article entitled "A Dialogue Between Two of the Presbyterians Meeting in this City." The first Presbyterian asked Rev. Hemphill's critic:

> S. I am sorry we should differ in Opinion upon any Account; but let us reason the Point calmly; what Offence does Mr. [Hemphill]. give you?
>
> T. Tis his Preaching disturbs me: He talks of nothing but the Duties of Morality: I do not love to hear so much of Morality: I am sure it will carry no Man to Heaven, and I do not think it fit to be preached in a Christian Congregation.
>
> S. I do not conceive then how you can dislike the Preaching of Morality, when you consider, that Morality made the principal Part of their Preaching as well as of Mr. [Hemphill's]. What is Christ's Sermon on the Mount but an excellent moral Discourse?[60]

However, in the end, Rev. Hemphill was convicted of heresy and run out of town. Franklin charged Hemphill's accusers with "pious fraud . . . bigotry, and prejudice" and left the church, never to return.[61]

Benjamin suffered another loss in 1735, when his brother James passed away. Benjamin and Deborah reached out to help provide aid to their brother's widow and James, Jr., their nephew. James, Jr. soon came to live with Benjamin and Deborah for more than the next ten years. Benjamin continued to provide financial assistance to his brother's widow and family for three decades.

Death visited the Franklin family again. On November 21, 1736, Benjamin and Deborah buried their four-year-old son, Francis Folger Franklin, at Christ Church cemetery. He reportedly died from smallpox. The parents took the loss of "Little Franky" especially hard, because they had failed to provide their son with the new smallpox inoculation. They commissioned a portrait painting of their departed son so that his image might live on forever.

Benjamin thrust himself into civil service. He became clerk of the Pennsylvania General Assembly and Deputy Postmaster-General. He planned the city police department and founded the Union Fire Company of Philadelphia.

In 1738, he wrote a letter to his father, explaining his religious views:

> I think vital religion has always suffered when orthodoxy is more regard-
> ed than virtue. The scriptures assure me that at the last day we shall not
> be examined on what we thought but what we did.[62]

Benjamin's comments reflected his sentiments in the wake of the Rev. Hemphill affair. Franklin hit a brick wall against the staunch position of orthodox Presbyterian leaders. He believed in free speech for ministers and encouraged themes of morals and virtues as beneficial to a positive public spirit.

REV. GEORGE WHITEFIELD AND THE GREAT AWAKENING

In the summer of 1739, Benjamin Franklin printed "The Art of Preaching" and Elizabeth's Rowe's *History of Joseph*, in addition to *Poor Richard's Almanack* and the weekly *Pennsylvania Gazette*. Finally he began, by subscription, an extremely successful printing venture, the journals and sermons of Rev. George Whitefield (1714-1770), the charismatic traveling revivalist preacher.[63] Whitefield was a leader in the first religious revival movement called the "Great Awakening." In November of 1739, Rev. Whitefield preached for four nights in a row in front of the Philadelphia Courthouse, attracting crowds estimated at over 6,000 people. Earlier that summer he had addressed crowds upward of 23,000 in England, and since he had begun preaching three years earlier, an estimated two million people had listened to his message. The result was the establishment of hundreds of new churches and hundreds of thousands of followers, a fact that threatened the official leadership of the Church of England. Edward's wife Sarah wrote, "It is wonderful to see how he casts a spell over the audience by proclaim-ing the simplest truths of the Bible . . ."

On November 28 at his last Philadelphia sermon, the crowds swelled to over 10,000, requiring the gathering to be moved to larger open fields. A great dust cloud formed around the city, as thousands raced in on horseback from the countryside. Rev. Whitefield was said to be with God; therefore, the people swarmed to be in His presence, listening to the Reverend speak of Jesus Christ:

> Matthew 1:21, And she shall bring forth a Son, and then shalt call his Name Jesus: For he shall save his People from their Sins.
>
> The celebration of the birth of Christ hath been esteemed a duty by most who profess Christianity. When we consider the condescension and love of the Lord Jesus Christ, in submitting to be born of a virgin, a poor sinful creature; and especially as he knew how he was to be treated in this world; that he was to be despised, scoffed at, and at last to die a painful, shameful, and ignominious death; that he should be treated as though he was the off-scouring of all mankind; used, not like the son of man, and, therefore, not at all like the Son of God; the consideration of these things should make us to admire the love of the Lord Jesus Christ, who was so willing to offer himself as a ransom for the sins of the people, that when the fullness of time was come, Christ came, made [born] of a woman, made under the law: he came according to the eternal counsel of the Father; he came, not in glory or in splendor, not like him who brought all salvation with him: no, he was born in a stable, and laid in a manger; oxen were his companions. O amazing condescension of the Lord Jesus Christ, to stoop to such low and poor things for our sake. What love is this, what great and wonderful love was here, that the Son of God should come into our world in so mean a condition, to deliver us from the sin and misery in which we were involved by our fall in our first parents! And as all that proceeded from the springs must be muddy, because the fountain was so, the Lord Jesus Christ came to take our natures upon him, to die a shameful, a painful, and an accursed death for our sakes; he died for our sins, and to bring us to God: he cleansed us by his blood from the guilt of sin, he satisfied for our imperfections; and now, my brethren, we have access unto him with boldness; he is a mediator between us and his offended Father . . .[64]

Rev. Whitefield preached for over an hour, speaking with such powerful conviction as to excite his audience with feelings of spiritual exaltation and even ecstasy. He assured his followers that they could travel a path in life that would lead to freedom on Earth and eternal life in Heaven.

Benjamin Franklin met and befriended Rev. Whitefield. Franklin was so impressed that he contributed all the silver and gold coins in his pockets to Whitefield's humanitarian causes. Franklin recognized Rev. Whitefield as one of the "finest prose stylists," and agreed to print his journals and sermons. Franklin raced to set type for the presses and to advertise the series. By the time of Rev. Whitefield's farewell address, on November 28, Franklin had already sold over 200 subscriptions to the series. Sales soared quickly into the thousands, resulting in an "overnight bestseller."

Rev. Whitefield proceeded on his American tour, preaching along the Atlantic coast in almost "every Province in America." Hundreds of thousands were enraptured by his message, many became "reborn" as Christians, and hundreds of churches formed in his wake. America's first "born-again" religious movement became known as the "Great Awakening." Rev. Jonathan Edwards in Northampton, MA had ignited the movement five years earlier, in 1734. However, Rev. Whitefield accelerated and spread the movement through his successful evangelical tour.

By 1740, the population of the American colonies was estimated to be 889,000. Changes began to take place in locations where Rev. Whitefield had held his audiences "spellbound by his fervour and dramatic action." The powerful effect of Rev. Whitefield and the Great Awakening was to unite the "nation spiritually as community after community were moved by his sermons." His simple teachings of the gospel appealed to the masses and transcended denominational groups of Presbyterians, Congregationalists, Episcopalians, Catholics, Quakers, Moravians, and more. Rev. Whitefield overcame the old European religious divisions and united Americans behind a "common experience of faith."

On June 12, Benjamin Franklin reported in the *Pennsylvania Gazette* on the "Religious Mood in Philadelphia":

> During the Session of the Presbyterian Synod, which began on the 28th of the last Month, and continued to the third of this Instant, there were no less than 14 Sermons preached on Society-Hill to large Audiences, by the Rev. Messrs. the Tennents, Mr. Davenport, Mr. Rowland and Mr. Blair, besides what were delivered at the Presbyterian and Baptist Meetings, and Expoundings and Exhortations in private Houses. The Alteration in the Face of Religion here is altogether surprising. Never did the People show so great a Willingness to attend Sermons, nor the Preachers greater Zeal and Diligence in performing the Duties of their Function. Religion is become the Subject of most Conversations. No Books are in Request but those of Piety and Devotion; and instead of idle Songs and Ballads, the People are everywhere entertaining themselves with Psalms, Hymns and Spiritual Songs. All which, under God, is owing to the successful Labours of the Reverend Mr. Whitefield.[65]

In the year 1740, Franklin published over 40 imprints, mostly on religion, the largest number in his printing career. He printed two volumes of sermons and two volumes of journals written by Rev. Whitefield. Franklin also printed texts by six other ministers, including Gilbert Tennet, Samuel Finley, Sir Matthew Hale, Josiah Smith, and Isaac Watt.

"RELATING TO THE DIVINE PRESENCE"

Benjamin Franklin expanded his publishing efforts by creating a *General Magazine* for the American readers. In 1741, he published a letter under a pen name, Theophilus, "Relating to the Divine Presence":

> There is a Question in the Schools, and I think generally resolved in the Affirmative; Whether God concurs with all human Actions or not? . . . God acts directly and immediately in them and by them; that he pro-

duces all the Acts of Thinking, and all the Volitions or Acts of Willing; and that he has from all Eternity decreed . . . So that whoever denies God's immediate Concourse with every Action we produce, must of Consequence deny God's Foreknowledge.[66]

Franklin encouraged his readers to respond in creating a dialogue on the topic of God's "Divine Presence" and His daily influence on our lives. Franklin extended his theological beliefs to accept God's knowledge of the past, present, and future. He republished his philosophy on "Thirteen Virtues," reflecting his thinking that God's grace came through virtuous acts and good works.

Benjamin Franklin demonstrated his commitment to good works. He proposed an educational academy that led to the founding of the University of Pennsylvania, establishing an important institution for higher education. For the benefit of the common man, he invented the Franklin stove. This practical invention served Americans for generations. His good works brought many blessings, including greater prosperity and the birth of his daughter, Sarah, who became known as Sally Franklin.

On May 14, 1743, Benjamin Franklin published, "A Proposal for Promoting Useful Knowledge." This served as the founding document and prototype for the American Philosophical Society, an intellectual organization dedicated to the study of philosophy, theology, and science. The original members included nine from Philadelphia: lawyer Thomas Hopkinson served as President, Franklin was the first Secretary, along with botanist John Bartram, mathematician Thomas Godfrey, surveyor William Parsons, physicians Dr. Thomas Bond and Dr. Phineas Bond, merchant William Coleman, as well as Samuel Rhoads, who later served as a delegate to the Continental Congress. Four of the original members were from New Jersey: Chief Justice Morris, Mr. Home, John Coxe, and Mr. Martyn. Two members came from New York: Cadwallader Colden and William Alexander.[67]

EXPLAINING HIS RELIGIOUS BELIEFS TO HIS SISTER

On July 28, 1743, Benjamin Franklin wrote a response to his sister, Jane Mecom, who had expressed concern regarding her brother's religious beliefs. Franklin stated in part:

> Dearest Sister . . . You express yourself as if you thought I was against Worshipping of God, and believed Good Works would merit Heaven; which are both Fancies of your own, I think, without Foundation. I am so far from thinking that God is not to be worshipped, that I have [composed] and wrote a whole Book of Devotions for my own Use . . .Read the Pages of Mr. [Jonathan] Edward's late Book entitled SOME THOUGHTS CONCERNING THE PRESENT REVIVAL OF RELIGION IN NE. [New England] from 367 to 375; and when you judge of others, if you can perceive the Fruit to be good, don't terrify your self that the Tree may be evil, but be [assured] it is not so; for you know who has said, Men do not gather Grapes of Thorns or Figs of Thistles. I have not

time to add but that I shall always be Your affectionate Brother.[68]

Franklin defended his religious faith. He urged his sister not to believe rumors that came from his critics.

Franklin further urged her to read Jonathan Edwards' book on the religious revival in New England. If she followed his advice, she read from Edwards' text regarding the human soul:

> The soul often entertained, with unspeakable delight, the thoughts of heaven, as a world of love; where love shall be the saints' eternal food, where they shall dwell in the light, and swim in an ocean of love, and where the very air and breath will be nothing but love; love to the people of God, or God's true saints, as having the image of Christ, and as those who will in a very little time shine in his perfect image.[69]

Benjamin advocated the religious philosophy of the Great Awakening. He expressed his love for God, for the world and for his sister. He further joined Edwards in accepting Jesus Christ and seeking salvation for human souls.

In 1745, his family mourned two deaths. Benjamin's father, Josiah Franklin, passed away at the age of eighty-seven. His will divided his estate between his wife and nine children. His obituary appeared in the newspaper:

> Last night [16 Jan] died Mr. Josiah Franklin, Tallow-Chandler and Soap-maker. By the Force of a steady Temperance he had made a Constitution, naturally none of the strongest, last with comfort to the Age of Eighty-seven Years; and by an entire Dependence of his Redeemer and a constant Course of the strictest Piety and Virtue, he was enabled to die, as he [lived], with [cheerfulness] and Peace, leaving a numerous Posterity the Honour of being descended from a Person, who [through] a long Life supported the Character of an Honest Man.[70]

Benjamin's brother-in-law, Captain Robert Holmes, then drowned in a storm in the Boston harbor. Shortly thereafter, Benjamin thrust himself into his work and began his famous scientific experiments on electricity.

"APPRECIATION OF GEORGE WHITEFIELD"

In 1746, he published five sermons by Rev. George Whitefield, the charismatic Christian evangelist. On July 31, Franklin wrote a review in the *Pennsylvania Gazette* entitled "Appreciation of George Whitefield."

> On Sunday the 20th Instant, the Rev. Mr. Whitefield [preached] twice, [though] apparently much [indisposed], to large Congregations in the New-Building in this City, and the next Day set out for New-York. When we seriously consider how incessantly this faithful Servant (not yet 32 Years old) has, for about 10 Years past, laboured in his great Master's Vineyard, with an Alacrity and fervent Zeal, which an infirm Constitution, still daily declining, cannot abate; and which have triumphed over the most vigorous Opposition from whole Armies of invidious Preachers and

Pamphleteers; under whose Performances, the Pulpits and Presses, of Great Britain and America, have groaned; We may reasonably think with the learned Dr. Watts, "That he is a Man raised up by Providence in an uncommon Way, to awaken a stupid and ungodly World, to a Sense of the important Affairs of Religion and Eternity:" And the Lines of Mr. Wesley, concerning another young Methodist, may justly be applied to his dear Friend Whitefield.

> Wise in his Prime, he waited not for Noon,
> [Convinced] that Mortals never liv'd too soon;
> As if foreboding here his little Stay,
> He makes his Morning bear the Heat of Day.
> No fair Occasion glides unheeded by,
> Snatching the Golden Moments as they fly,
> He by few fleeting Hours ensures Eternity.

His Sermons here this summer have given general Satisfaction, and plainly proved the great Ability of the Preacher. His rich Fancy, sound and ripening Judgment, and extensive Acquaintance with Men and Books of useful Literature, have been [acknowledged] by every unprejudiced Person. Purity of Language, Perspicuity of Method, a ready Elocution, an engaging Address, and an apt Gesture, peculiar to this [accomplished] Orator, [considered] with his unspotted Character in private Life, have added Force to the plain strong Arguments, and [pathetic] Expostulations, wherewith his Discourses abounded. And, it cannot be doubted, that many have been [awakened] to a Sense of the Importance of Religion, and others have been built up in their most holy Christian Faith under his Ministry.[71]

The many readers of the *Pennsylvania Gazette* read Franklin's high praise of Rev. Whitefield. Its purpose was to address his critics and to promote the sale of his sermons and journals. Franklin's observation — that "many have been awakened" — exemplified the powerful religious movement, the "Great Awakening." As previously stated, thousands of people became more active Christians and hundreds of new churches were built throughout the American colonies. More religious writings were printed in America, as religion became more popular.

"NATURE OF THE HUMAN SOUL," "PLAIN TRUTH," AND "THE NECESSITY OF SELF-DEFENSE"

On October 16, Benjamin wrote a letter to Philadelphia lawyer and fellow Mason, Thomas Hopkinson. The topic of Franklin's letter was a refutation of Andrew Baxter's "Enquiry into the Nature of the Human Soul" [1737]. Baxter's subtitle was "Wherein the Immateriality of the Soul Is Evinced from the Principles of Reason and Philosophy." Franklin expounded on his own theories regarding the "Creation of the World."

If God was before all Things, and [filled] all Space; then, when he [formed] what we call Matter, he must have done it out of his own Thinking immaterial Substance. The same, [though] he had not [filled] all Space; if it be true that Ex nihilo nihil fit [Nothing begets nothing]. From hence may we not draw this Conclusion, That if any Part of Matter does not at present act and think, 'tis not from an Incapacity in its Nature but from a positive Restraint.[72]

Baxter was a moral and natural philosopher from Scotland. His thesis was articulated by Lord Woodhouselee, "There is a resistance to any change of its present state, either of rest or motion, essential to matter, which is inconsistent with its possessing any active power." Franklin countered that he believed that all matter possessed "active power" in the form of a "positive restraint." This idea would later relate to his study of electricity.

On December 29, Benjamin Franklin wrote *Plain Truth* and published an anonymous letter, "The Necessity of Self-Defense," in support of his organization of the first Pennsylvania militia. The letter used religious precedence from Rev. George Tennent's recent sermon to justify the establishment of the militia:

When it is considered that some Kinds of War were held lawful amongst the primitive Christians, as appears evidently from many of the ancient Martyrs, who suffered Torture and Death, for their Faith in Jesus, and Constancy to the Christian Religion . . . Use was to be made of Swords; but it has been already shewn that Christianity was not to be forced upon People by the Sword: What better Use then remains, than the [defense] of our Country, and the Protection of the Helpless and Innocent?[73]

The issue of establishing a public militia grew controversial among various religious groups. The Quakers generally opposed a standing army on religious grounds. Political forces mounted in support of the plan. When the militia was created, Franklin declined a position as colonel, saying he was too inexperienced, and instead accepted the rank of common soldier.

PERSONAL SUCCESS & PUBLIC SERVICE

On January 1, 1748, Benjamin Franklin formed a partnership in his printing business with David Hall who assumed management of the print shop. Hall did the work, and they split the profits. Franklin became financially secure from the combined income of his half interest in the printing business added to his income from real estate investments and his salary as postmaster. His annual gross income in the coming years grew to over 5,000 pounds sterling per annum.

Benjamin devoted his time to two major activities: scientific/scholarly studies and public service. He served on the Common Council, the Pennsylvania Assembly, and Commission on the Peace.

In 1748, at the age of forty-two, Franklin proposed a public day of fasting. He delivered his most famous quote on religion when he stated:

It is the duty of mankind on all suitable occasions to acknowledge their dependence on the Divine Being . . .[74]

This quote appears frequently in the literature in defense of public prayer. Because public prayer later became, and remains today, an important Constitutional issue, Franklin's sentiments have been judged germane to the topic.

Examination of the larger quote further illuminates Franklin's feelings that faith in God might help end wars between nations:

> Almighty God would mercifully interpose and still the rage of war among the nations and would put a stop to the effusion of Christian blood . . . [that] He would take this province under His protection, confound the designs and defeat the attempts of its enemies, and unite our hearts and strengthen our hands in every undertaking that may be for the public good, and for our defense and security in this time of danger.[75]

Recognizing that more people have been killed in the name of religion than perhaps any other reason, Franklin called upon God's mercy to stop the bloodshed. Conflicts with European roots had spilled over into the American colonies. His study of history had taught him the importance of seeking the public good, and he recognized the relevance of fasting and prayer as a means of achieving those laudable ends. As he matured, Franklin clearly changed his religious viewpoints from deism to more complex religious beliefs. He concluded that God would intercede in the affairs of humanity.

MORAL TEACHINGS OF RELIGIOUS REFORMERS: FROM JESUS CHRIST TO CONFUCIUS

A sense of optimism swept over Franklin in 1749 as he began to ponder how men of power might be influenced to become more moral. He wanted powerful men to act more for the common good of society instead of their own selfish ends for power and wealth. He wondered if dynamic religious leaders could influence powerful civic leaders to become better public servants. He considered the effectiveness of religious reformers throughout history from Jesus Christ to Confucius.

On July 6, 1749, Benjamin Franklin penned his ideas to Rev. George Whitefield:

> I am glad to hear that you have frequent opportunities of preaching among the great. If you can gain them to a good and exemplary life, wonderful changes will follow in the manners of the lower ranks; for, ad Exemplum Regis, &c. On this principle Confucius, the famous eastern reformer, proceeded. When he saw his country sunk in vice, and wickedness of all kinds triumphant, he applied himself first to the grandees; and having by his doctrine won them to the cause of virtue, the commons followed in multitudes. The mode has a wonderful influence on mankind; and there are numbers that perhaps fear less the being in Hell, than out of the fashion! Our more western reformations began with the ignorant mob; and when numbers of them were gained, interest and party-views

drew in the wise and great. Where both methods can be used, reformations are like to be more speedy. O that some method could be found to make them lasting! He that shall discover that, will, in my opinion, deserve more, ten thousand times, than the inventor of the longitude.[76]

Thus, Franklin concluded that a religious reformation in which good men were inspired to be good public servants might have a more beneficial influence on society as a whole, even greater than the impact of important scientific inventions.

To cultivate a society of good men who acted as good public servants, Franklin promoted the establishment of a Pennsylvania academy dedicated to public education. He advocated a liberal education on "everything useful," including writing, drawing, accounting, geometry, astronomy, grammar, reading the Classics and great writers, public speaking, history, chronology, geography, morality, foreign languages, and more. In his 1749 essay on "Proposals Relating to the Education of Youth in Pennsylvania," Franklin wrote in part:

> History will also afford frequent Opportunities of showing the Necessity of a [Public] Religion, from its Usefulness to the [Public]; the Advantage of a Religious Character among private Persons; the Mischiefs of Superstition . . . and the Excellency of the CHRISTIAN RELIGION above all others [ancient] or modern.[77]

Benjamin Franklin directly stated that Christianity, in his personal opinion, was "above all others." His advocacy held special weight because he chose to include it in his proposal for creating a public school. The institution grew into the University of Pennsylvania. America's early colleges, including Harvard, Yale, and others, were established as Christian colleges where ministers were trained along with future lawyers, politicians, and members of other professions.

FRANKLIN AS INDIAN AFFAIRS COMMISSIONER

In furtherance on his public service, Benjamin Franklin accepted an important appointment as Commissioner to trade with American Indians. On March 20, 1750, Franklin wrote a letter on the significance of Indian affairs to James Parker, his printing partner in the *New York Gazette:*

> . . . securing the Friendship of the Indians is of the greatest Consequence to these Colonies; and that the surest Means of doing it, are, to regulate the Indian Trade, so as to convince them, by Experience, that they may have the best and cheapest Goods, and the fairest Dealing from the English; and to unite the several Governments, so as to form a Strength that the Indians may depend on for Protection, in Case of a Rupture with the French; or apprehend great Danger from, if they should break with us.[78]

Franklin's prominent role in colonial Indian affairs has been well documented. He generally advocated fair dealings with American Indians, in contrast with the shameless record of other colonial authorities who broke treaties, stole lands, raped, and pillaged Native Americans with general impunity from the law. The most despicable early acts included offering cash bounties for Indian scalps, kidnapping, enslavement, torture, and murder. Franklin sought to replace policies of genocide with policies of fair trade, honest dealings, peace, and friendship.[79]

The early history of Indian affairs from 1492 to 1750 has not yet been fully written, but was a topic of great interest to Benjamin Franklin.[80] His knowledge was developed by his publication of the transcripts of colonial Indian treaties. He printed numerous letters, reports, and articles on Indian affairs in the *Pennsylvania Gazette*. He also printed some of the writings of Count Nicolaus Ludwig von Zinzendorf (1700-1760), a preacher of the United Brethren of Moravian missionaries, German speaking Protestant pacifists. Moravian missionaries, including Rev. David Zeisberger and Rev. John Heckewelder, lived with the Indians, compiled dictionaries and translated Biblical teachings into various Indian languages. They kept detailed diaries of their centers of refuge for displaced Christian Indians, providing a fascinating historical record of daily life on the frontier.[81]

Franklin personally met with Christian Indians, as well as with many delegations of traditional American Indian leaders who regularly visited Philadelphia to meet and negotiate with the Governor and the Pennsylvania Assembly. He learned that American Indians spoke many different languages and were from hundreds of different tribes or nations. The Iroquois Confederacy of Six Nations, as well as the Lenni Lenape [Delawares] and their Algonquian allies, were the most powerful American Indians related to his role as Pennsylvania's Commissioner to trade with American Indians. Indian trade goods included the finest deerskin for covering leather-bound books and herbal medicines for treating scores of different illnesses and medical conditions. Medicinal remedies were personally important to Franklin, who suffered from an inflammation of the joints called gout and other illnesses.

In return, Euro-Americans offered American Indians manufactured goods such as pots, pans, knives, blankets, cloth, sewing kits, silver jewelry, trade beads, and guns. Franklin's professional experience as an international importer made him ideal as an Indian trade commissioner. His interest in the history, manners, and customs of different American Indian cultures reflected both his intellectual curiosity regarding the origins of humanity in North America, as well as his need to better understand the people with whom he was trading. Disruptions in American Colonial — Indian relations were due largely to greed for Indian land and ignorance of Native American cultures. Here was found the root of racism. The solution to ignorance in colonial society, Franklin concluded, was public education.[82]

FRANKLIN ON THE IMPORTANCE OF PUBLIC EDUCATION

He continued his pursuit of promoting public education throughout the rest of his life. On August 23, 1750, from Philadelphia, Franklin wrote to Dr. Samuel Johnson (October 14, 1696-January 6, 1772), the first President of

King's College (now Columbia University), regarding education:

> I think with you, that nothing is of more importance for the public weal,
> than to form and train up youth in wisdom and virtue . . . I think also,
> general virtue is more probably to be expected and obtained from the
> education of youth, than from the exhortation of adult persons; bad habits
> and vices of the mind being, like diseases of the body, more easily prevent-
> ed than cured. I think, moreover, that talents for the education of youth
> are the gift of God; and that he on whom they are bestowed, whenever a
> way is opened for the use of them, is as strongly called as if he heard a
> voice from heaven.[83]

In 1751, Benjamin Franklin published his essay, "Observations Concerning
the Increase of Mankind," perhaps the most influential essay written by an
American colonist. In comparing the growth of Europe with growth in North
America, Franklin observed:

> Europe is generally full settled with Husbandmen, Manufacturers, etc. and
> therefore cannot now much increase in People: America is chiefly occupied
> by Indians, who subsist mostly by Hunting. But as the Hunter, of all Men,
> requires the greatest Quantity of Land from whence to draw his
> Subsistence, (the Husbandman subsisting on much less, the Gardner on
> still less, and the Manufacturer requiring least of all), The Europeans
> found America as fully settled as it well could be by Hunters; yet these
> having large Tracks, were easily [prevailed] on to part with Portions of
> Territory to the new Comers, who did not much interfere with the
> Natives in Hunting, and [furnished] them with many Things they
> wanted.[84]

Colonial Indian treaties addressed two main negotiations: trade and land.
Franklin recognized that these treaties were important to the future growth of
American colonies. His essay was like a blueprint for promoting peaceful future
development, a subject of great value and interest to his readers.

ELECTRICITY AND OTHER SCIENTIFIC EXPERIMENTS

In 1751, Benjamin Franklin also found a large audience for his book,
Experiments and Observations on Electricity. His practical solution to the dangers
of lightning was the invention of a lightning rod with proper grounding. His
experiments had not been without risk, as he suffered several severe electrical
shocks. The following year he performed his famous kite experiment, proving that
lightning was an electrical discharge.

In 1752, Benjamin Franklin acknowledged his study of a treatise, "An
Explication of the First Causes of Action in Matter" by the American philosopher Dr. Cadwallader Colden (1688-1776). In a pursuit to understand the
physics of matter, Dr. Colden theorized:

> All our knowledge of things consists in the perception of the power, or
> force, or property, or manner of acting of that thing . . . Every thing, that

we know, is an agent, or has a power of acting: for as we know nothing of any thing but its action, and the effects of that action, the moment any thing ceases to act it must be annihilated as to us: we can have no kind of idea of its existence.[85]

Franklin shared with Dr. Colden an interest in the nature of power. What is power or the force that acts within the universe? This was a mystery they sought to understand. Franklin balanced his scientific experiments with the study of political science.

Franklin was elected to the Pennsylvania Assembly and served as an alderman of Philadelphia. In his continued public service, he founded the first American fire insurance company. He also worked toward the establishment of the Pennsylvania Hospital. Growing respect for his service to his community, colony, and nation was a source of pride for his family. He saved his brother John's life by designing a flexible catheter to help him pass a bladder stone. However, he found no cure for old age, and his mother Abiah Folger Franklin passed away on May 8, 1752 at the age eighty-four.

For his revolutionary scientific discoveries on the study of electricity, Benjamin Franklin was awarded in 1753 the prestigious Copley Medal, the highest award from the Royal Society of London. The award was comparable to winning a Nobel Prize. Franklin received Master's degrees from Yale and Harvard. He also was appointed joint Postmaster-General.

FRANKLIN'S RELIGIOUS VIEWS IN 1753

On June 6, 1753, Franklin wrote a letter on his religious views to his Pennsylvanian friend, Joseph Huey:

> For my own part, when I am employed in serving others, I do not look upon myself as conferring favours, but as paying debts. In my travels and since my settlement I have received much kindness from men, to whom I shall never have any opportunity of making the least direct return. And numberless mercies from God, who is infinitely above being benefited by our services. These kindnesses from men I can therefore only return on their fellow-men; and I can only show my gratitude for those mercies from God, by a readiness to help his other children and my brethren. For I do not think that thanks, and compliments, though repeated weekly, can discharge our real obligations to each other, and much less those to our Creator?[86]

Public service was performed with God's mercy. Helping others was a way of showing gratitude "for those mercies from God." Franklin criticized those who thought that simply going through the motions would suffice, and challenged them to perform true acts of kindness.

Benjamin explained his personal views regarding "good works." He advocated sincere charity with a lively "publick spirit":

> The faith you mention has doubtless its use in the world; I do not desire

> to see it diminished, nor would I endeavour to lessen it in any man. But I
> wish it were more productive of good works than I have generally seen it:
> I mean real good works, works of kindness, charity, mercy, and publick
> spirit; not holiday-keeping, sermon-reading or hearing, performing
> church ceremonies, or making long prayers, filled with flatteries or com-
> pliments, despised even by wise men, and much less capable of pleasing
> the deity. The worship of God is a duty, the hearing and reading of sermons
> may be useful; but if men rest in hearing and praying, as too many do, it
> is as if a tree should value itself on being watered and putting forth leaves,
> though it never produced any fruit.[87]

Franklin was direct in challenging local religious leaders to speak to the needs of
the common man. Their intellectual sermons were out of pace with the growing
American society. Americans should not rest on their laurels; they should multiply
and bear fruit.

Franklin divided people into to groups — the "hearers" and the "doers." It
was not enough to simply listen to sermons; they must do something to benefit
society:

> Your great Master thought much less of these outward appearances and
> professions than many of his modern disciples. He preferred the doers of
> the word to the mere hearers; the son that seemingly refused to obey his
> Father and yet performed his commands, to him that professed his readiness
> but neglected the works; the heretical but charitable Samaritan, to the
> uncharitable though orthodox priest and sanctified Levite; and those who
> gave food to the hungry, drink to the thirsty, raiment to the naked, enter-
> tainment to the stranger, and relief to the sick, etc. though they never
> heard of his name, he declares shall in the last day be accepted, when those
> who cry Lord, Lord; who value themselves on their faith though great
> enough to perform miracles but have neglected good works shall be
> rejected.[88]

Franklin recounted the unselfish acts of the Good Samaritan. This kind and
sincere person was a good role model for Pennsylvanians. How would society
change for the better if more people became Good Samaritans?

THE 1753 CARLISLE INDIAN TREATY

In the autumn of 1753, Benjamin Franklin, Richard Peters, and Isaac Norris
were called into service to represent Pennsylvania at an important treaty conference
with American Indian leaders. The main topic was the need for a mutual defense
against the French. Reports from young George Washington and others warned
that the French were establishing military forts in the rich Ohio River Valley. In
the competition between France and Great Britain over the most bountiful lands
in America, the territory held strategic importance to the military. For real estate
developers, who were behind the scenes, the Ohio lands potentially were worth
a fortune. Franklin and the Pennsylvania delegation's primary concern was to
protect Pennsylvania's western frontier. Franklin advocated a defensive alliance

and fair trade agreements with the Indians.

The Indian leaders who attended the treaty conference, September 26-October 4, 1753, complained that the French forts constituted an invasion of sovereign Indian lands. French forces had directly attacked a village of Twightwees [Miami] Indians. The Oneida Indian Chief Scarroyady [meaning "From the Other Side of the Sky"] represented the Iroquois Confederacy of Six Nations. The old chief complained also about unscrupulous traders and bootleggers who were corrupting the Indians:

> Your traders now bring us scarce any Thing but Rum and Flour. They bring us little Powder and Lead, or other valuable Goods. The rum ruins us. We beg you would prevent its coming in such Quantities, by regulating the Traders . . . We desire it be forbidden, and none sold in the Indian Country . . . Those wicked Whiskey Sellers, when they have once got the Indians in Liquor, make them sell their very Clothes from their Backs.[89]

Franklin and the Pennsylvania delegation agreed with Scarroyady's assessment, reporting "That the traders are under no Bonds . . . and by their own Intemperance, unfair Dealings and Irregularities will, it is to be feared, entirely estrange the affections of the Indians from the English."

After Franklin returned to Philadelphia, he published in November the proceedings of the 1753 Carlisle Treaty conference. The experience marked the beginnings of Franklin's diplomatic career. The outcome of the treaty underscored the need for the American colonies to unite in a defensive alliance. In an earlier letter to James Parker, Franklin recognized that the Iroquois Six Nations had succeeded in creating a model alliance of United Nations:

> It would be a very strange thing if Six Nations of [so-called] Ignorant Savages should be capable of forming a Scheme for such an Union and be able to execute it in such a manner, as that it has subsisted Ages, and appears indissoluble, and yet a like Union should be impracticable for ten or a dozen English colonies.[90]

Franklin had observed firsthand how intelligent and powerful the Iroquois really were. He had his tongue in his cheek when he called them "Ignorant Savages," a derogatory phrase used by colonial racists. He sought to challenge other Americans to unite in a way the Indians proved possible. The political structure of the Iroquois Confederacy was in fact a participatory democracy. Franklin and other colonial Americans did not have to look to European philosophers who only dreamed of popular liberty. The model for a united democratic government was there in America for all to see among the Iroquois and other democratic Indian governments. Franklin had read a history of the Iroquois written by Dr. Cadwallader Colden, the American philosopher and scholar:

> Each [Iroquois] nation is an absolute republic by itself, governed in all public affairs of war and peace by the Sachems of old men whose authority and power is gained by, and consists wholly in, the opinions of the rest of the Nation in their wisdom and integrity. They never execute their resolutions

by compulsion or force upon any of their people. Honor and esteem are their principle rewards as shame and being despised are their punishments.[91]

Franklin praised the Iroquois, noting, "Happiness is more generally and equally diffused . . . than in our [so-called] civilized societies."[92]

ALBANY PLAN OF UNION

In 1754, as the French and Indian Wars entered their final chapter, both the French and English forces recognized the importance of the Iroquois, the Lenni Lenape, and their other Indian allies to the balance of power on the American frontier. Benjamin Franklin studied and reported on Indian affairs extensively. Franklin listened carefully to eloquent Iroquois leaders like the elderly Oneida Chief Scarroyady, who, after the Carlisle Treaty, traveled to negotiate successfully the release of Shawnee Indian hostages with the Governor of Virginia. The wise old sachem visited Philadelphia on his return trip, giving Franklin another opportunity to learn about the remarkable Iroquois history and culture. Their religion and democratic government was based on teachings of the "Great Law of Peace" laid down by the "Great Peacemaker," who inspired their warriors to "bury the hatchet" and to plant a sacred "Tree of Peace." Franklin and other colonials recognized the powerful symbolism of the story in creating their "Tree of Liberty." Within the Great Law of Peace is laid out the original plans for establishing a native "United Nations." Within their Grand Council of 50 chiefs and clan mothers one finds a three-part structure, a model for executive, legislative, and judicial branches of government with a system of checks and balances. The Great Law of Peace was brilliant and later was officially recognized by the United States Congress as a model for the United States Constitution. The Peacemaker's plan to unite the Iroquois nations bears striking parallels with Benjamin Franklin's ideas in shaping the Albany Plan of Union.[93]

Franklin took the position that if the Iroquois could create and maintain for centuries a united Six Nations, then the American colonists should be able to create a "United Colonies." In 1754, Franklin was appointed to be one of the Commissioners from Pennsylvania to the Colonial Congress at Albany, New York, located near the site of the Iroquois Grand Council at Onondaga. In June, the representatives from seven colonies convened for the purpose of uniting in a common defense against French advances on the frontier and in Canada. Franklin proposed a plan to unite the colonies in the form of a "Grand Council," borrowing the name of the Iroquois governing body.[94]

The Albany Plan initially was adopted at the conference but later faced stiff opposition by British and Colonial officials who feared the plan to unite the colonies. Franklin encouraged the colonies to unite when he published one of the first political cartoons, a snake cut in pieces with a caption, "Join or Die." Despite political lobbying efforts, seven colonial assemblies and the British government rejected the plan.

FRANKLIN ACTS TO CHANGE SOCIETY

Franklin began protesting against colonial "taxation without representation." He also criticized the English Welfare Act for making people dependent on the State, taking away "all inducements to industry, frugality and sobriety." He encouraged people around the world to immigrate to America and to join Americans in building a better society. He reassured foreigners that America was a land of religious freedom:

> ... serious religion, under its various denominations, is not only tolerated, but respected and [practiced]. Atheism is unknown there; Infidelity rare and secret...And the Divine Being seems to have manifested his approbation of the mutual forbearance and kindness with which the different sects treat each other; by the remarkable prosperity with which he has been pleased to favor the whole country.[95]

Franklin recognized the importance of religious freedom in attracting foreign settlement in America. He welcomed immigration as a means of achieving faster growth of the American population.

By inviting people to establish and practice their religions freely in America, Franklin made it clear that he did not advocate an official state religion. He also advised against the State funding churches. He believed in the old-fashioned collection plate:

> When a religion is good, I conceive it will support itself; and when it does not support itself, and God does not care to support it, so that its professors are obliged to call for the help of the civil power, 'tis a sign, I apprehend, of its being a bad one . . . God helps them that help themselves.[96]

While Franklin advocated voluntary donations for churches, he supported public funding for a general hospital. He had been working for five years to help establish a facility to provide medical care for the poor and mentally ill. On May 28, 1755, the cornerstone was laid for the Pennsylvania Hospital. Chiseled into the stone were these words composed by Benjamin Franklin:

> In the year of Christ, 1755 . . . this building, by the bounty of the Government and of many private persons, was piously founded, for the relief of the sick and miserable. May the God of mercies bless the undertaking![97]

Franklin soon wrote, "Some Account of the Pennsylvania Hospital . . ." He concluded with a sermon on the subject of charity, preached by Rev. Thomas Hartley that illustrated the biblical foundations on which the hospital was built: "But prove yourselves doers of the Word and not merely hearers who delude themselves." (James 1:22).

The narrative states: "Being in company with a Reverend gentleman who was expatiating largely on the importance of a uniformity in religious worship; Franklin told him he could find something in the Bible which seemed opposed to his opinion; and taking one down from a shelf, opened it and read as follows:

1. And it came to pass after these Things, that Abraham sat in the Door of his Tent, about the going down of the Sun.

2. And behold a Man, bowed with Age, came from the Way of the Wilderness, leaning on a Staff.

3. And Abraham arose and met him, and said unto him, Turn in, I pray thee, and wash thy Feet, and tarry all Night, and thou shalt arise early on the Morrow, and go on thy Way.

4. And the Man said, Nay, for I will abide under this Tree.

5. But Abraham pressed him greatly; so he turned, and they went into the Tent; and Abraham baked unleavened Bread, and they did eat.

6. And when Abraham saw that the Man blessed not God, he said unto him, Wherefore dost thou not worship the most high God, Creator of Heaven and Earth?

7. And the Man answered and said, I do not worship the God thou speakest of; neither do I call upon his Name; for I have made to myself a God, which abideth always in mine House, and provideth me with all Things.

8. And Abraham's Zeal was kindled against the Man; and he arose, and fell upon him, and drove him forth with Blows into the Wilderness.

9. And at Midnight God called unto Abraham, saying, Abraham, where is the Stranger?

10. And Abraham answered and said, Lord, he would not worship thee, neither would he call upon thy Name; therefore have I driven him out from before my Face into the Wilderness.

11. And God said, Have I born with him these hundred ninety and eight Years, and nourished him, and [clothed] him, notwithstanding his Rebellion against me, and couldst not thou, that art thyself a Sinner, bear with him one Night?

12. And Abraham said, Let not the Anger of my Lord wax hot against his Servant. Lo, I have sinned; forgive me, I pray Thee:

13. And Abraham arose and went forth into the Wilderness, and sought diligently for the Man, and found him, and returned with him to his Tent; and when he had entreated him kindly, he sent him away on the Morrow with Gifts.

14. And God spake again unto Abraham, saying, For this thy Sin shall thy Seed be afflicted four Hundred Years in a strange Land:

15. But for thy Repentance will I deliver them; and they shall come forth with Power, and with Gladness of Heart, and with much Substance.[98]

The Reverend reportedly "expressed great surprise that he should have forgot this account and enquired what Chapter contained it." Franklin referred him to the 27th Chapter of Genesis. Franklin actually invented the story "to impress the duty of religious toleration on his antagonist."[99]

In October of 1755, Franklin was chosen colonel by a regiment of foot soldiers recruited in Philadelphia. The passage of Franklin's Militia Bill on November 25 approved raising the militia in defense against a feared French invasion. Two days later, Franklin and his son William rode horseback into the frontier to build forts and organize defenses.

FRANKLIN'S VIEWS ON LIFE, DEATH, AND HEAVEN

On February 22, 1756, shortly after his 50th birthday, Benjamin Franklin wrote a letter of condolence to Elizabeth Hubbart, his brother John Franklin's stepdaughter. She was grieving the death of her father when Benjamin explained his personal views on life death, and heaven:

> DEAR CHILD, PHILADELPHIA, February 22, 1756.
> "I condole with you, we have lost a most dear and valuable relation, but it is the will of God and Nature that these mortal bodies be laid aside, when the soul is to enter into real life; 'tis rather an [embryo] state, a preparation for living; a man is not completely born until he be dead: Why then should we grieve that a new child is born among the immortals? A new member added to their happy society? We are spirits. That bodies should be lent us, while they can afford us pleasure, assist us in acquiring knowledge, or doing good to our fellow creatures, is a kind and benevolent act of God — when they become unfit for these purposes and afford us pain instead of pleasure — instead of an aid, become an [encumbrance] and answer none of the intentions for which they were given, it is equally kind and benevolent that a way is provided by which we may get rid of them. Death is that way. We ourselves prudently choose a partial death. In some cases a mangled painful limb, which cannot be restored, we willingly cut off — He who plucks out a tooth, parts with it freely since the pain goes with it, and he that quits the whole body, parts at once with all pains and possibilities of pains and diseases it was liable to, or capable of making him suffer.
> "Our friend and we are invited abroad on a party of pleasure — that is to last forever — His chair was first ready and he is gone before us — we could not all conveniently start together, and why should you and I be grieved at this, since we are soon to follow, and we know where to find him. Adieu, Benjamin Franklin[100]

Franklin's views had changed fundamentally from his earlier beliefs in deism and polytheism to a worldview that embraced a benevolent God, salvation, and a happy afterlife. The fact that he believed in God and did not fear death gave him courage.

FRANKLIN NEGOTIATES 1756 INDIAN PEACE TREATY WITH LENNI LENAPE

Franklin's courage was tested in 1756, when Great Britain formally declared war on the French. Recognizing that the Indian nations influenced the balance of power, Governor Morris and the Pennsylvania Assembly sent Benjamin Franklin and other commissioners to negotiate with the Lenni Lenape [Delaware] Indians at the 1756 Treaty of Easton negotiations. On November 8, the nine-day conference commenced "with colors flying, drums beating, and music playing." The imposing Indian Chief Teedyuscung spoke on behalf of the

Lenni Lenape and other nations, recounting the history of broken promises, land rip-offs, and major crimes against Indian people. He was said to have supported the rights and claims of the Indians in a dignified and spirited manner. Chief Teedyuscung reassured Benjamin Franklin and the commissioners that the Indians were glad "to meet their old friends, the English, to smoke the pipe of peace with them, and hoped that justice would be done to them, for all the injuries they had received." The colorful Indian chief spoke frankly:

> There are many reasons why the Indians have ceased to be the friends of the English. The [Indians] had never been satisfied with the conduct of the English after the treaty of 1737, when their fathers, Tishekunk and Nutimus, sold them the lands upon the Delaware: that although the rights of the purchase were to extend "as far as a man can go in a day and a half," from Neshamony Creek, yet the man who was appointed to go over the ground, did not walk, but ran.[101]

Chief Teedyuscung related the facts of the infamous "Walking Purchase," when trained colonial runners raced along a pre-cut path to claim for Pennsylvania millions of acres of Indian land. William Penn's unscrupulous sons were involved in the land fraud.

Chief Teedyuscung continued to recount the next thirty years of fraudulent land transactions and broken treaties between the English and the Indians. After nine days of negotiations, Franklin and the commissioners convinced Chief Teedyuscung, the Lenni Lenape and Shawnee Nations to accept the 1756 Treaty of Easton. They encouraged the Indians to maintain peace with the English and to not join the French. The Indians agreed, not because they trusted the English, but because the French already had attacked and burned Indian villages and posed a more direct threat.

The Lenni Lenape War Chief, Shingas, offered an additional proposal to promote peace between his nation and the English colonies. He suggested "The English send five Men" to live with his tribe "at the Indians' expense." These men were to be expert craftsmen, metalsmiths, and gunsmiths. Spinning and weaving wool also would be encouraged to make blankets and clothing. Shingas proposed a social experiment to see if Euro-Americans and American Indians could "live together in love and friendship and become one people."[102] The experiment was attempted later with positive results, as non-Indian people lived with Indians, resulting in both learning to better respect one another.

At a subsequent meeting with the Lenni Lenape, one of the Indian elders raised his hands toward Heaven and prayed "God would have mercy upon them and help . . . to bring them and the English together again, and establish an ever-lasting Ground and Foundation for Peace between them."[103] Franklin and other colonial Indian commissioners observed firsthand that American Indians were a spiritual people. If given a chance, the overwhelming majority preferred to live in peace and friendship under the grace of God.

In 1757, Philadelphia silversmith Mr. Duffield created a silver medal to commemorate the Treaty of Easton. The design portrays Benjamin Franklin passing a peace pipe to Chief Teedyuscung underneath a Tree of Peace. The caption reads: "Let us look to the most high who blessed our fathers with peace." The "most high" was God, who "blessed" the original 1682 Treaty of Peace and Friendship formed between Chief Tamanend and William Penn beneath the "Shackamaxon Elm" tree in Philadelphia. It was said to be "the only treaty that was never signed and never broken" for as long as these two leaders lived.[104] William Penn's greedy sons were guilty of breaking the treaty and fraudulently claiming Indian lands. The 1758 Treaty of Easton reversed these unscrupulous actions in part by deeding back to the Indians lands west of the Susquehanna River in Pennsylvania. The return of Indian lands by the colonials, proving their good faith, had a powerful effect on the Indians. The Appalachian ridge of the Allegheny then was established as the dividing line between the colonies and sovereign Indian nations.

THE WAY TO WEALTH

Benjamin Franklin challenged his fellow colonials to recognize that there were better, more ethical ways to become wealthy than cheating the poor Indians out of their lands. In 1757, while Franklin was sailing to England on a new diplomatic mission as Pennsylvania Colonial Agent, he penned an essay entitled, "The Way to Wealth":

> This doctrine, my friends, is reason and wisdom; but after all, do not depend too much upon your own industry, and frugality, and prudence, though excellent things, for they may all be blasted without the blessing of Heaven; and therefore, ask that blessing humbly, and be not uncharitable to those that at the present seem to [lack] it, but comfort and help them. Remember, Job suffered, and was afterwards prosperous.[105]

God's blessing was the key ingredient in "The Way to Wealth." He further encouraged public charity, along with industry, frugality, and prudence. While in England for several years, Franklin espoused these moral principles in advocating the rights of Pennsylvanians before the British Court. He also tried to negotiate with descendants of William Penn who claimed a proprietary interest in the colony.

IN SUPPORT OF DIVINE PROVIDENCE AND SELF EXAMINATION

On December 13, 1757, Benjamin Franklin wrote a critique of an unnamed manuscript against the doctrine of "Divine Providence." Franklin criticized the author:

> . . . you strike at the Foundation of all Religion: For without the Belief of a Providence that takes Cognizance of, guards and guides and may favour particular Persons, there is no Motive to Worship a Deity, to fear its Displeasure, or to pray for its Protection . . . He that spits against the

Wind, spits in his own Face. But were you to succeed, do you imagine any Good would be done by it?[106]

Franklin explained that society needed religion. One should consider the welfare of the general public. Religion, Franklin argued, provided essential benefits to people in their lives and their salvation.

In August of 1758, Franklin wrote a letter in the voice of the biblical figure Abraham to his son Isaac. The theme was the benefits of "SELF-EXAMINA-TION, by the Lights of Reason, Conscience, and the Word of GOD." Speaking as a father to his son, Franklin advised:

> . . . set apart a Portion of every Day for the Purpose of *Self-Examination*, and trying your daily Actions by that Rule of Rectitude implanted by GOD in your Breast. The properest Time for this, is when you are retiring to Rest; then carefully review the Transactions of the past Day; and consider how far they have agreed with *what you know of* your Duty to God and to Man . . . you will find (through God's Grace assisting) that your Faults are continually diminishing, and your Stock of Virtue increasing; in Consequence of which you will grow in Favour both with GOD and Man.[107]

Franklin noted that the origin of this self-examination exercise came from the Greek philosopher and mathematician Pythagoras. The technique was "practiced since in every Age, with Success, by Men of all Religions."

DR. FRANKLIN IN LONDON

In 1759, at the age of fifty-three, Benjamin Franklin received an honorary doctorate degree from St. Andrews University in Scotland. From this time forward, he was addressed as Dr. Franklin. In September, Dr. Franklin received word that Great Britain had defeated the French on the Plains of Abraham at Quebec, ending the war between England and France.

In 1760, the population of the American colonies reportedly grew to over 1,610,000 people. In March, Dr. Franklin was elected chairman of a philanthropic organization that sponsored schools for African Americans in Philadelphia, New York, Rhode Island, and Williamsburg, Virginia. The organization was named after Reverend Thomas Bray (1656-1730), an Anglican minister who established thirty-nine public libraries in America. He also established the Society for the Propagation of Christian Knowledge.[108]

In 1761, Dr. Franklin maintained from London an active role in the "Friends of Dr. Bray." As a member of the Society of Arts, he promoted innovative farming methods and the introduction of new crops. Useful plants developed by American Indians included corn, beans, squash, melons, and more. Dr. Franklin also became an active member of the Royal Society of London, the "premier scientific society of the day." In September, he witnessed the coronation of George III, who was the King of England through the American Revolution.

In his leisure time Dr. Franklin enjoyed the study of music. He learned to play the guitar, harp, violin, and viola da gamba. He then invented a new instrument called an "armonica," a device that used tuned wine glasses filled with water to make music.[109] Mozart and Beethoven later wrote compositions for it. One night, while his wife was asleep, Franklin reportedly went to the attic and played his armonica with "angelic strains." His wife awoke thinking that she had "died and got to heaven and was listening to the music of the angels."[110]

In 1762, Dr. Franklin was honored with Doctorate of Law degrees from Oxford and Edinburgh colleges. However, he was frustrated by the breakdown in his negotiations to get William Penn's sons to recognize the rights of the colony of Pennsylvania. When news arrived that the Pennsylvania Legislature had elected him in honor of his efforts, Dr. Franklin sailed from London, arriving in Philadelphia on the first of November.

DR. FRANKLIN RETURNS TO PHILADELPHIA & DEFENDS MINORITIES

In 1763, Dr. Franklin resumed his position as Deputy Postmaster General. For five months he toured the northern colonies, inspecting post offices in New Jersey, New York, and New England. He established 24-hour mail service between the major cities of Philadelphia, Boston, and New York. During this time period, the Treaty of Paris was signed, ending the Seven Years' War. France thereby ceded to Great Britain the territory of Canada. Irate American Indians, led by the Ottawa Chief Pontiac, demanded sovereign rights and defense of Indian nations. They sought Indian independence.

After visiting one of the African American schools supported by Dr. Franklin and the "Friends of Dr. Bray," he stated that he, "conceived a higher Opinion of the natural Capacities of the black Race, than I had ever before entertained."[111] Dr. Franklin fundamentally changed his views from owning slaves earlier in his life to becoming an abolitionist. He began to long for the day when all African Americans would enjoy freedom and concluded, "Slavery is . . . an atrocious debasement of human nature."[112]

Franklin continued to advocate for the rights of Native Americans as well as African Americans. He was shocked and outraged on December 14, 1763, when news arrived that a group of armed colonial men had attacked and murdered a group of "innocent" and "peaceful" Christian Indians. These Conestoga Indians were related to the Iroquois and were killed by the notorious Paxton Boys, a vigilante group of Indian haters.

The surviving Conestoga Indians, who were not present at the first massacre, were granted safe sanctuary at nearby Lancaster. However, on the night of December 27th, fifty armed men attacked the supposed safe house and murdered the remaining 14 Conestoga Indians. Franklin reported, ". . . They all received the Hatchet! — Men, Women and little Children — were every one inhumanly murdered! — in cold Blood!"

Dr. Franklin went on to charge the mob of anti-Indian colonists:

The barbarous Men who committed the atrocious Fact, in Defiance of Government, of all Laws human and divine, and to the eternal Disgrace of their Country and Colour, then mounted their Horses, huzza'd in Triumph, as if they had gained a Victory, and rode off — unmolested!

The Bodies of the Murdered were then brought out and exposed in the Street, till a Hole could be made in the Earth, to receive and cover them.

But the Wickedness cannot be covered, the Guilt will lie on the whole Land, till Justice is done on the Murderers. THE BLOOD OF THE INNOCENT WILL CRY TO HEAVEN FOR VENGEANCE.[113]

The Pennsylvania Governor offered a cash bounty for the identification and arrest of the murderers. No one stepped forward. Other Christian Indians, from the Moravian Mission near Bethlehem, Pennsylvania, sought refuge in Philadelphia from the murderous mob.

At midnight, as the mob advanced toward the outskirts of Philadelphia, the Governor called Benjamin Franklin for advice. Dr. Franklin called out the city militia and led them to the city limits. He personally confronted the mob and talked them down, convincing them to return to their homes. Dr Franklin later wrote and published, "A Narrative of the Late Massacres, in Lancaster County, of a Number of Indians, Friends of this Province, by Persons Unknown With Some Observations on the Same." Dr. Franklin stated in part:

On Wednesday, the 14th of December, 1763, Fifty-seven Men . . . all well-mounted, and armed with Firelocks, Hangers and Hatchets, having travelled through the Country in the Night, to Conestogoe Manor. There they surrounded the small Village of Indian Huts, and just at Break of Day broke into them all at once . . . These poor defenseless Creatures were immediately fired upon, stabbed and hatcheted to Death! The good Shehaes [their elderly leader], among the rest, cut to Pieces in his Bed. All of them were scalped, and otherwise horribly mangled. Then their Huts were set on Fire, and most of them burnt down.[114]

After laying down the facts of the case, Dr. Franklin proceeded to explain why this criminal act was so very wrong.

With his usual rational and logical thought, Franklin addressed colonists whose families had been attacked or threatened by individual American Indians, families who sought revenge against all Indian people. He rationalized:

If an Indian injures me, does it follow that I may revenge that injury on all Indians? . . . If it be right to kill men for such a reason, then, should nay man with a freckled face and red hair kill a wife or child of mine, it would be right for me to revenge it by killing all the freckled red-haired men, women and children I could afterwards anywhere meet with.[115]

Dr. Franklin's reasoning against prejudice and revenge was so logical as to defy debate. He displayed a tremendous amount of courage when he stood up, face-to-face, against the mob of Indian haters. He placed his life in danger, as he stood bravely between the mob and the Christian Indians who remained hidden in Philadelphia. Dr. Franklin convinced the angry mob to present their grievances, and then to return to their homes.

What Dr. Franklin may have not realized at the time was that the heirs of William Penn were privately behind the scenes advocating the elimination of all Indians in Pennsylvania to clear their land title. Dr. Franklin's support for Indian rights marked him as a political barrier and targeted him personally for political elimination. The Penns mounted a campaign to smear Franklin's reputation through character assassination. Franklin wrote and published essays in his own defense. At first, things seemed to be going his way, as he was elected the presiding officer and speaker of the legislature. He pressed against the oppressive Stamp Act. However, on October 1, 1764, Dr. Franklin was defeated in his bid for reelection to the Assembly. Rev. George Whitefield wrote to Franklin in his support, and Dr. Franklin replied, "Your frequently repeated Wishes and Prayers for my Eternal as well as temporal Happiness are very obliging. I can only thank you for them, and offer you mine in return."[116]

His party did manage to retain a majority in the legislature, and three weeks later they commissioned Dr. Franklin to make a direct appeal to King III to take away the proprietorship from the Penns. They sought to reestablish Pennsylvania under a Royal Charter.

While on board a ship bound for England, Dr. Franklin wrote a letter to his 22-year-old daughter, Sarah:

> My dear child, the natural prudence and goodness of heart God has blessed you with, make it less necessary for me to be particular in giving you advice. I shall therefore only say, that the more attentively dutiful and tender you are towards your good mamma, the more you will recommend yourself to me. But why should I mention me, when you have so much higher a promise in the commandments, that such conduct will recommend you to the favor of God.[117]

Dr. Franklin's letter reflects a parent's care and concern for his child. He left his wife and daughter in God's care, as he embarked on a long and dangerous mission to London.

Franklin correctly predicted that the campaign to smear his reputation would continue in his absence:

> You know I have many enemies, all indeed on the public account, (for I cannot recollect, that I have in a private capacity given just cause of offence to any one whatever,) yet they are enemies, and very bitter ones; and you must expect their enmity will extend in some degree to you, so that your, slightest indiscretions will be magnified into crimes, in order the more sensibly to wound and afflict me. It is, therefore, the more necessary for you to be extremely circumspect in all your [behavior], that no advantage may be given to their malevolence.[118]

He feared that his daughter might become entangled in the web of political intrigue. Her every action might be scrutinized and maligned. She needed to be on her guard.

Dr. Franklin recommended to his daughter that she attend church and pray to God:

> Go constantly to church, whoever preaches. The act of devotion in the Common Prayer Book is your principal business there, and, if properly attended to, will do more towards amending the heart than sermons generally can do. For they were composed by men of much greater piety and wisdom, than our common composers of sermons can pretend to be; and therefore I wish you would never miss the prayer days; yet I do not mean you should despise sermons, even of the preachers you dislike; for the discourse is often much better than the man, as sweet and clear waters come through very dirty earth. I am the more particular on this head, as you seemed to express, a little before I came away, some inclination to leave our church, which I would not have you do.[119]

Here we see further evidence of Dr. Franklin's changing religious views from his earlier beliefs in deism and polytheism. At the age of fifty-eight he recommended the "Common Prayer Book" and attendance in church. He did not go so far as to advocate blind acceptance of sermons, as he suggested a more personal relationship with God.

DR. FRANKLIN'S MISSION TO EUROPE: 1765-1775

After surviving a thirty-day, storm-filled voyage, Dr. Franklin landed on December 9, 1764 at Portsmouth, England, and quickly proceeded to London. When the news of his safe arrival reached Philadelphia, "his friends celebrated by the ringing of bells and other demonstrations of joy."[120] He boldly embarked on his diplomatic mission

What Franklin did not realize was that his planned 6-month stay would stretch into ten years of diplomatic service in Europe. Whether he liked it or not, he was to assume the role of principal spokesperson for the American Colonies before the crown heads of Europe. He officially represented the colonies of Pennsylvania, Massachusetts, New Jersey, and Georgia. Dr. Franklin embodied the American call for greater liberties.

Meeting first with powerful Parliamentary leaders, he advocated the importance of the American colonies. Dr. Franklin's first petition to King George III was flatly denied. The king and his agents were trying to get the American colonists to pay for the high costs of the French and Indian Wars. The Stamp Tax imposed duties on newspapers, pamphlets, legal documents and similar items. He argued, "There is not gold and silver enough in the colonies to pay the stamp duty for one year." Dr. Franklin challenged the British position by explaining that the colonists had performed many duties in trying to keep the peace on the frontier. The rallying cry against the Stamp Tax was "No Taxation Without Representation." The Americans were being taxed, but they had no representation in the British Parliament. Sam Adams and the Sons of Liberty called for a boycott of British goods. Dr. Franklin lobbied the British government successfully, winning support from British merchants. When the Stamp Act was repealed in March of 1766, Dr. Franklin was celebrated, his reputation soaring throughout Europe and America. In the summer of 1766, he traveled with his good friend, Sir John Pringle, to Germany where Franklin was elected to the Royal Academy of Sciences.

In 1767, the King and his agents renewed their attempts to extract taxes from the American colonies. Dr. Franklin and Sir John Pringle traveled to Paris to seek support from the French court. Franklin was presented to King Louis XV at the Palace of Versailles. He was recognized for his "meritorious achievements in the field of science." He also laid the diplomatic groundwork for France to become a powerful ally to the American colonies, much to the dismay of the British.

In the same year, Franklin traveled to Ireland where he witnessed the Irish patriot movement which called for British troops and officials to be sent back to England. These Irish patriots found common ground with the Americans, since both were suffering from British oppression. The British Parliament sanctioned the Declaratory Act, claiming legal jurisdiction to pass any laws affecting the American colonies. This was followed by passage of the repressive Townsend Acts which imposed on the American colonists import duties on "tea, glass, oil, lead, paper, and paint." The Americans responded by calling on Americans to produce local alternatives to British goods.

Dr. Franklin wrote a letter to his Scottish friend, Lord Kames, describing the current political atmosphere: "America, an immense territory, favored by nature with all advantages of climate, soils, great navigable rivers, and lakes, must become a great country, populous and mighty...the seeds of liberty are universally found there, and nothing can eradicate them."[121] He concluded that Americans would "be able to shake off any shackles that may be imposed upon her."

On January 7, 1768, Franklin wrote an historical review of British-American relations entitled, "Causes of the American Discontents Before 1768." His essay soon was published in the *London Chronicle newspaper*. He blasted the Quartering Act that claimed to give the British generals authority for "quartering of the troops" in the private homes of Americans against their will.[122] As Secretary of State for America, Lord Hillsborough was given almost sole authority over the American Colonies. Dr. Franklin met with him and expressed concerns over American liberties.

When word reached Dr. Franklin that two regiments of British troops had landed in Boston on October 1, all he could do was pray. He actually took the time to write a version of the "Lord's Prayer" for the common man:

> Heavenly Father, may all revere thee, and become thy dutiful Children and faithful Subjects; may thy Laws be obeyed on Earth as perfectly as they are in Heaven: Provide for us this Day as thou hast hitherto daily done: Forgive us our Trespasses, and enable us likewise to forgive those that offend us. Keep us out of Temptation, and deliver us from Evil.[123]

The fact that Dr. Franklin was thinking so much about the "Lord's Prayer" during this time of peril is worthy of note.

On January 1, 1769, Franklin wrote a letter to Lord James on the future advancement of society:

> The moral character and happiness of mankind, are so interwoven with the
> operation of government, and the progress of the arts and sciences is so
> dependent on the nature of our political institutions, that it is essential to the
> advancement of civilized society to give ample discussion to these topics.[124]

Politics and government, Dr. Franklin concluded, affected science, the arts and
the social well being of society. He contemplated what course was best for the
future of America.

On April 4, 1769, Franklin wrote an essay on three ways for a nation to
acquire wealth:

> Finally, there seem to be but three Ways for a Nation to acquire
> Wealth. The first is by War as the Romans did in plundering their con-
> quered [Neighbors]. This is Robbery. The second by Commerce which is
> generally Cheating. The third by Agriculture the only honest Way; wherein
> Man receives a real Increase of the Seed thrown into the Ground, in a kind
> of continual Miracle wrought by the Hand of God in his Favour, as a
> Reward for his innocent Life, and virtuous Industry.[125]

Dr. Franklin concluded that American farmers were the best role models. They
represented an honest means to prosperity. American farmers were not afraid of
an honest day's work. Blessed by God's grace, American farmers represented the
backbone of America.

By 1770, the population of the American colonies grew to over two million
people. The cry for greater freedom and liberty was growing ever louder. Dr.
Franklin remained in Europe as the principal voice of the American people. On
March 5, the dispute between America and Great Britain turned to bloodshed,
when British troops fired on a crowd of protesters resulting in the Boston
Massacre. Three men were killed instantly and two others soon died from their
mortal wounds. Two British soldiers later were found guilty of manslaughter,
branded on their thumbs and discharged from the army.[126]

Dr. Franklin's protests were finally heard on April 12, when the British
Parliament repealed the Townsend duties on all goods except tea. This tax
remained a symbol of British sovereignty claims over America. This stubborn
demand would become the cause of the Boston Tea Party three years later.
During this calm before the storm, Franklin began writing his famous
Autobiography. At the age of sixty-five, he began to think of his own mortality.
In 1771, he traveled around the countryside, visiting old friends and making new
ones. He enjoyed happy times with Dr. Jonathan Shipley (1712-1788), the
Anglican Bishop of St. Asaph in Wales, who was an avid supporter of American
independence. Dr. Franklin is believed to have written part of his *Autobiography*
while visiting the Shipley family at their summer residence, Twyford House in
Hampshire County.[127]

By 1772, Dr. Franklin was elected to the French Academy, adding to his list
of distinguished associations with scientific and literary societies throughout
Europe and America. He was a member of the American Academy of Arts and

Sciences at Boston; the Royal Societies of London and Goettingen; the Royal Academy of Sciences in Paris, the Philosophical Societies of Rotterdam, Edinburgh, and Manchester; the Academy of Sciences, Belles Lettres, and Arts at Lyons; the Academy of Sciences and Arts at Padua; the Royal Academy of History in Madrid; the Patriotic Society of Milan, the Imperial Academy of Sciences at St. Petersburg; the Medical Society of London; the Royal Medical Society of Paris; and others.

On June 3, 1772, Franklin wrote a letter signed "New England Man" to the *London Packet* newspaper, defending dissenters from the established Church. He pointed out:

> If we look back into history for the character of present sects in Christianity, we shall find few that have not in their turns been persecutors, and complainers of persecution. The primitive Christians thought persecution extremely wrong in the Pagans, but practiced it on one another. The first Protestants of the Church of England, blamed persecution in the Roman church, but practiced it against the Puritans: these found it wrong in the Bishops, but fell into the same practice themselves both here and in New England.[128]

Dr. Franklin explained in plain English the facts regarding the history of religious persecution. He observed how history repeated itself with each group not wanting to be personally persecuted, but then continuing to persecute other groups. The problem rested on ". . . every sect believing itself possessed of all truth, and that every tenet differing from theirs was error . . ." Some groups believed that is was their "duty" to persecute errors deemed "heresy."

Dr. Franklin expressed hope that the cycles of religious conflict might subside:

> By degrees more moderate and more modest sentiments have taken place in the Christian world; and among Protestants particularly all disclaim persecution, none vindicate it, and few [practice] it. We should then cease to reproach each other with what was done by our ancestors, but judge of the present character of sects or churches by their present conduct only.[129]

He offered a common sense approach. Judge churches based on their present conduct, not on their past transgressions. This was easier said than done, but he deserves credit for attempting to moderate the situation.

Dr. Franklin then turned specifically to the history of religious dissenters in America:

> They went from England to establish a new country for themselves, at their own [expense], where they might enjoy the free exercise of religion in their own way. When they had purchased the territory of the natives, they granted the lands out in townships, requiring for it neither purchasemoney nor quit-rent, but this condition only to be complied with, that the freeholders should for ever support a gospel minister (meaning probably one of the then governing sects) and a free-school within the township. Thus, what is commonly called Presbyterianism became the established religion of that country.[130]

He explained clearly how early American Christians paid for their churches and schools through local community support and property taxes.

In time, American Christians began to diversify into an increasing number of different Christian groups. The question then arose over how these different groups would be supported.

> All went on well in this way while the same religious opinions were general, the support of minister and school being raised by a proportionate tax on the lands. But in process of time, some becoming Quakers, some Baptists, and, of late years some returning to the Church of England (through the laudable [endeavors] and a proper application of their funds by the society for propagating the gospel) objections were made to the payment of a tax appropriated to the support of a church they disapproved and had forsaken.[131]

A source of discontent arose when individual Christians were required to provide support for religious groups other than their own. In some cases, these were the very churches that they had left in the past, and they no longer wanted to be compelled to support them through tax dollars.

However, the collection of tax dollars was placed in the hands of civil government officials. The tax collectors didn't want to hear any excuses. They just demanded the taxes be paid:

> The civil magistrates, however, continued for a time to collect and apply the tax . . . thinking it just and equitable that the holders of lands should pay what was contracted . . . as a perpetual [encumbrance] on the estate . . . a payment which it was thought no honest man ought to avoid under the pretence of his having changed his religious persuasion.[132]

Religious dissenters now were challenging the original financing of early American churches through property taxes. The idea of their tax money or tithes going to support rival churches outraged them.

In Massachusetts, Dr. Franklin pointed out, the matter of religious taxes was resolved by allowing the money to be paid not to the civil tax collectors, but rather directly to the minister of their choice. The stated purpose of religious taxes was to "improve the morals of the people, and promote their happiness, by supporting among them the public worship of God and the preaching of the gospel . . ."

In New England, Dr. Franklin continued, the colonial legislatures were comprised of men who were "dissenters from the Church of England." In Virginia, most citizens were Episcopalians or Anglicans in support of the Church of England. Americans generally did not support the idea of a European Bishop seeking to control America and money from religious taxes.

The institution of the European class system also did not survive in America. In 1773, Harvard College stopped ranking students by social prominence. In that year, an African American woman, Phyllis Wheatly, witnessed the publication of her book, *Poems on Various Subjects*. A new French edition of Dr. Franklin's philosophical writings was published in two volumes, while a fifth edition was published simultaneously in London.

On February 14, 1773, Dr. Franklin wrote a letter to Rev. William Marshall on "The Increase of Religious as Well as Civil Liberty." He addressed the issue of religious oaths and called for "the Increase of Religious as well as Civil Liberty [throughout] the World . . . "[133] Later that summer, Franklin abridged a new edition of the "Book of Common Prayer." He also contributed to the construction of Theophilus Lindsey's Essex House Chapel, the first enduring Unitarian congregation in England.

On July 7, 1773, Franklin wrote a letter to Rev. Samuel Mather regarding the petition of religious dissenters. Benjamin wrote in part:

> It should be no Wonder therefore if among so many Thousand true Patriots as New England contains there should be found even Twelve Judases, ready to betray their Country for a few paltry Pieces of Silver. Their Ends, as well as their Views, ought to be similar. But all these Oppressions evidently work for our Good. Providence seems by every Means intent on making us a great People. May our Virtues publick and private grow with us, and be durable, that Liberty Civil and Religious, may be [secured] to our Posterity, and to all from every Part of the old World that take Refuge among us.[134]

Dr. Franklin's patriotism sparked a passion in his writings. Further British oppression seemed to only fuel greater determination among Americans to be free and throw off the yoke of British colonialism at every opportunity. The change came again on December 16, 1773, when a group of 150 colonial patriots dumped 342 chests of tea into Boston Harbor. The fact that the protesters dressed up as "Mohawk Indians" reveals how the image of American Indians then was used to symbolize an act for "freedom and liberty."

The British Parliament responded harshly on March 31, 1774 with the passage of the first of the "Intolerable Acts." Boston Harbor was blockaded and ordered closed. Full payment was demanded for losses from the destroyed tea. The second "Intolerable Act" revoked the right of assembly. The third allowed capital trials involving British officials to be remanded to other colonies or back to England at the will of British officials. The "Quartering Act" was reinstated in May, requiring American citizens to feed and quarter British troops upon command. The English cracked their whips on the backs of Americans.

The time arrived to unite America. On September 5, 1774, the First Continental Congress convened in Philadelphia. All American colonies except Georgia were represented at the initial gathering. Their first order of business was to organize opposition against the Intolerable Acts. Dr. Franklin was working feverishly, lobbying the British Parliament when bad news arrived that his wife, Deborah Franklin, aged sixty-six, had suffered a stroke and died on December 19. She was buried at Christ Church in Philadelphia.

After ten years of diplomatic service in Europe, Franklin came to accept that his attempts to forge a reconciliation with England were coming to an end. He was thousands of miles from his homeland, when Paul Revere (1735-1818) made his famous ride, shouting, "The British are coming! The British are coming!"

Dr. Franklin also was not in attendance when Patrick Henry gave his stirring speech at St. Johns Episcopal Church in Richmond, VA: "Is life so dear, or peace so sweet, as to be purchased at the price of chains and slavery? Forbid it, Almighty God. I know not what course others may take, but as for me, give me liberty or give me death."[135]

However, from Dr. Franklin's diplomatic quarters in London, he did hear "the shot heard around the world" at Lexington and Concord. There now would be no turning back. War seemed inevitable. He quickly prepared to set sail for home on the eve of the American Revolution.

DR. FRANKLIN AND THE DAWN OF THE AMERICAN REVOLUTION

On May 5, 1775, Dr. Franklin's ship cruised into Philadelphia harbor. The city was abuzz with the chatter of revolution. There was no time to rest. This was a time for action. The very next morning he was elected unanimously to the Continental Congress. Sam Adams, John Adams, John Hancock, Patrick Henry, and George Washington were among his fellow delegates. Charles Thomson, who later translated the Greek Bible into English, served as secretary. The delegates of the Continental Congress were largely Christians.

For a month they debated what course they should chart for America. Was it really too late for reconciliation? If they chose to plunge forward, how could they pay for a revolutionary army? Who would be their leader? The latter question was answered on June 17, when George Washington was officially commissioned General and Commander-in-Chief.

In July, Dr. Franklin worked on writing "Articles of Confederation," that soon would serve as the first model of the U.S. Constitution.[136] He strongly asserted America's political sovereignty, their right to determine their own future. He proposed to unite the thirteen colonies under a single national confederation called the "United Colonies of North America." He called for free trade and an end to all trade duties. However, Congress was not yet ready to take such·a bold stand.

An anonymous document was written in July entitled, "Declaration of the Causes and Necessity of Taking Up Arms." The document began:

> If it was possible for men, who exercise their reason to believe, that [God] the divine Author of our existence intended a part of the human race to hold an absolute property in, and an unbounded power over others, marked out by his infinite goodness and wisdom, as the objects of a legal domination never rightfully resistible, however severe and oppressive, the inhabitants of these colonies might at least require from the parliament of Great-Britain some evidence, that this dreadful authority over them, has been granted to that body. But a reverence for our Creator, principles of humanity, and the dictates of common sense, must convince all those who reflect upon the subject, that government was instituted to promote the welfare of mankind, and ought to be administered for the attainment of

that end.[137]

Before they plunged the whole nation into war, they decided to give peace one last chance. Prior to the end of summer, the "Olive Branch Petition" was written and signed by Congress.[138] However, when word returned from London that King George III refused to even read the petition, Congress began working on the "Declaration of Independence." On August 23, the King proclaimed that the American colonies were in a state of "rebellion," thus authorizing the British Army to shoot at Americans.

In October, Dr. Franklin and a Congressional committee traveled to confer with General George Washington at his Massachusetts headquarters. Franklin soon returned to Philadelphia, bringing with him Jane Mecom, his sister, who had fled occupied Boston.

In November, Dr. Franklin was re-elected as a delegate to Congress and assumed position on several important committees. At the end of the month, he was appointed to the Standing Committee of Secret Correspondence, forerunner of the State Department, to deal with foreign affairs. He met secretly in December with an agent of the French court. However, before recognizing public support, France wanted to make certain that the Americans actually had a chance of winning the war.

THOMAS PAINE'S *COMMON SENSE*

Toward the end of 1775, Thomas Paine was putting the finishing touches on his revolutionary pamphlet, "Common Sense." Dr. Franklin had encouraged this fiery Englishman to come to America and had written him a letter of recommendation. Paine wrote in part:

> The cause of America is in a great measure the cause of all mankind . . . The laying of a Country desolate with Fire and Sword, declaring War against the natural rights of all Mankind, and extirpating the Defenders thereof from the Face of the Earth, is the Concern of every Man to whom Nature hath given the Power of feeling . . .[139]

"Common Sense" was published on January 10, 1776 and within three months it sold over 100,000 copies. The pamphlet was a revolutionary best seller and exerted a powerful influence over the minds and hearts of the American public.

DR. FRANKLIN AND JEFFERSON'S IDEAS FOR THE NATIONAL SEAL

Dr. Franklin also turned his pen to writing essays, songs, and a mock epitaph in support of the war effort. He was asked to give suggestions for a national seal. His proposed design, from the Old Testament Book of Exodus, portrays Moses freeing the slaves, symbolizing America. King George was depicted as the evil Egyptian Pharaoh:

Moses standing on the Shore, and extending his Hand over the Sea, thereby causing the same to overwhelm Pharaoh who is sitting in an open Chariot, a Crown on his Head and a Sword in his Hand. Rays from a Pillar of Fire in the Clouds reaching to Moses, to express that he acts by Command of the Deity.[140]

He concluded with a phrase, "Rebellion to Tyrants is Obedience to God." Thomas Jefferson liked Franklin's words so much he was said to have adopted it as his personal motto. Jefferson revised Franklin's design for the opposite side of the final national seal with the motto, "E Pluribus Unum," meaning "Out of Many, One." The motto appears on the back of a $1 bill.[141]

Regarding the question of how the Americans were going to pay for the war, Dr. Franklin was appointed to a committee authorized to print money. Given his experience in printing colonial bills, he was well trained for the task. In the summer of 1775, the first Continental bills were printed and distributed. It was said that they never would run out of money, as long as they didn't run out of paper and ink. Franklin's old printing firm, now called Hall & Sellers, was hired to print the bills. Continental coins also were minted in silver, brass, and pewter. While the coins held their value, the paper money was subject to inflation, because there was no gold to back it up. Long term financing of the war required foreign aid and a creative combination of domestic sources.[142]

In the spring of 1776, Congress imposed upon the seventy-year-old Franklin to make a long and dangerous journey to Canada. The purpose of his mission was to seek an alliance with French Canadians. Still under British rule, the French Canadians refused the American offer. Dr. Franklin returned to Philadelphia tired and empty-handed.

Congress set May 17, 1776 as a "day of Humiliation, Fasting and Prayer" throughout the colonies. Congress urged Americans to "confess and bewail our manifold sins and transgressions, and by a sincere repentance and amendment of life, appease his [God's] righteous displeasure, and through the merits and mediation of Jesus Christ, obtain his pardon and forgiveness." Massachusetts added the motto "God Save This People" as a substitute for "God Save the King."[143]

THE DECLARATION OF INDEPENDENCE

With no time to rest, Dr. Franklin went to work with a committee to draft a "Declaration of Independence." John Adams, Robert Livingston, Roger Sherman, and Thomas Jefferson joined him. Jefferson penned the original draft that was revised first by Adams and Franklin, and then by the full committee. Jefferson's original phrase, "reduce them to arbitrary power" was strengthened by Dr. Franklin to read "reduce them to absolute Despotism." Dr. Franklin made at least four other changes. Forty-seven alterations were made in total, including the insertion of three complete paragraphs before June 28, when the text was presented to Congress.[144]

On July 2, Dr. Franklin voted in favor of Richard Henry Lee's motion for independence, which passed. Congress made thirty-nine additional changes before its final adoption on the morning of July 4. Contrary to public myth, all of the delegates did not sign the "Declaration of Independence" on July 4th, but the Congress did "adopt" the document on that date.

On July 9, 1776, Rev. Jacob Duché (1738-98), a Philadelphia Anglican priest from Christ's Church, was elected the first chaplain of the Continental Congress. In an earlier sermon, he called upon the members of Congress, "Go on, ye chosen band of Christians."[145] On that same day, General George Washington issued general orders:

> The Hon. Continental Congress having been pleased to allow a Chaplain to each Regiment . . . The Colonels or commanding officers of each regiment are directed to procure Chaplains accordingly; persons of good Characters and exemplary lives — To see that all inferior officers and soldiers pay them a suitable respect and attend carefully upon religious exercises. The blessing and protection of Heaven are at all times necessary but especially so in times of public distress and danger — The General hopes and trusts, that every officer and man, will endeavour so to live, and act, as becomes a Christian Soldier defending the dearest Rights and Liberties of his country.[146]

General Washington cast the American Revolution as a crusade carried on by Christian soldiers. They were to be ministered to by regimental chaplains, praying to God for divine "blessing and protection." Taking on the British Army, then considered the greatest in the world, required God's aid.

At 6 p.m. that evening, General Washington paraded his troops before Independence Hall in Philadelphia. The "Declaration of Independence" was read to the public. General Washington hoped:

> . . . This important Event will serve as a fresh incentive to every officer, and soldier, to act with Fidelity and Courage, as knowing that now the peace and safety of his Country depends (under God) solely on the success of our arms: And that he is now in the service of a State, possessed of sufficient power to reward his merit, and advance him to the highest Honors of a free Country.[147]

Freedom, General Washington concluded, would be achieved with God's help and man's "fidelity and courage."

Dr. Franklin was elected president of the Pennsylvania convention to approve the "Declaration of Independence." On July 20, he was chosen to sign the document on behalf of Pennsylvania, one of the original thirteen states. In August, Dr. Franklin and other members of Congress actually signed the "Declaration of Independence."

Dr. Franklin's Revolutionary Diplomacy

On September 11, 1776, Dr. Franklin met with the British commanding officer, General Lord Howe, on Staten Island. Franklin wanted Great Britain to cede Canada and the United States, an optimistic idea the British curtly rejected.

Howe responded by attacking General George Washington on Long Island and in New York City. Dr. Franklin, along with Silas Deane and Arthur Lee, then were elected as commissioners to France and directed to negotiate a treaty with that nation.

The United States was desperately in need of money and troops to support the Revolutionary War. On October 27, Dr. Franklin set sail for France on this clandestine diplomatic mission. His two grandsons, William Temple Franklin (William's illegitimate son), and Benjamin Franklin Bache (eldest of Sarah's children), accompanied their grandfather on the greatest adventure of their lives. They arrived on December 3 and proceeded to Paris. On December 28, Dr. Franklin met secretly with the French Foreign Minister, Charles Gavier, Comte de Vergennes. The French nobleman directed foreign policy for the French court. His main concern was what would happen if the French openly allied with the United States, and then the Americans resolved their differences with Great Britain. However, the French diplomat did agree to make small contributions of cash and supplies under the table. Dr. Franklin used his considerable diplomatic skills to win support from members of the French Court. He also employed his charm to attract the favor of French noblemen's wives who urged their husbands to support the American cause for liberty. British spies monitored Franklin's every move.

Dr. Franklin succeeded in winning the aid of two foreign military officers — Marquis de Lafayette and Friedrich Wilhelm, also known as Baron von Steuben. The two soldiers soon departed for America. The Marquis served as a tactical aide to General Washington, while Baron von Steuben drilled the untrained Continental Army at its winter headquarters at Valley Forge. The winter was a hard one for Washington's troops and the American Revolutionaries. Thomas Paine offered a new publication, *The Crisis*, which began, "These are the times that try men's souls."[148]

On January 13, 1777, Dr. Franklin and the Americans received a verbal promise of two million livres in French aid. News of the American victory at Saratoga proved to the French court that the Americans could win the war. This advanced diplomatic negotiations, leading to an alliance between France and the United States of America.

Dr. Franklin also sought aid from Spain and the Netherlands. He played these nations like he was playing chess, his favorite game. Franklin dangled before them the potential prizes of lucrative American trade, Caribbean island paradises, and a chance to knock Great Britain off the top of the mountain in the larger game of world domination. He wrote the French Foreign Minister, recognizing that "the influence of every power is measured by the opinion one has of its intrinsic force."[149] Dr. Franklin herein distinguished himself as a true political scientist.

The United States of America gained new identity before the court of world opinion. On June 14, 1777, Congress authorized a new symbol for their new nation. The official U.S. flag was unfurled, displaying 13 red and white stripes and 13 white stars on a field of blue. The number 13 symbolized the original 13 states.

Congress further determined the need for one essential item withheld by the British — the Holy Bible. On September 11, they authorized the importation of 20,000 Bibles from "Scotland, Holland or elsewhere" and later sanctioned the printing of the Old and New Testament by Philadelphia printer Robert Aitken (1734-1802). Congress resolved that they "highly approve the pious and laudable undertaking of Mr. Aitken, as subservient to the interest of religion . . . in this country, and . . . they recommend this edition of the bible to the inhabitants of the United States."[150]

Toward the end of the year, Congress declared that December 18th would be "Thanksgiving Day." On this day, the proclamation read, the American people "may express the grateful feelings of their hearts and consecrate themselves to the service of their divine benefactor" and they might "join the penitent confession of their manifold sins . . . that it may please God, through the merits of Jesus Christ, mercifully to forgive and blot them out of remembrance." Congress also recommended that Americans petition God "to prosper the means of religion for the promotion and enlargement of that kingdom which consisteth in righteousness, peace and joy in the Holy Ghost."[151]

On February 6, 1778, Dr. Franklin negotiated and signed a "Treaty of Alliance" between France and the United States. The treaty formed a defensive alliance, opened formal diplomatic relations and cooperative trade. France agreed to contribute to the American war effort an estimated 12,000 soldiers and 32,000 sailors. The treaty read in part:

> The most Christian King and the United States of North America . . . having this Day concluded a Treaty of amity and Commerce . . . to maintain effectually the liberty, Sovereignty, and independence absolute and unlimited of the said United States.[152]

The fact that King Louis XIV was Catholic, and not Protestant, as were most the American Revolutionaries, created a bridge between the two religions. A month later, Dr. Franklin proclaimed in a letter to the French Ministry, "Whoever shall introduce into public affairs the principles of primitive Christianity will change the face of the world."[153]

Throughout French high society, Dr. Franklin was celebrated as a diplomat, scientist, and philosopher. He embodied an American manifestation of Rousseau's "Natural Rights" philosophy. He promoted "natural religion," viewing God as the "Great Architect of the Universe." His American ideology advocated "liberty, equality, and fraternity." In the "Age of Reason," he advanced "scientific, political, and constitutional" approaches to the problems of the world. Dr. Franklin's perspectives attracted supporters among intellectuals of the "Enlightenment" movement. His association with the international fraternal order of the Freemasons expanded his influence. At the same time among the French bourgeoisie, Dr. Franklin and the American Revolutionaries represented proof that social equality was possible. He inspired the French to admire the republican qualities of Americans who sought "freedom, liberty and justice for all." They admired the courage of Americans who were willing to fight and die for their noble cause against the tyranny and imperialism of the British Empire. Americans were not afraid to take a stand to change their destiny to a future blessed with liberty. This fact fueled the beginnings of the French Revolution.[154]

By 1780, the population of America grew to an estimated 2,781,000. The tide of the Revolutionary War, with the support of France and Spain, was beginning to flow in America's favor. The convictions and determinations of Americans were growing stronger. Regarding freedom of religion, Dr. Franklin wrote to his Quaker friend, Richard Price, on October 9th:

> I am fully of your opinion respecting religious tests . . . if we consider what that people were 100 years ago, we must allow they have gone great lengths in liberality of sentiment on religious subjects . . . If Christian preachers had continued to teach as Christ and his Apostles did, without salaries, and as the Quakers now do, I imagine tests would never have existed; for I think they were invented, not so much to secure religion itself, as the emoluments [profits] of it. When a religion is good, I conceive that it will support itself; and, when it cannot support itself, and God does not take care to support, so that its professors are obliged to call for the help of the civil power, it is a sign, I apprehend, of its being a bad one.[155]

Dr. Franklin stood strong in his convictions that religions should be supported through personal contributions, not by public tax money collected by the State. As the American Revolution was drawing to a close, men of ambition, both civil and religious, were jockeying for position in the new nation.

U.S. ARTICLES OF CONFEDERATION

On March 1, 1781, the Articles of Confederation, which Dr. Franklin had begun drafting five years earlier, finally were ratified. The document stated in part:

> The said States hereby severally enter into a firm league of friendship with each other, for their common defense, the security of their liberties, and their mutual and general welfare, binding themselves to assist each other, against all force offered to, or attacks made upon them, or any of them, on account of religion, sovereignty, trade, or any other pretense whatever . . . And Whereas it hath pleased [God] the Great Governor of the World to incline the hearts of the legislatures we respectively represent in Congress, to approve of, and to authorize us to ratify the said Articles of Confederation and perpetual Union.[156]

The "Articles of Confederation" represented the first U. S. constitutional agreement. The purpose was to provide a governing document for the United States.

THE BATTLE OF YORKTOWN AND
THE END OF THE REVOLUTIONARY WAR

Early in October 1781, General George Washington and the Continental Army together with allied French soldiers, an estimated force of 17,000 troops, encircled a 9,700-man British army at Yorktown, VA. After five days of bombardment, the battle was over. Dr. James Thatcher of the Continental Army provided an eyewitness account of the surrender ceremony:

> At about twelve o'clock, the combined army was arranged and drawn up in two lines extending more than a mile in length. The Americans were drawn up in a line on the right side of the road, and the French occupied the left. At the head of the former, the great American commander [George Washington], mounted on his noble courser, took his station, attended by his aides. At the head of the latter was posted the excellent Count Rochambeau and his suite. The French troops, in complete uniform, displayed a martial and noble appearance; their bands of music, of which the timbrel formed a part, is a delightful novelty, and produced while marching to the ground a most enchanting effect.[157]

During the surrender ceremony a British band played the song, "The World Turned Upside Down." With the surrender of General Cornwallis and his troops, the Revolutionary War effectively ended. The United States won a final victory few outside observers would have thought possible only two or three years earlier.

THE PARIS PEACE TALKS

In 1782, at the age of seventy-six, Dr. Franklin was called upon to help negotiate the final peace terms between Great Britain and the United States and her allies. On February 28 in Paris, he and his fellow commissioners held informal peace talks with British emissaries. A diplomatic chess game commenced. On April 28, Dr. Franklin suggested Great Britain cede Canada to the United States. Great Britain balked. As the talks dragged on over the summer, Dr. Franklin suffered inflamed joints from a gout attack and passed a painful stone through his urinary tract. Unwilling to yield to his body's call for rest, he pressed forward with the negotiations. In the autumn, John Adams arrived to reinforce Dr. Franklin, joining the peace negotiators. However, the two men did not get along personally. John Jay also joined the American side of the table. The British negotiator was Richard Oswald, who, on September 21, conceded that Great Britain was effectively recognizing the United States as a nation. Dr. Franklin made a misstep when he suggested terms for peace to the British without first consulting the French. Articles for a peace treaty were drafted and sent to England. Dr. Franklin apologized to the French foreign minister Vergennes and also renewed the American request for more aid. His apology was accepted; ruffled French feathers were preened. Dr. Franklin's success was reflected in Vergennes' assurance of an additional six million livres loan.

Dr. Franklin published, and may have had a hand in writing, a bold and ambitious plan to create a form of United Nations. He sent a copy of the plan, "A Project of Universal and Perpetual Peace," to the brother of the French King Louis XVI. Proposed earlier by Saint-Simon, the plan called for "a permanent European Congress, headed by a President and containing one mediator for each sovereign."[158] This revolutionary plan to reform Europe was suppressed by the European heads of state, who saw it as a threat to their hold on power. However, it sowed seeds in the minds of Europeans that they too might throw off the imperial yokes, exciting thoughts of liberty. Also in 1782, J. Hector St. John de Crevecoeur published his *Letters from an American Farmer*, which asked the question on the minds of Europeans and people around the world: "What is an American, this new man?"[159]

On September 3, 1783, Dr. Franklin, along with John Adams, John Jay, and D. Hartley, signed the Treaty of Paris. Great Britain officially recognized the sovereignty of the United States of America. Dr. Franklin made certain that his country was not made subordinate to France or Spain. The articles of the treaty addressed territorial boundaries, fishing rights, financial and property settlement, an end to confiscations and persecutions, promises against looting, and open navigation of the Mississippi River. While the United States claimed sovereignty westward to the Mississippi, the Native Americans were not party to the treaty. If their sovereign rights to lands within this territory had been recognized respectfully, a century of Indian wars could have been averted. A series of Indian treaties were made and broken. It took over 150 years for the United States to admit that they fraudulently took Indian lands, but the Indians were only offered cash settlement in the 1950s at the value of the land at the time it was taken, often less than a dollar per acre. At the end of the American Revolution, the United States treasury was nearly broke, and the truth is that the eventual financial recovery was due largely to the sale and settlement of western Indian lands.

During the next two years, Dr. Franklin negotiated treaties with Sweden, Prussia and other European nations. The toast of European courts, he was crowned with laurel and myrtle at the Museum of Paris. Franklin witnessed the flying of the first hot air balloon by the Montgolfier brothers. He also met with a Vatican representative regarding the Roman Catholic Church in United States, and recommended John Carroll to be their American representative.

DR. FRANKLIN'S ADVICE TO HIS DAUGHTER

On January 26, 1784, Dr. Franklin yearned to return home and wrote a long letter to his daughter, Sarah, now the wife of Richard Bache, who had taken Franklin's old job as U.S. Postmaster General. Dr. Franklin addressed his daughter's concern over the formation in America of a secret society of self-proclaimed nobility who called themselves "hereditary knights" of "Cincinnati."

My DEAR CHILD,
I only wonder that, when the united wisdom of our nation had, in the

articles of confederation, manifested their dislike of establishing ranks of nobility, by authority either of the Congress or of any particular State, a number of private persons should think proper to distinguish themselves and their posterity, from their fellow citizens, and form an order of hereditary knights [Cincinnati], in direct opposition to the solemnly declared sense of their country![160]

Dr. Franklin didn't want a noble class of people in America. He observed first-hand the gap between the "haves and the have-nots" in Europe and in America. He sought to establish greater social equality for his country.

Dr. Franklin did strongly support "honor" in American society. However, he looked for his model of honor not from Europe, but from Asia. He greatly admired the Chinese philosophy that "honor does not descend, but ascends."

> Thus among the Chinese, the most ancient, and from long experience the wisest of nations, honor does not descend, but ascends. If a man from his learning, his wisdom, or his valor, is promoted by the Emperor to the rank of Mandarin, his parents are immediately entitled to all the same ceremonies of respect from the people, that are established as due to the Mandarin himself; on the supposition that it must have been owing to the education, instruction, and good example afforded him by his parents, that he was rendered capable of serving the public.
>
> This ascending honor is therefore useful to the state, as it encourages parents to give their children a good and virtuous education. But the descending honor, to a posterity who could have no share in obtaining it, is not only groundless and absurd, but often hurtful to that posterity, since it is apt to make them proud, disdaining to be employed in useful arts, and thence falling into poverty, and all the meannesses, servility, and wretchedness attending it; which is the present case with much of what is called the noblesse in Europe.[161]

Dr. Franklin felt it was unhealthy for people to be born into a noble class. In America he envisioned a society in which anyone could become a productive and honored citizen.

Franklin supported effective child rearing and strong family values. He believed that children should honor their parents:

> It would also be a kind of obedience to the fourth commandment, in which God enjoins us to honor our father and mother, but has nowhere directed us to honor our children. And certainly no mode of honoring those immediate authors of our being can be more effectual, than that of doing praiseworthy actions, which reflect honor on those who gave us our education; or more becoming, than that of manifesting, by some public expression or token, that it is to their instruction and example we ascribe the merit of those actions.[162]

Public education would give every child the freedom to make achievements for the benefit of one's family and community. Parents often work so hard to raise their children, and thus he believed families should be celebrated.

Dr. Franklin ended the letter to his daughter by his often quoted comparison of the eagle vs. the turkey:

> For in truth, the turkey is in comparison [with the eagle] a much more respectable bird, and withal a true original native of America . . . He is, besides, (though a little vain and silly, it is true, but not the worse emblem for that,) a bird of courage, and would not hesitate to attack a grenadier of the British guards, who should presume to invade his farm-yard with a red coat on.[163]

Which was a more appropriate national bird — the eagle or the turkey? The "Native American" turkey received Franklin's vote. He most admired turkeys for their courage. Furthermore, turkeys had been served at the first Thanksgiving between the Pilgrims of Massachusetts Bay Colony and the Wampanoag Indians back in the 1620s.

DR. FRANKLIN ON AMERICAN INDIANS BEFORE THE U.S. CONSTITUTION

Later in the year, Dr. Franklin took time to record some of his recollections of American Indians. He wrote with admiration for their political system of government and their skill as great orators. They chose the wisest men and women as leaders to govern through a system of participatory democracy:

> The Indian men, when young, are hunters and warriors, when old, counselors; for all their government is by counsel of the sages; there is no force, there are no prisons, no officers to compel obedience, or inflict punishment. Hence they generally study oratory, the best speaker having the most influence.[164]

Instead of prisons, Indian nations offered counseling and support from family, clan, and nation to develop good and positive members of society. People who acted out of the norm were teased by the parodies of the clowns, and the laughter of the people had a powerful impact on human behavior. To be on the "Good Road" of life was reinforced through careful childbearing, traditional education, and spiritual ceremonies.

Dr. Franklin noted the remarkable role of Indian women serving as teachers for their children and as the oral history record-keepers for their clans and nations:

> Having frequent occasions to hold public councils, they have acquired great order and decency in conducting them. The old men sit in the fore-most ranks . . . warriors in the next, and the women and children in the hindmost. The business of the women is to take exact notice of what passes, imprint it in their memories (for they have no writing), and com-municate it to their children. They are the records of the council, and they preserve traditions of the stipulations in treaties 100 years back; which, when we compare with our writings we always find exact.[165]

The separation of Church and State was not necessary in Indian nations because their religions were not institutionalized. Thus, a spiritual person was deemed natural for leadership. Their councils began and ended by praying to the Creator. They prayed openly and often in the Council Houses that were used both for political meetings and religious ceremonies. Dr. Franklin observed Indian council meetings to be a model of harmony, noting, "How different this is from the conduct of a polite British House of Commons, where scarce a day passes without some confusion, that makes the speaker hoarse in calling to order . . ."[166]

Dr. Franklin recognized that Indian traditions related and supported many of the same "rules of common civility." They believed that it was possible for both cultures to respect the universal nature of their mutual social and religious teachings. Indian people generally found it difficult to accept white people who prayed one day per week, then sinned the other six. Everyday was a sacred day according to Native American teachings. "In the beginning, the white man had the book [Bible] and the Indians had the land. However, soon Indians had the book, and the white man had their lands." This old Indian joke summarized their colonial experience.

DR. FRANKLIN RETURNS TO AMERICA AND RECEIVES A HERO'S WELCOME

In 1785, Dr. Franklin passed the diplomatic baton to Thomas Jefferson as Ambassador to France. As a parting gift, Franklin received from King Louis XVI his portrait painting by Louis Sicardy (1746-1825) in a frame inlaid with over 408 diamonds. Dr. Franklin later willed the priceless treasure to his daughter with a promise that she would never reset the diamonds into regal jewelry. She later sold many of the diamonds to finance travel to France, but the original painting is preserved today at the American Philosophical Society in Philadelphia.[167]

On July 28, 1785, Dr. Franklin sailed home to America. He wore his latest invention — bifocal glasses. During the voyage he took notes on how to make ships sail faster, while keeping "Maritime Observations" of the course, velocity, and temperature of the Gulf Stream. He even designed a new anchor to hold a ship steady in a storm. As the ship neared Philadelphia harbor, the roar of a huge welcoming crowd rose up. They gave him a hero's welcome, "cannon salutes, pealing bells, and cheering crowds."[168]

A month after Dr. Franklin's return, he was elected to the Supreme Executive Council of Pennsylvania. On October 14, 1785, he was elected President [Governor] of Pennsylvania and re-elected unanimously the next two years. Generously, he donated his salary to charity.

Dr. Franklin was also was elected President of the Pennsylvania Society for Promoting the Abolition of Slavery. He founded the Society for Political Enquiries, dedicated to political reform and improvement. He built a new addition onto his home and a library to organize his more than 4,000 books.

DR. FRANKLIN AND THE U.S. CONSTITUTION

In 1787 at the age of eighty-one, Dr. Franklin served as a Pennsylvania delegate to the Federal Constitutional Convention. Their purpose was to write a "Constitution of the United States of America." George Washington presided over the convention in Philadelphia, and James Madison took the lead in drafting the U.S. Constitution. Dr. Franklin commanded the respect of all present as the senior statesman.

The Constitutional convention opened on May 28 and got off to a rocky start. Strong divisions surfaced when they debated how to unite the states under one constitution. The main point of contention was the separation of powers between the states and the federal government. Dr. Franklin grew concerned that the wealthiest Americans would monopolize the power, thus controlling both federal and state governments. On June 2, the elder statesman rose before the Constitutional Convention and proposed that politicians should be true public servants without greed for money or power. Warning against the "Dangers of a Salaried Bureaucracy," Dr. Franklin proclaimed:

> IT IS with reluctance that I rise to express a disapprobation of any one article of the plan for which we are so much obliged to the honorable gentlemen who laid it before us. From its first reading I have borne a good will to it, and, in general, wished it success. In this particular of salaries to the executive branch, I happen to differ; and, as my opinion may appear new and chimerical, it is only from a persuasion that it is right, and from a sense of duty, that I hazard it. The committee will judge of my reasons when they have heard them, and their judgment may possibly change mine. I think I see inconveniences in the appointment of salaries; I see none in refusing them, but, on the contrary, great advantages.[169]

Franklin was concerned that high salaries might corrupt the executive branch of government. He observed firsthand how wealth was concentrated in European monarchies, and he sought to discourage the emergence of a wealthy ruling class in America.

Dr. Franklin focused attention on the "dangers" of creating a vast federal bureaucracy:

> Sir, there are two passions which have a powerful influence in the affairs of men. These are ambition and avarice; the love of power and the love of money. Separately, each of these has great force in prompting men to action; but, when united in view of the same object, they have, in many minds, the most violent effects. Place before the eyes of such men a post of honor, that shall, at the same time, be a place of profit, and they will move heaven and earth to obtain it. The vast number of such places it is that renders the British Government so tempestuous. The struggles for them are the true source of all those factions which are perpetually dividing the nation, distracting its councils, hurrying it sometimes into fruitless and mischievous wars, and often compelling a submission to dishonorable terms of peace.[170]

He reiterated that government officials should not profit from public service. Understanding much about human nature, he sought to limit temptations of money and power among federal officials. Left unchecked, greedy men would cause disruptive factions which could lead to "fruitless and mischievous wars."

Beware of "bold" and "violent" men, Dr. Franklin warned. If not guarded against, these selfish men will seek political positions with hidden agendas to enrich themselves and their associates:

> And of what kind are the men that will strive for this profitable pre-eminence, through all the bustle of cabal, the heat of contention, the infinite mutual abuse of parties, tearing to pieces the best of characters? It will not be the wise and moderate, the lovers of peace and good order, the men fittest for the trust. It will be the bold and the violent, the men of strong passions and indefatigable activity in their selfish pursuits. These will thrust themselves into your government, and be your rulers. And these, too, will be mistaken in the expected happiness of their situation, for their vanquished competitors, of the same spirit, and from the same motives, will perpetually be endeavoring to distress their administration, thwart their measures, and render them odious to the people.[171]

Men who lust for power and wealth should not be the rulers of America, Dr. Franklin asserted. He and James Madison united in their stand against factions and divisive party politics. They sought to avoid the old civil "warfare" between the people and their government:

> Hence, as all history informs us, there has been in every state and kingdom a constant kind of warfare between the governing and the governed; the one striving to obtain more for its support, and the other to pay less. And this has alone occasioned great convulsions, actual civil wars, ending either in dethroning of the princes or enslaving of the people. Generally, indeed, the ruling power carries its point, and we see the revenues of princes constantly increasing, and we see that they are never satisfied, but always in want of more. The more the people are discontented with the oppression of taxes, the greater need the prince has of money to distribute among his partisans, and pay the troops that are to suppress all resistance, and enable him to plunder at pleasure.[172]

Franklin's explanation of the "oppression of taxes" became a battle cry for tax protesters. He warned against federal armed troops being directed against American citizens.

Dr. Franklin was determined to protect the rights of the people against tyrants like the King of England. The American Revolution was a popular movement to bring freedom and liberty to the people. The elder statesman did not want to see their higher purpose slip away now that the war had been won and they were drafting the U.S. Constitution. Franklin pointed out how absolute power corrupted leaders:

> There is scarce a king in a hundred, who would not, if he could, follow the example of Pharaoh, - get first all the people's money, then all their

lands, and then make them and their children servants forever. It will be said that we do not propose to establish kings. I know it. But there is a natural inclination in mankind to kingly government. It sometimes relieves them from aristocratic domination. They had rather have one tyrant than five hundred. It gives more of the appearance of equality among citizens; and that they like. I am apprehensive, therefore, - perhaps too apprehensive, - that the government of these States may, in future times, end in a monarchy.[173]

Dr. Franklin feared the danger of a powerful President acting like a king. America, he asserted, should be a government of the people. Politicians were to be civil servants, not dictators or monarchs who ruled the people.

Franklin believed that Presidents and their cabinet secretaries should perform their duties freely as a public service:

> It may be imagined by some that this is an Utopian idea, and that we can never find men to serve us in the executive department without paying them well for their services. I conceive this to be a mistake . . . the pleasure of doing good and serving their country, and the respect such conduct entitles them to, are sufficient motives with some minds to give up a great portion of their time to the public, without the mean inducement of pecuniary satisfaction.[174]

People should seek public office not to enrich themselves, but rather to sincerely serve their country for the common good of the people. Dr. Franklin expressed faith that enough good and honest men existed to fill these positions. Politicians who sought to line their pockets with gold need not apply.

Franklin asked the members of the Constitutional Convention to consider the laudable practices of the Quakers, who sought to resolve problems through town meetings and public councils:

> Another instance is that of a respectable society who have made the experiment and practiced it with success now more than a hundred years. I mean the Quakers. It is an established rule with them that they are not to go to law, but in their controversies they must apply to their monthly, quarterly, and yearly meetings. Committees of these sit with patience to hear the parties, and spend much time in composing their differences. In doing this, they are supported by a sense of duty and the respect paid to usefulness. It is honorable to be so employed, but it was never made profitable by salaries, fees, or perquisites. And, in deed, in all cases of public service, the less the profit, the greater the honor.[175]

Dr. Franklin practiced what he preached. Leading by example, he donated his Governor's salary to public charity. Politicians, he believed, should be honorable and earn the trust of the people.

George Washington shared Dr. Franklin's views of pro bono public service. Men like Washington and Franklin did not do what they did for money. They looked to higher purposes:

> To bring the matter nearer home, have we not seen the greatest and

most important of our offices, that of general of our armies, executed for eight years together, without the smallest salary . . . ? And shall we doubt finding three or four men in all the United States with public spirit enough to bear sitting in peaceful council . . . and see that our laws are duly executed? Sir, I have a better opinion of our country. I think we shall never be without a sufficient number of wise and good men to undertake and execute well and faithfully the office in question.[176]

Dr. Franklin challenged the members of the Constitutional Convention to stop their wrangling over money and power. It was better to place the public good in the forefront.

Being a good businessman, he also knew there was little money in the federal treasury. He contended that his purpose was not to be so frugal, but rather to prevent the designs of men greedy for money and power from ever getting control of the Office of the Presidency:

> Sir, the saving of the salaries, that may at first be proposed, is not an object with me. The subsequent mischiefs of proposing them are what I apprehend. And, therefore, it is that I move the amendment. If it be not seconded or accepted, I must be contented with the satisfaction of having delivered my opinion frankly and done my duty.[177]

After due consideration, the signers of the U.S. Constitution did decide to allow some "compensation" for the President. Article II, Section 1, Clause 7 reads:

> The President shall, at stated Times, receive for his Services, a Compensation, which shall neither be increased nor diminished during the Period for which he shall have been elected, and he shall not receive within that Period any other Emolument from the United States, or any of them.[178]

Although George Washington stated that he did not wish to receive a salary, Congress insisted that he receive $25,000/year to cover all expenses of the Presidential household and official entertaining, as well as personal expenses. The present Presidential salary is $400,000/year, plus a $50,000 expense account.[179]

DR. FRANKLIN RECOMMENDS PRAYER AT CONSTITUTIONAL CONVENTION

On Thursday, June 28, 1787, Dr. Franklin addressed the Constitutional Convention to call for an end to the factionalism that threatened the establishment of the U.S. Constitution. The main divisive issue revolved around how each state would be represented in the new government. The interests of large states were pitted against smaller states which prompted some delegates to leave the Convention in disgust. Dr. Franklin rose to quell the moment of crisis:

> The small progress we have made after 4 or five weeks attendance & continual reasonings with each other - our different sentiments on almost every question, several of the last producing as many noes and ayes, is methinks a melancholy proof of the imperfection of the Human Understanding. We indeed seem to feel our own want of political wisdom, some we have been running about in search of it. We have gone back to ancient history for models of Government, and examined the different forms of those Republics which having been formed with the seeds of their own dissolution now no longer exist. And we have viewed Modern States all round Europe, but find none of their Constitutions suitable to our circumstances.[180]

The models for the U.S. Constitution have long been debated. Some point to ancient Greece, looking back to Plato's Republic. However, Greek government was a dictatorship, not a democratic republic. The Greek empire collapsed. Some point to ancient Rome, but a system that encouraged Christians to be eaten by lions for sport hardly qualified as a suitable model for America. Others point to French philosophers, such as Locke and Montesquieu. Their original sources featured the diaries of French missionaries to the Iroquois Indians, later published in 73 volumes entitled, *Jesuit Relations*.[181]

Just as the Iroquois Grand Council began and ended their councils in prayer, Dr. Franklin recommended to the delegates of the Constitutional Convention that they seek to resolve their differences by praying to God for His divine assistance:

> In this situation of this Assembly, groping as it were in the dark to find political truth, and scarce able to distinguish it when presented to us, how has it happened, Sir, that we have not hitherto once thought of humbly applying to the Father of lights [God] to illuminate our under-standings? In the beginning of the Contest with G. Britain, when we were sensible of danger we had daily prayer in this room for the divine protection. Our prayers, Sir, were heard, and they were graciously answered. All of us who were engaged in the struggle must have observed frequent instances of a Superintending providence in our favor. To that kind providence we owe this happy opportunity of consulting in peace on the means of establishing our future national felicity. And have we now forgotten that powerful friend?[182]

God was their "powerful friend," Dr. Franklin proclaimed. He reminded his fellow statesmen that they had sought God's help from the early days of the American Revolution. They should not forget this fact. Now, in this time when unity was needed most, God would help them through divine providence.

Dr. Franklin appeared as a wise octogenarian in his personal testimony of his faith in God:

> I have lived, Sir, a long time, and the longer I live, the more convinc-ing proofs I see of this truth-that God governs in the affairs of men. And if a sparrow cannot fall to the ground without his notice, is it probable that an empire can rise without his aid? We have been assured, Sir, in the sacred

writings, that "except the Lord build the House they [labor] in vain that build it." [Psalm 127] I firmly believe this; and I also believe that without his concurring aid we shall succeed in this political building no better than the Builders of Babel [Genesis 11:1-9]: We shall be divided by our little partial local interests; our projects will be confounded, and we ourselves shall become a reproach and bye word down to future ages. And what is worse, mankind may hereafter from this unfortunate instance, despair of establishing Governments by Human Wisdom and leave it to chance, war and conquest.[183]

Franklin quoted the scriptures to make his point that the United States of America could — with the help of God — establish a lasting Constitution. If they did not unite at this crucial moment in history, the very foundation of America was in danger of collapsing.

At the climax of his oration, Dr. Franklin called for daily prayer to open the proceedings of the Constitutional Convention each morning:

> I therefore beg leave to move-that henceforth prayers imploring the assistance of Heaven, and its blessings on our deliberations, be held in this Assembly every morning before we proceed to business, and that one or more of the Clergy of the City be requested to officiate in that service.[184]

Franklin did not seek to prohibit prayer in public buildings, a hot issue to our present day. Quite the contrary, he highly recommended that the delegates of the Constitutional Convention pray to God — publicly, openly, every day.

Former Superior Court Judge Roger Sherman from Connecticut seconded the motion for public prayer at the Constitutional Convention. He had served in the Continental Congress from the beginning, and he remembered that Dr. Franklin was correct in recollecting how they had prayed for the success of the American Revolution. Alexander Hamilton from New York expressed "apprehensions" over public prayer, because he feared criticism and public embarrassment that the convention had sunk so low that they needed to pray to God to raise themselves out of the quagmire. Dr. Franklin, Mr. Sherman, and others pointed out that public prayer was for the purpose of carrying out their duty. Furthermore, "omission of a duty could not justify a further omission." However, Dr. Hugh Williamson, a Scots-Irish doctor from North Carolina, suggested that they could explain their omission of prayer by the fact that the Convention had no money to pay a minister to lead them in prayer. Although the excuse seemed weak, the proposal for prayer was tabled at first. On the draft of his speech, Dr. Franklin wrote, "The convention, except three or four persons, thought prayer unnecessary."[185]

Just when it seemed the proposal for prayer was doomed, Virginia's Edmund Randolph offered a counterproposal. He recommended that a "sermon be preached at the request of the convention on the 4th of July, the anniversary of Independence, & thence forward prayers be used in ye Convention every morning." Mr. Randolph had served in the war as General Washington's aide-de-camp. He also was the former Attorney General of Virginia and later would become the Attorney General of the United States. Although he was only thirty-three years old in 1787, his strong advocacy for amendments did not go unheard. According to one account, General Washington led most of the Convention delegates to a nearby church where Rev. James Campbell, a Lutheran minister, delivered a sermon:[186]

> [We] fervently recommend to thy fatherly notice . . . our federal convention . . . [Favor] them, from day to day, with thy inspiring presence; be their wisdom and strength; enable them to devise such measures as may prove happy instruments in healing all divisions and prove the good of the great whole . . . that the United States of America may form one example of a free and virtuous government . . . May we . . . continue, under the influence of republican virtue, to partake of all the blessings of cultivated and Christian society.[187]

Dr. Franklin's proposal for daily prayer finally was adopted at the first Constitutional Congress. The House and the Senate appointed two chaplains of different denominations with a salary of $500 each. The Chaplaincy program exists to this day.

THE GREAT COMPROMISE IN APPROVING THE U.S. CONSTITUTION

On July 16, 1787, Dr. Franklin supported the "Great Compromise" over the composition of the Congress. In the U.S. Senate each state would have two senators. In the U.S. House of Representatives representation would be proportional to each state's population. Oliver Ellsworth and Roger Sherman, the Connecticut judge who had seconded Dr. Franklin's proposal for prayer, engineered the compromise. The measure passed by only one vote.

On September 17, 1787, Dr. Franklin prepared a speech in support of passage of the U.S. Constitution. Because he was feeling ill, his dear friend James Wilson delivered the speech. It was his final address to the Constitutional Convention:

> Mr. President:
> I confess that I do not entirely approve of this Constitution at present; but, sir, I am not sure I shall never approve it; for, having lived long, I have experienced many instances of being obliged, by better information or fuller consideration, to change my opinions even on important subjects, which I once thought right, but found to be otherwise. It is therefore that, the older I grow, the more apt I am to doubt my own judgment of others. Most men, indeed, as well as most sects in religion, think themselves in possession of all truth, and that wherever others differ from them, it is so far error . . .[188]

The wise old Dr. Franklin harmonized a resonating tone of reason with the main causes of social conflict — religious schisms, and political factions. When men grew entrenched within their positions, society failed to move forward.

They must move forward, Dr. Franklin asserted, to make the Constitution be like a "blessing" for the people. "We, the People" needed a Constitutional government:

> In these sentiments, sir, I agree to this Constitution, with all its faults-if they are such; because I think a general government necessary for us, and there is no *form* of government but what may be a blessing to the people if well administered; and I believe, farther, that this is likely to be well administered for a course of years, and can only end in despotism, as other forms have done before it, when the people shall become so corrupted as to need despotic government, being incapable of any other. I doubt, too, whether any other Convention we can obtain may be able to make a better constitution; for when you assemble a number of men to have the advantage of their joint wisdom, you inevitably assemble with those men all their prejudices, their passions, their errors of opinion, their local interests, and their selfish views. From such an assembly, can a perfect production be expected? It therefore astonishes me, sir, to find this system approaching so near to perfection as it does; and I think it will astonish our enemies, who are waiting with confidence to hear that our councils are confounded like those of the builders of Babel, and that our States are on the point of separation, only to meet hereafter for the purpose of cutting one another's throats.[189]

In powerful, dramatic form — that would have done Rev. George Whitefield proud — Dr. Franklin hearkened back to the Book of Genesis to make his case. The United States of America could not be a "Tower of Babel," vulnerable to destruction. They must unite.

Dr. Franklin urged his colleagues to accept the Constitution. They must organize behind a common goal, " . . . securing the happiness of the people." He rallied them in support of the Constitution:

> Thus I consent, sir, to this Constitution, because I expect no better, and because I am not sure that it is not the best. The opinions I have had of its *errors* I sacrifice to the public good. I have never whispered a syllable of them abroad. Within these walls they were born, and here they shall die. If every one of us, in returning to our constituents, were to report the objections he has had to it, and endeavor to gain partisans in support of them, we might prevent its being generally received, and thereby lose all the salutary effects and great advantages resulting naturally in our favor among foreign nations, as well as among ourselves, from our real or apparent unanimity. Much of the strength and efficiency of any government, in procuring and securing the happiness to the people, depends on *opinion*, and the general opinion of the goodness of that government, as well as of the wisdom and integrity of its governors. I hope, therefore, for our own sakes, as a part of the people, and for the sake of our posterity, that we shall act heartily and unanimously in recommending this Constitution, wherever our influence may extend, and turn our future thoughts and endeavors to the means of having it *well administered.*[190]

American citizens deserved to feel confident in the "goodness" of their government. Their leaders needed to be wise men of integrity.

Good administration was a key to good government. And, good government was the goal. Finally, he called on every member who still had objections to recognize that they were not "infallible":

> On the whole, sir, I cannot help expressing a wish that every member of the Convention who may still have objections to it, would with me on this occasion doubt a little of his own infallibility, and, to make *manifest our unanimity,* put his name to this instrument.[191]

Sign the Constitution of the United States of America! Endorse this document was Dr. Franklin's parting recommendation. After surviving more that eight decades, Benjamin Franklin, led the campaign to win endorsement and ratification of the country's seminal document. He was tired. He was weak. But, he expressed himself with the eloquence of an Iroquois Chief.

On September 28, Congress agreed to pass the U.S. Constitution on to the states, so each could debate it in separate ratifying conventions. Nine states had to agree to the new Constitution for it to go into effect. As Dr. Franklin was departing from Independence Hall, the elder statesman reportedly was approached by a woman who asked him, "Dr. Franklin, what have you given us?" "A republic," he replied. "If you can keep it."[192]

NORTHWEST ORDINANCE: THE FUTURE OF THE WEST

During the summer of 1787, Congress also passed the "Northwest Ordinance" to govern western territories north of the Ohio River. The "Northwest Ordinance" provided for a plan of government, the creation of states, the acceptance of each new state as an equal of the original states, freedom of religion, right to a trial by jury, public support of education, and the prohibition of slavery. Article 3 addressed religion, education, and American Indians:

> Religion, morality, and knowledge, being necessary to good government and the happiness of mankind, schools and the means of education shall forever be encouraged. The utmost good faith shall always be observed towards the Indians; their lands and property shall never be taken from them without their consent; and, in their property, rights, and liberty, they shall never be invaded or disturbed, unless in just and lawful wars authorized by Congress; but laws founded in justice and humanity, shall from time to time be made for preventing wrongs being done to them, and for preserving peace and friendship with them.[193]

If Article 3 of the "Northwest Ordinance" had been honored, the history of America would have changed fundamentally. However, the ratification of the U.S. Constitution now was the main focus of attention. Those who supported the Constitution were called "Federalists." Seventy-seven articles in support of the Constitution were entitled the "Federalist Papers." Their opponents were dubbed the "Anti-Federalists." The debate between the two groups raged from state to state. On June 29, 1788, New Hampshire became the ninth state to ratify the U.S. Constitution — by a vote of 57 to 47 — marking its official adoption into law.

DR. FRANKLIN'S VISION FOR THE CREATION OF A UNITED NATIONS

In 1788 at the age of 83, Dr. Franklin continued writing his *Autobiography.* An important theme emerged in his writings — the spread of "virtue" from an individual to a worldwide basis.

Franklin wrote with his quill pen about "a great and extensive project" that he had envisioned. At the age of twenty-five, while reading in a library, a powerful idea came to him. The establishment of a "United Nations." If founded on principles of "virtue," this "United Party" might change the history of the world:

> There seems to me at present to be great occasion for raising a United Party for Virtue, by forming the virtuous and good men of all nations into a regular body, to be governed by suitable good and wise rules, which good and wise men may probably be more unanimous in their obedience to, than common people are to common laws. I at present think that whoever attempts this aright, and is well qualified, cannot fail of pleasing God and of meeting with success.[194]

Dr. Franklin believed that a "United Nations" not only would be successful and help the whole world, but moreover, it would please God. Franklin had witnessed the united Six Nations of the Iroquois Confederacy. Over forty years earlier, he had noted the remarkable unity of their system of government. If the Indians could create a "United Nations," why then could not this powerful idea help unify the world?

While he was writing his visions of the future, Dr. Franklin also wrote his last will and testament on July 17, 1788. He left most of his estate to his daughter, Sarah Bache, while also making endowments to different states. To his son, William, who had betrayed the Revolution by siding with the British, he left little.

DR. FRANKLIN'S RETIREMENT AND THE INAUGURATION OF PRESIDENT GEORGE WASHINGTON

On October 14, 1788, Benjamin Franklin retired from his last public office as President of the Supreme Executive Council of Pennsylvania. The position was comparable to governor. Over his long and illustrious public career, he had served as Indian treaty negotiator, Postmaster General, Ambassador to France, member of the Continental Congress, delegate to the Constitutional Convention, and more.

On April 30, 1789, George Washington was inaugurated as the first President of the United States. He swore an oath of office upon a bible that came from New York's St. John's Masonic Lodge. The ceremony was held in New York City on the balcony of the Senate Chamber at Federal Hall on Wall Street. He joked as he prepared to take office, "My movement to the chair of Government will be accompanied by feelings not unlike those of a culprit who is going to the place of his execution." As President Washington traveled to New York, thousand of people reportedly lined his route, singing and dancing in celebration. When he arrived to a hero's welcome in the city, the "bells rang and cannons boomed, the streets were gay with flags, and crowded with people, and as he passed along cheer upon cheer thundered and echoed over the city."[195]

President George Washington said in part in his "First Inaugural Address:"

> . . . It would be peculiarly improper to omit in this first official act my fervent supplications to that Almighty Being who rules over the universe, who presides in the councils of nations, and whose providential aids can supply every human defect, that His benediction may consecrate to the liberties and happiness of the people of the United States . . . No people can be bound to acknowledge and adore the Invisible Hand which conducts the affairs of men more than those of the United States.[196]

Washington's public acknowledgment of God set a religious tone for the establishment of government. Dr. Franklin later met with Washington and personally praised him for his laudable public service.

In the summer of '89, crowds numbering over 20,000 strong stormed the Bastille royal fortress in Paris. A month later, the French National Assembly issued the "Declaration of the Rights of Man," Perhaps inspired by the "Declaration of Independence," they proclaimed the "legal equality of all citizens and freedom of speech, press, assembly, and religion." In the wake of the Revolution, Dr. Franklin concluded, " . . . in this world nothing can be said to be certain, except death and taxes."[197]

DR. FRANKLIN'S PROPOSED 11TH AMENDMENT: ABOLITION OF SLAVERY

On September 25, 1789, the United States Congress adopted the "Bill of Rights." The document featured the first ten amendments to the U.S. Constitution. Congress sent it to the states to be ratified. While Dr. Franklin supported the "Bill of Rights," he thought there should have been an eleventh amendment. He wrote "An Address to the Public Concerning Slavery."

> It is with peculiar satisfaction we assure the friends of humanity, that, in prosecuting the design of our association, our endeavours have proved successful, far beyond our most sanguine expectations. Encouraged by this success, and by the daily progress of that luminous and benign spirit of liberty, which is diffusing itself throughout the world, and humbly hoping for the continuance of the divine blessing on our labours, we have ventured to make an important addition to our original plan, and do, therefore, earnestly solicit the support and assistance of all who can feel the tender

emotions of sympathy and compassion, or relish the exalted pleasure of beneficence.[198]

Franklin asked God for a "divine blessing" to help them in the future development of America. Their "original plan" of the U.S. Constitution was succeeding. The powerful ideas embodied in liberty and freedom were spreading around the world.

Dr. Franklin appealed to the American citizens to feel "sympathy and compassion" for those who were not free. The distinguished retired statesman called for an end to slavery:

> Slavery is such an atrocious debasement of human nature, that its very extirpation, if not performed with solicitous care, may sometimes open a source of serious evils. The unhappy man, who has long been treated as a brute animal, too frequently sinks beneath the common standard of the human species. The galling chains, that bind his body, do also fetter his intellectual faculties, and impair the social affections of his heart. Accustomed to move like a mere machine, by the will of a master, reflection is suspended; he has not the power of choice; and reason and conscience have but little influence over his conduct, because he is chiefly governed by the passion of fear. He is poor and friendless — perhaps worn out by extreme labour, age, and disease.[199]

Franklin painted a realistic picture of the horrors of slavery. He portrayed the tortured lives of slaves in graphic language. The practice of slavery, he asserted, needed to come to an end.

While calling for the emancipation of African American slaves, Dr. Franklin reassured people that the process could be done in a secure way. Abolishing slavery, he insisted, was our "serious duty." Freeing the slaves, needed to be done "to the best of our judgment and abilities."

Dr. Franklin called for public education and free advice to help Black people adjust to their new lives in freedom:

> To instruct, to advise, to qualify those, who have been restored to freedom, for the exercise and enjoyment of civil liberty, to promote in them habits of industry, to furnish them with employments suited to their age, sex, talents, and other circumstances, and to procure their children an education calculated for their future situation in life; these are the great outlines of the annexed plan, which we have adopted, and which we conceive will essentially promote the public good, and the happiness of these our hitherto too much neglected fellow-creatures.[200]

Franklin proposed a job-training program for adult African Americans. He sought free education for their children. While President of the Pennsylvania Society for Promoting the Abolition of Slavery, he developed a detailed plan.

To help finance the cost of freeing the slaves and helping them adjust to free and productive lives, Dr. Franklin called for a national fund-raising campaign:

> A plan so extensive cannot be carried into execution without considerable pecuniary resources, beyond the present ordinary funds of the society. We

hope much from the generosity of enlightened and benevolent freemen, and will gratefully receive any donations or subscriptions for this purpose, which may be made to our treasurer, James Starr, or to James Pemberton, chairman of our committee of correspondence.[201]

Dr. Franklin, Mr. Starr, and Mr. Pemberton, along with Dr. Benjamin Rush, Jonathan Penrose, and Tench Coxe were officers of the Pennsylvania Society for Promoting the Abolition of Slavery. Their constitution read in part:

> It having pleased the Creator of the world, to make of one flesh all the children of men — it becomes them to consult and promote each other's happiness, as members of the same family, however diversified they may be, by colour, situation, religion, or different states of society. It is more especially the duty of those persons, who profess to maintain for themselves the rights of human nature, and who acknowledge the obligations of Christianity, to use such means as are in their power, to extend the blessings of freedom to every part of the human race; and in a more particular manner, to such of their fellow creatures, as are entitled to freedom by the laws and constitutions of any of the United States, and who, notwithstanding, are detained in bondage, by fraud or violence. From a full conviction of the truth and obligation of these principles — from a desire to diffuse them, wherever the miseries and vices of slavery exist, and in humble confidence of the favor and support of the Father of Mankind, the subscribers have associated themselves, under the title of the Pennsylvania Society for promoting the Abolition of Slavery, and the Relief of free Negroes unlawfully held in Bondage.[202]

This vein held that God made all people to be like one great family in diversity. Franklin pointed to those of his own faith, Christianity, and called upon them to accept their civil and religious duties. Free the slaves! Free the slaves! Free the slaves! God, the "Father of Mankind," would "favor and support" their just actions. The worldview of one great extended family in diversity was fundamental to Iroquois and other Native American philosophies. Their people were not enslaved, but rather adopted into Indian families sometimes to take the place of a departed loved one. In contrasting Indian and non-Indian ways, Native elders warned that if some White People enslaved the Black People, then it was only a matter of time until those same White People tried to enslave the Red People.

Congress responded that each state could decide whether they would be a "Slave State" or a "Free State." Their decision divided the country on this issue. One can only wonder, if wiser men had accepted Dr. Franklin's call for abolition in 1789, perhaps the Civil War, 75 years later, would have been avoided and millions of lives would have been saved.

On November 26, 1789, Congress established "Thanksgiving Day." The nation needed a day of thanksgiving, a time to pause and reflect upon all the things for which we have to be thankful. The Iroquoian response was that it should be "Thanksgiving everyday" because every day is sacred in the eyes of the Creator.

DR. FRANKLIN'S FINAL
WRITTEN STATEMENT ON RELIGION

In January of 1790, Benjamin Franklin turned eighty-four. The population of the United States had grown to almost four million people. Two months later, the President of Yale College, Dr. Ezra Stiles (1727-1795), corresponded with Dr. Franklin regarding his religious views. Franklin's religious views evolved many, many times during his lifetime. He had examined deism, polytheism, Greek and Roman mythology, ancient European and Asian religions, The Old Testament, early Christianity, Catholicism, Protestantism, Calvinism, Quakerism, Episcopalism, Presbyterianism, Evangelicalism, and Native American religions. History is fortunate that Dr. Ezra Stiles preserved the letter from Dr. Franklin that expressed his final written views on religion:

> I believe in one God, the Creator of the universe; that he governs it by his Providence; that he ought to be worshipped; that the most acceptable service we can render to him is doing good to his other children; that the soul of man is immortal, and will be treated with justice in another life respecting its conduct in this. These I take to be the fundamental points of all sound religion, and I regard them as you do, in whatever sect I meet with them.[203]

Franklin embraced the fundamental principles of universal religion. He accepted God as the "Creator of the universe." His method of governance was through divine "Providence." God was the "caretaker" of all life. He exercised care and foresight of the future.

Dr. Franklin believed the religion and morals of Jesus Christ to be the "best in the world." However, he was critical of men who corrupted Christianity for their own selfish gains:

> As to Jesus of Nazareth, my opinion of whom you particularly desire, I think his system of morals and his religion, as he left them to us, the best the world ever saw, or is like to see; but I apprehend it has received various corrupting changes, and I have, with most of the present Dissenters in England, some doubts as to his divinity; though it is a question I do not dogmatize upon, having never studied it . . . [204]

Was Jesus the "Son of God" or a "great teacher" or both? Dr. Franklin never resolved this question in writing. He humbly confessed to not having studied the question fully enough to compose a final statement. He left future generations to ponder such profound questions.

Benjamin Franklin knew that the end of his life was near when he wrote that all of his questions about God and Jesus were about to be answered:

> I expect soon an opportunity of knowing the truth with less trouble. I see no harm, however, in its being believed, if that belief has the good consequence, as probably it has, of making his doctrines more respected and more observed; especially as I do not perceive, that the Supreme takes it

amiss, by distinguishing the unbelievers in his government of the world with any peculiar marks of his displeasure.[205]

Dr. Franklin believed that God loved all his children, whether they believed in Him or not. In the end, each would receive an opportunity for salvation.

Franklin gave God credit for helping to conduct him through life. He had no doubt in the existence of Heaven.

> I shall only add, respecting myself, that having experienced the goodness of that Being in conducting me prosperously through a long life, I have no doubt of its continuance in the next, without the smallest conceit of meriting it . . . .All sects here, and we have a great variety, have experienced my good will in assisting them with subscriptions for building their new places of worship; and, as I never opposed any of their doctrines, I hope to go out of the world in peace with them all.[206]

Dr. Franklin felt good about having contributed to the building and support of many places of worship. He sought to be at peace with all different religious denominations.

THE DEATH OF BENJAMIN FRANKLIN

On the evening of April 17, 1790, Benjamin Franklin died at the age of 84 surrounded by his grandchildren in Philadelphia. The cause of death was pleurisy, an inflammation of the lungs. Over twenty thousand citizens gathered to pay tribute to this great American hero. The entire clergy of Philadelphia led his funeral procession to Old Christ Church cemetery. Influential civic and business leaders acted as pallbearers. He was lauded as "the harmonious human multitude." Dr. Franklin was buried in a plot beside his wife, Deborah, and son, Francis. Franklin's tombstone reads: "Benjamin and Deborah Franklin — 1790." This phrase exemplifies his style as a "Common Man," plain and simple.

People around the world mourned for Benjamin Franklin. He touched the lives and won the respect of hundreds of thousands of people from America and abroad. Thomas Jefferson felt the need to express a few words in remembrance of his dear old friend in "On Benjamin Franklin":

> I feel both the wish and the duty to communicate, in compliance with your request, whatever, within my knowledge, might render justice to the memory of our great countryman, Dr. Franklin, in which Philosophy has to deplore one of its principal luminaries extinguished.[207]

Jefferson noted how Dr. Franklin's witty sayings charmed every society. Jefferson recollected when they were together in Paris, and Franklin was winding up his diplomatic affairs and scientific experiments.

The French loved Franklin and highly valued his friendship. Jefferson appraised Dr. Franklin's international stature:

> I can only therefore testify in general, that there appeared to me more

respect and veneration attached to the character of Doctor Franklin in France, than to that of any other person in the same country, foreign or native.[208]

Jefferson related how the ministers of France were "impressed with the talents and integrity of Dr. Franklin." The French foreign minister, Count de Vergennes, ". . . gave me repeated and unequivocal demonstrations of his entire confidence in him."

Jefferson, who followed Franklin as Ambassador to France, admitted how hard it would be to try to fill Franklin's shoes:

> The succession to Dr. Franklin, at the court of France, was an excellent school of humility. On being presented to any one as the minister of America, the commonplace question used in such cases was "c'est votts, Monsieur, qui remplace le Docteur Franklin?" "It is you, Sir, who replace Doctor Franklin?" I generally answered, "No one can replace him, Sir. I am only his successor.[209]

Jefferson was astute in recognizing Benjamin Franklin as a unique figure in history. He was happy that his colleague was able to live long enough to see the birth of the United States of America.

Although Franklin, Jefferson, and Madison exerted their influence on the development of the U.S. Constitution and the first ten Amendments, Dr. Franklin did not live long enough to witness the final approval of the Bill of Rights. By December 15, 1791, three quarters of the states had ratified the Bill of Rights, guaranteeing the freedoms of speech, religion, and assembly, the right to a jury trial and more. Now it was up to Thomas Jefferson, James Madison, and all Americans to make their "grand design" a reality.

Thomas Jefferson to James Madison,
"Bill of Rights Needed" (1787),
Library of Congress.

Thomas Jefferson,
"Lord's Prayer in secret code,"
Manuscript Division, Library of Congress,
(LCMS-27748-276).

Thomas Jefferson,
"An Act for Establishing Religious Freedom" (1786),
Broadside Collection, Rare Book and Special Collections Division,
Library of Congress.

Chapter Two

"THOMAS JEFFERSON ON RELIGION AND THE STATE"

This chapter traces the life and times of Thomas Jefferson (1743-1826), who served as a public official for half a century and is respected as one of America's most important philosophers and early founders. He was the author of the Declaration of Independence and the Statute of Virginia for Religious Freedom, as well as the third President of the United States. He believed strongly in the free exercise of religion and the separation of Church and State.[1]

THE ROOTS OF THOMAS JEFFERSON

On April 13, 1743, Jefferson was born at Shadwell plantation along the banks of the Rivanna River in Virginia. His father, Peter Jefferson, was a planter, mapmaker, justice of the peace, county justice, sheriff, and a lieutenant colonel in the militia. He also was the fourth generation in his family to serve in the Virginia House of Burgesses. Family lore related that he was descended from a line of Welsh kings. In fact, his great-great grandfather John Jefferson emigrated from Gwynedd, Wales to Virginia sometime before 1653 and was a direct descendent of Sir Walkelin de Arderne (ca. 1217-1265).[2]

Thomas Jefferson's mother, Jane Randolph (1720-1776), was born in London, the daughter of a prominent family resettled in Virginia as part of the landed gentry. Her aristocratic family tree originated in Old England and Scotland ranging as far back as Charlemagne (742-814), Emperor of the Holy Roman Empire. One genealogist documented her as a direct descendant of both King Henry III Plantagenet (1207-1272) of England and King Ferdinand III de Castille (1201-1252) of Spain.[3]

Thomas was a redheaded, freckled-faced boy. From age two to nine, he lived with his mother's relatives, the Randolphs, on the Tuckahoe estate in Virginia. He attended their family schoolhouse, educated by private tutors, along with his brothers, sisters, and the Randolph children.

At the age of nine, he and his family returned to the Shadwell estate. Young Jefferson began attending a local school run by the Scottish American Reverend William Douglas, famous for his detailed register of genealogical information. He taught Thomas to speak French with a Scottish accent. Although tall and gangly, Jefferson displayed musical talent and was taught to play the violin by Francis Alberti, the noted Italian American violinist in Williamsburg.[4]

In 1757, when Thomas was fourteen, tragedy struck. His father died at the age of fifty, leaving a wife, six daughters, and two sons. Peter Jefferson specifically left his books and surveying equipment to Thomas. One of the interests he had instilled in his son was a love for horsemanship. As the eldest son, Thomas eventually inherited much of the family estate. A thousand acres of patent land later became the grounds of Monticello, the Thomas Jefferson estate. He generously gave his younger brother, James, the rich riverfront property known as Snowden, named after Snowden Mountain in northern Wales where the Jefferson family originated.[5]

JEFFERSON'S HIGHER EDUCATION

In 1758, Jefferson advanced to the school of the Episcopal Reverend James Maury (1717-1769) in Fredericksville Parish, twelve miles from Shadwell. He boarded with Maury's family, who were descended from French Huguenots who fled in 1713 from Normandy to Virginia. The Huguenots, as French Protestants, left to escape religious persecution by French Catholics. Reverend Maury preached that Christians should be free to worship as they pleased.[6]

Rev. Maury followed a classical curriculum focused on the language arts. As a serious student and avid reader, Jefferson began keeping a literary common-place book, writing extracts in it from Greek, Latin, and English literature. He further developed his language skills in French, Italian, and Spanish.

In 1760, at the age of sixteen, Jefferson traveled 150 miles to Williamsburg, where he commenced his higher education at William and Mary College. At the School of Philosophy, he completed his undergraduate work in two and a half years. His graduate education and legal training took much longer; five years, under the guidance of law professor George Wythe, who later assisted Jefferson in writing the Virginia legal code. Wythe introduced Jefferson not only to law and political theory, but also to the works of the famous European philosophers Locke, Rousseau, Montesquieu, and Voltaire.[7]

Jefferson's college days were not focused entirely on his studies. He became obsessed with Rebecca Burwell, a sixteen-year-old local beauty. In 1764, when she dismissed his proposal in favor of a younger lover, Jefferson was emotionally devastated. He was struck with migraine headaches from which he suffered off and on for the rest of his life.[8]

Jefferson soothed his broken heart by traveling. He toured the mid-Atlantic colonies, visiting New York, Philadelphia, Annapolis, and Maryland. In Annapolis he witnessed a session of the Maryland legislature, an experience that sparked his political interests. While in Massachusetts, he made friends with Elbridge Gerry, who later would join him in the Continental Congress. Jefferson returned to complete his law school training at William & Mary College. In 1767, he passed the bar and became an attorney in Williamsburg, VA. He returned frequently to his family homestead, where he began clearing the land for his future mansion at Monticello ["little mountain" in Italian].[9]

THE BEGINNINGS OF JEFFERSON'S POLITICAL CAREER

Thomas Jefferson's political career began in 1769, when he became the Albemarle County Representative to the House of Burgesses. Following his family tradition, Jefferson entered public service in the lower chamber of the Virginia colonial legislature. However, only nine days after his arrival, the

Virginia House of Burgesses was dismissed by the royal governor, Baron de Botetourt, the former constable of the Tower of London. His act of colonial oppression was prompted by a reaction to the legislature's attempt to assume legal jurisdiction over taxation and judiciary appointments. Jefferson and the Virginia colonials, outraged by the heavy-handedness of the royal governor, met privately at Raleigh Tavern. They responded by organizing a boycott against British imported goods. Here we find the seeds of protest that led to the American Revolution.[10]

Jefferson returned home for the summer and immersed himself in reading about politics, history, and law. In the autumn, he was elected for a second term to the House of Burgesses. This time he was fired up with revolutionary fervor. His bold proposal to liberalize colonial slave policies caught the attention of the royal governor. However, before any formal action was taken against him, Governor Baron de Botetourt died from unknown causes.[11]

On February 1, 1770, Jefferson's home burned to the ground. He lost most of his library and early writings in the fire. His treasured Italian violin somehow survived the blaze. Undaunted, Jefferson orchestrated the architectural design and construction of his new mansion at Monticello. With equal passion, he began courting 23-year-old Martha Wayles Skelton. She was a young widow trying to overcome her sorrows. She was blessed with a fine voice and sang while Jefferson played his violin or the piano. Despite objections from her father, Martha and Thomas were married on New Year's Day, 1772. Eighteen months later, Martha's father died, leaving her and Thomas a 10,000-acre estate, as well as 130 slaves. Among them was Betty Hemings, the mistress and mother of perhaps six children from Martha's father. One of the six children, Sally Hemings, the half-sister of Martha, purportedly became mistress to Thomas Jefferson in later years.[12]

Nevertheless, Jefferson loved his wife dearly, as evidenced by the fact that he spent more time with her than he did in the state legislature. About nine months after their marriage, they were blessed with a baby girl. Her formal name was Martha, but she became known as Patsy. She was to be the first of six children.

In September of 1775, the Jeffersons lost their second daughter, Jane, who died at the age of three. Then in March of 1776, Jefferson's mother, Jane Randolph Jefferson, passed away from a sudden stroke. She was only fifty-seven. Jefferson went into mourning and suffered from persistent migraine headaches.

Premature deaths plagued the Jefferson family. Only one other of their six children, Maria, whom they nicknamed Polly, ultimately survived to adulthood. However, before Polly was born, Jefferson was called away by the Virginia legislature to help draft a new state constitution.

"LIBERTY OF RELIGIOUS OPINION": THE 1776 VIRGINIA STATE CONSTITUTION

Jefferson's three drafts of the 1776 Virginia Constitution are important in helping to establish an understanding of his early ideas about government and the impending Declaration of Independence. The Virginia Constitution represents a practical application of his political theories.

Regarding religious freedom, Jefferson wrote in his first draft:

> All persons shall have full & free liberty of religious opinion, nor shall any be compelled to frequent or maintain any religious service or institution (but seditious behavior to be punble [punishable] by civil magistrate accdg [according] to the laws already made or hereafter to be made.)[13]

Jefferson made the end phrase parenthetical because it was optional or open to question. Should the civil magistrate, meaning a state judge, have jurisdiction over the "seditious behavior" of a religious group?

In the second draft, Jefferson made some modifications to his tentative end phrase:

> RELIGION
> All persons shall have full & free liberty of religious opinion: nor shall any be compelled to frequent or maintain any religious institution. *[But this shall not be held to justify any seditious preaching or conversation against the authority of the civil government.]*[14]

Here Jefferson momentarily considered limiting the free exercise of religion. He apparently was concerned about religious groups who might conspire to overthrow the civil government. He further considered limiting freedom of speech in such cases.

However, in his third draft, Jefferson deleted the end section, thus eliminating a statement that would have given jurisdiction by the state over religious groups:

> RELIGION
> All persons shall have full and free liberty of religious opinion; nor shall any be compelled to frequent or maintain any religious institution.[15]

The final statement recognized the people's "free liberty of religious opinion." This was not as far as James Madison was willing to go in extending freedom to "exercise" religious practices. Jefferson also recognized the people's freedom not to join any particular church. Thus he supported Madison's position against religious establishments of a state-recognized religion, like the Church of England. He further shared Madison's viewpoint against the state "maintaining" or providing tax dollars to support religious institutions. They believed in supporting churches through the collection plate.

Jefferson's extraordinary abilities as a writer and statesman were further called upon when he was chosen to be a representative of Virginia in the Continental Congress. On May 14, 1776, he arrived in Philadelphia. Congress recently had adopted a resolution to begin functioning as a government separate from England. The Virginia Convention had just made its historic call for independence. On May 16, Jefferson penned a letter to fellow Virginia delegate to the Continental Congress Thomas Nelson (ca. 1738-89) expressing the importance of framing a new government:

. . . the whole object of the present controversy; for should a bad government be instituted for us in future it had been as well to have accepted at first the bad one offered to us from beyond the water without the risk and [expense] of contest.[16]

In creating a new government, Jefferson also sought to change the aristocratic structure of society. Even though he was born into the upper class of the landed gentry, he embraced a government based on the popular sovereignty of the people.

"ALL MEN ARE EQUALLY ENTITLED TO THE FREE EXERCISE OF RELIGION . . . "

Jefferson's writings related to the Virginia Constitution further illuminate the main principles that guided his career. He believed strongly in a government "of the people, for the people and by the people." He defended "public liberty" and the rights of the individual against government intrusions impacting personal freedoms. The thought crossed his mind of how this might affect cases of suspected sedition, but Jefferson soon deleted such clauses from his drafts.

He believed that the number of Congressional representatives should be fair for each state. He advocated U.S. policy toward Indians should be more fair and honest and that Indian tribes should be respected as sovereign nations. He supported liberal immigration policies and protection of rights for foreign naturalized citizens. He reversed British policy, extending civil authority over the military. He advocated separation of powers within government and a clear separation between Church and State.

However, the Virginia legislature was not ready to accept many of Jefferson's more revolutionary reforms of government and social structure. They resisted many of his principles for creating a democratic republic. George Mason's draft, strongly influenced by the writings of John Adams, was more favorably accepted. After a long debate over the successive drafts, a final version was composed by taking parts from various authors. On June 29, 1776, the Constitution of Virginia was approved. The law regarding religious freedom now read:

> SEC. 16. That religion, or the duty which we owe to our Creator, and the manner of discharging it, can be directed only by reason and conviction, not by force or violence; and therefore all men are equally entitled to the free exercise of religion, according to the dictates of conscience; and that it is the mutual duty of all to practice Christian forbearance, love, and charity towards each other.[17]

The final draft actually expanded religious liberty from Jefferson's freedom of religious "opinion" to the Virginia legislature's full recognition of the "free exercise of religion." This is important because Virginians then were not just free to think and pray, but also free to practice their religions as they saw fit. However, the Virginia legislature did delete Jefferson's clause regarding one's right not to "be compelled to frequent or maintain any religious institution."

Change did not come fast enough for Jefferson. Undaunted by the stubborn posture of conservative Virginians, he set upon the task of reframing the entire body of law. What he could not fully achieve in Constitutional reform, Jefferson sought to do step by step through a barrage of new legislation.

THE DECLARATION OF INDEPENDENCE

While the Virginia legislature was finalizing the law regarding religious freedom, Jefferson threw himself into drafting the Declaration of Independence. His strong democratic convictions came through clearly. For eighteen days, between June 11 and June 28, 1776, he labored over the text of what would come to be recognized as one of America's most valued symbols of liberty. His words expressed the hopes and aspirations of American people to be able to live in a free and independent country. Drawing from the ideas of European Enlightenment philosophers and American Revolutionary writers, Jefferson set forth a list of grievances against British oppression and then proclaimed the right of Americans to be free. Few other documents in the history of the United States have become so engrained in the hearts and minds of American people. On July 4, 1776, Congress unanimously passed the resolution declaring an independent United States:

> When in the Course of human events, it becomes necessary for one people to dissolve the political bands which have connected them with another, and to assume among the powers of the earth, the separate and equal station to which the Laws of Nature and of Nature's God entitle them, a decent respect to the opinions of mankind requires that they should declare the causes which impel them to the separation.[18]

The Declaration of Independence could be viewed as America's case before the world court of public opinion. Jefferson sought to justify the American Revolution by outlining the causes for the break between the American colonies and Great Britain.

The Declaration of Independence presented a philosophy of freedom based on "self-evident truths":

> We hold these truths to be self-evident, that all men are created equal, that they are endowed by their Creator with certain unalienable Rights, that among these are Life, Liberty and the pursuit of Happiness. — That to secure these rights, Governments are instituted among Men, deriving their just powers from the consent of the governed.[19]

Jefferson proclaimed that the Creator endowed people with their fundamental religious and civil rights. The people were to enjoy divine rights previously claimed by kings. The purpose of a democratic government was to protect the rights of the people. Furthermore, the power rested with the people, while government officials would function as public servants with the consent of the people.

Jefferson asserted that the American people had a right to abolish the old British rule and replace it with a new form of government:

> That whenever any Form of Government becomes destructive of these ends, it is the Right of the People to alter or to abolish it, and to institute new Government, laying its foundation on such principles and organizing its powers in such form, as to them shall seem most likely to effect their Safety and Happiness.[20]

Tyranny must be overthrown to protect the rights of the people against oppression. The purpose of government - to insure the "safety and happiness" of the people — must never be lost.

Jefferson accused the King of England of "despotism," acts of harsh absolute power and tyranny. The term originally was used to describe the Byzantine emperor and was also applied to domineering bishops of the Greek Church:

> But when a long train of abuses and usurpations, pursuing invariably the same Object evinces a design to reduce them under absolute Despotism, it is their right, it is their duty, to throw off such Government, and to provide new Guards for their future security. — Such has been the patient sufferance of these Colonies; and such is now the necessity which constrains them to alter their former Systems of Government.[21]

The American Revolution not only was their "right," according to Jefferson, it was their "duty." Their security demanded a change in civil government. Jefferson and the members of the Continental Congress were determined not to just reform the government, but rather to create a new form of government called "democracy."

"Let history be the judge," states a wise proverb. The history of the British King, Jefferson asserted, marked an intolerable record of crimes against humanity. The result was a state of "tyranny," a Greek term used by Greek slaves to describe their cruel masters. He charged:

> The history of the present King of Great Britain is a history of repeated injuries and usurpations, all having in direct object the establishment of an absolute Tyranny over these States. To prove this, let Facts be submitted to a candid world.[22]

As an attorney of law, Jefferson laid out the facts, compiling a long list of 26 specific civil and criminal charges against the King, British colonial officials and the British military. In short, the King had created a military dictatorship over the American colonies. He had obstructed justice, suspended colonial legislatures, prevented lawful elections, and given the military authority over civil government. Furthermore, the King and British officials had created a series of acts resulting in taxation without representation, quartering troops in American homes, creating mock trials, depriving Americans of trial by a jury of their peers, and more. Serious criminal charges were filed as a result of British orders that American towns were to be burned, American ships plundered, and American citizens murdered. Jefferson finally described King George III as a tyrant "unfit to be the ruler of a free people."

Americans, Jefferson concluded, were faced with no other choice but to declare their independence and to proclaim their freedom to the world:

> We, therefore, the Representatives of the United States of America, in General Congress, Assembled, appealing to the Supreme Judge of the world for the rectitude of our intentions, do, in the Name, and by Authority of the good People of these Colonies, solemnly publish and declare, That these United Colonies are, and of Right ought to be Free and Independent States; that they are Absolved from all Allegiance to the British Crown, and that all political connection between them and the State of Great Britain, is and ought to be totally dissolved; and that as Free and Independent States, they have full Power to levy War, conclude Peace, contract Alliances, establish Commerce, and to do all other Acts and Things which Independent States may of right do. And for the support of this Declaration, with a firm reliance on the protection of divine Providence, we mutually pledge to each other our Lives, our Fortunes and our sacred Honor.[23]

Americans no longer were going to rely on the graces of a despotic king. Americans, Jefferson asserted, were determined to rely on the "protection of divine Providence," meaning the care God shows over the universe. In short, Americans placed their faith in God, not kings. To this end, Americans were willing to stake their honor and fortunes, and were ready to lay their lives on the line for freedom, liberty and justice.

John Hancock, President of the Continental Congress, was the first to sign the Declaration of Independence. His signature is written in a large script, reportedly big enough to make certain the King could read it. Hancock encouraged the members of Congress to remain united, "For if we do not hang together, we surely will hang separately." The resolution passed unanimously. However, if the American Revolution was not won, Hancock, Jefferson, Madison, Franklin, and other revolutionary leaders realized that they would be charged with treason, sedition, and conspiracy — all hangable offenses under the British system of capital punishment.[24]

Jefferson stayed in Philadelphia through the summer. He participated in the debates that would lead to the "Articles of Confederation," forerunner of the U.S. Constitution. During this period, he became friends with a fellow Virginian, James Madison. Thus began a lifelong friendship between the two men.

On August 13, 1776, Jefferson penned a letter to Edmund Pendleton, a fellow Virginian Congressman, in which he gave a status report on General George Washington and his troops:

> The General has by his last return, 17000 some odd men, of whom near 4000 are sick & near 3000 at out posts in Long Island &c. So you may say he has but 10000 effective men to defend the works of New York. His works however are good & his men in spirits, which I hope will be equal to an addition of many thousands.[25]

Jefferson also wrote about the importance of supporting foreign immigration to increase the population of the United States. He considered offering foreign immigrants a small tract of land and a little money to help get them started as naturalized American citizens. Full rights of citizenship would be guaranteed to them.

JEFFERSON'S EARLY ATTEMPTS TO ENSURE RELIGIOUS FREEDOM

Sometime before November 19, 1776, Jefferson worked on a draft of a bill regarding religious freedom in America. His legislation proposed to achieve two major points. First, he sought an end to the Church of England being the official church of the United States of America. Second, he was determined to repeal all colonial laws that might interfere with their "Freedom of Worship": Jefferson sought an end to "punishments for the offence of opinions deemed heretical." This referred to that European and old colonial practice of branding political opponents as "heretics," meaning anyone who holds religious opinions contrary to the fundamental doctrines and tenets of the Church.[26]

Jefferson then took the leap from "freedom of religious opinions" to "free exercise of religion." He called for an end to all criminal penalties and punishments regarding "exercising any mode of worship . . ." This placed him in full alignment with James Madison on this issue. He then championed Madison's cause to end the "establishment of the Church of England." This would terminate Anglican supremacy in America and clearly warn the civil government not to provide tax dollars nor official sanctions for favored religious groups. Jefferson made his position clear:

> . . . no pre-eminence may be allowed to any one Religious sect over another, is reasonable; & therefore that the several laws establishing the [said] Church of England, giving peculiar privileges to [the] it's ministers [thereof], & levying for the support thereof [the same] contributions on the people independent of their good will ought to be repealed . . . [27]

Churches should be supported through the good will of the collection plate, Jefferson asserted, and no church should receive a favored position from the civil government.

Jefferson must have written his draft prior to November 19, 1776, because on that date Congress adopted a similar resolution:

> *Resolved,* that all and every act or statute, either of the parliament of *England or of Great Britain,* by whatever title known or distinguished, which renders criminal the maintaining any opinions in matters of religion, forbearing to repair to church, or the exercising any mode of worship whatsoever, or which prescribes punishments for the same, ought to be declared henceforth of no validity or force within this Commonwealth.[28]

This clause of the resolution originally did not pass, but was added in the amendments.

Historian Bernard Bailyn, in his Pulitzer Prize-winning book, *The Ideological Origins of the American Revolution,* laid out the evidence to document the development of American convictions against religious establishments.[29] He pointed out the contradictions between minority religious leaders, who advocated a clear separation of Church and State vs. majority Anglican religious leaders, who wanted to maintain their favored status with the State. In the end, the minority camp won and American society was the beneficiary of a firm principle separating Church and State.

Jefferson's second resolution regarding religion was struck down. Congress was not prepared to repeal all laws regarding the "suppression of vice" and laws against "blasphemous, wicked, and dissolute persons." Jefferson's third resolution passed regarding tax-exemptions for churches. The fourth resolution insured that civil government should not restrain religious matters, except in cases of "publick assemblies." The fifth resolution brought an end to the use of public money to pay the salaries of the clergy. Jefferson's sixth and final resolution clarified the disposition of church lands. Lands and assets bestowed by the King were to be recognized as a life estate. However, in the case of lands and assets bestowed by private American citizens, the recognition of title would be in perpetuity.

In a fragment of a Jefferson document is found the presumed introduction to his resolutions. Jefferson wrote that the purpose of his religious resolutions was "for restoring to the *[Inhabitants]* Citizens of this Comm'w [Commonwealth], the right of maintaining their religious opinions, & of worshipping God in their own way; for releasing them from all legal obligations to frequent churches or other places of worship, *[&]* for exempting them from contributions for the support of any *[church]* religious society independent of their good will, *[&]* for discontinuing the establishment of the Church of England by *[thereby]* taking away the privilege & pre-eminence of one religions sect over another, and thereby *[establish* [several words illegible] & *equal rights among all]*."[30]

Regarding Jefferson's position on the separation of Church and State, a second fragmentary document in his hand, originally crossed out but still legible, reads:

> For discontinuing the establishment of the English church by law, taking away all privilege & pre-eminence of one religious sect over another; & totally and eternally restraining the civil magistrate from all pretensions of interposing his authority or exercise in matter of religion.[31]

Jefferson made his strongest statement to date regarding three major points: First, Americans should end official recognition of the Church of England. Second, the civil government should favor no single religion. Third, and most important, no civil government official or even a judge should have any authority whatsoever in matters of religion.

A LAW TO STOP FUNDING THE CHURCH OF ENGLAND WITH AMERICAN TAXES

On November 30, 1776, Jefferson drafted a "Bill for Exempting Dissenters from Contributing to the Support of the Church." No American, Jefferson asserted, should be forced to give money to the Church of England:

> Whereas, it is represented by many of the Inhabitants of this Country who dissent from the Church of England as by Law established that they consider the Assessments and Contributions which they have been hitherto obliged to make towards the support and Maintenance of the said Church and its Ministry as grievous and oppressive, and an Infringement of their religious Freedom.[32]

Jefferson clearly stated that religious assessments were a violation of religious freedom. He sought to protect Americans from being forced to give money to support religious groups. In his opinion, such contributions should be voluntary.

DANGERS OF THE STATE FAVORING SELECT RELIGIOUS GROUPS

Jefferson saw the dangers of civil government officials using favored religious groups to support their political ends. If the Church and State were not kept separated, the leaders of the two bodies might conspire to keep one another in power. The rights of the people could then be squashed and the result would be oppression.

Jefferson proclaimed the solution to the problem was to guarantee the people that their religious and civil liberties would be protected and honored:

> For Remedy whereof and that equal Liberty as well religious as civil may be universally extended to all the good People of this Common Wealth, Be it Enacted by the General Assembly of the Common Wealth of Virginia and it is hereby Enacted by the Authority of the same that all Dissenters of whatever Denomination from the said Church shall from and after the passing this Act be totally free and exempt from all Levies Taxes and Impositions whatever towards supporting and maintaining the said Church.[33]

At a time when the United States was newly forming, Jefferson sought to set a precedent regarding the religious and civil liberties of the American people. No levies. No taxes. No impositions whatever would be permitted in the United States regarding public money going to religious groups.

The collecting of funds to support religious groups, Jefferson acknowledged, must be done "within their respective Parishes." Payments to ministers must be done legally and in accordance to agreements within each religious group. Charitable contributions to the poor could continue according to local custom. Existing church lands and property would "be saved and reserved to the use of such Parishes as may have received private Donations for the better support of the said Church and its Ministers the perpetual Benefit and enjoyment of all such Donations."[34]

To help insure the passage of the bill, Jefferson left open to future debates in Congress issues related to dissenting denominations outside the Church of England. The importance of the bill to Jefferson is reflected in the copious notes he compiled to help him prepare for the debates in Congress. What follows is a detailed account of his research on the topic of religious dissent. First, he composed four pages outlining his position in support of the resolution. He began by pointing to instances in ancient history regarding oppressive acts by civil governments against religious liberty. He used examples from ancient Greek and Latin texts as a comparison with similar acts of oppression in colonial American history. People who asserted their religious freedom sometimes were branded "heretics." What follows is Jefferson's detailed study of "dissenters" and "heretics." If the American Revolutionaries were ever criticized by the British with these labels, Jefferson wanted their defense well prepared.[35]

RELIGIOUS DISSENTERS:
FROM THE ARIANS TO THE QUAKERS

Some American dissenters, like those in ancient times, were imprisoned for publicly expressing their views on religion. Others were imprisoned for not conforming to the demands of civil government. Jefferson used for examples, the Arians of ancient Europe and the Quakers of colonial America. The Arians of the Roman Empire did not believe that Christ was divine. When they dissented from the Athanasians, they were called heretics and suffered a fiery persecution.[36]

The Quaker religion was inspired in 1650 by an English judge, George Fox, who bade his followers to tremble or quake "at the word of the Lord." They suffered religious persecution as Protestant pacifists and resettled mostly in Pennsylvania, becoming known as the Society of Friends. Quaker meetings are noted for sitting in silence, "waiting upon the Spirit." They repudiated ritual, formal sacraments, oaths, and war.

Jefferson cited both groups as examples of dissenters who were fined, imprisoned, and oppressed for their religious views. Both were persecuted as heretics, non-conformists who held beliefs contrary to the official doctrines of the dominant church. With the passage of Jefferson's bill, Americans were declaring themselves dissenters from the Church of England.

He called forth the example of two 16th century Italian reformers, Faustus and Laelius, theologians who challenged beliefs in the devil and the idea of eternally burning in hell. They taught that human beings were not naturally depraved. Their philosophy was called Socinian.

Jefferson continued to cite examples of groups throughout history who had suffered from religious persecution. He pointed out that their religious rights need not be surrendered in the process of guaranteeing civil rights. Religious freedom, Jefferson argued, was an "unalienable right." Religious people ultimately were "answerable to God."

GALILEO GALILEI: A LESSON ON THE IMPORTANCE OF "FREE ENQUIRY"

Jefferson made a case for the importance of "free enquiry," the freedom to question things in society. As an example, he cited the lack of "free enquiry" for the Italian astronomer, Galileo Galilei (1564-1642). His invention of the telescope initially was viewed as a threat by the established church. Because the telescope was used to prove that the earth revolved around the sun, and official church doctrine then held that the universe revolved around the earth. With the publication of his book, *Two Chief World Systems,* Galileo was convicted of heresy by church inquisitors and condemned to house arrest for the remainder of his life. Galileo should have had a right to "free enquiry," Jefferson advanced. Because of men like Galileo, the world benefits from scientific knowledge. He made major contributions to several fields of science including astronomy and mechanics, Jefferson acknowledged. Within a free society, the growth of knowledge may be encouraged to progress. "Free enquiry," Jefferson proclaimed, was an important principle to be protected, if American society was to be free.[37]

SIR ISAAC NEWTON: A LESSON ON "SCIENTIFIC REASONING"

The well-studied Virginia statesman followed with the example of Sir Isaac Newton (1642-1727). Beyond his famous theories on gravity and optics, Newton pioneered a form of scientific reasoning that revolutionized scientific inquiry. He presented his methodology as a set of "four rules for scientific reasoning." In his treatise, *Principia,* Newton proposed that "(1) we are to admit no more causes of natural things such as are both true and sufficient to explain their appearances, (2) the same natural effects must be assigned to the same causes, (3) qualities of bodies are to be esteemed as universal, and (4) propositions deduced from observation of phenomena should be viewed as accurate until other phenomena contradict them." This revolutionary scientific approach to analysis excited Jefferson.[38]

The Virginia statesman challenged the concept of a state religion. In his view, its purpose was to create "uniformity." He pointed to Galileo and Newton as examples from history of important individuals who were not uniform. In fact, they were non-conformists. Because they strove for freedom of expression, the world benefited by their unique contributions to knowledge. "Uniformity" had a "suffocating" effect on "free enquiry." Therefore, he concluded, a state religion would be stifling to the progress of society.

Jefferson cited tragedies in history when the Church attempted to force society to accept "uniformity." During the past two centuries, European society had suffered from the "Inquisition." Church officials engaged in a "witch hunt" against anyone who defied their authority. Resisters were burned at the stake as heretics. Non-conformists were tortured and imprisoned. "Christianity flourished

for 300 years without establishment," he pointed out. With the onset of establishments such as the Church of England, the result was a "decline from purity."

Jefferson warned that some people tend to believe that only their religion is
right. Rather than officially recognize only one religion as being supreme, he
suggested that society would benefit more by recognizing all religions to be free.
He challenged the claim of "infallibility," as being unprecedented in history. He
queried, "Has God stamped us with [his] mark, [making us] whiter, handsomer,
more athletic or wiser?" The answer was no. Equal rights for citizens should be
extended to equal rights for churches.

JEFFERSON AGAINST TAX DOLLARS
BEING PAID TO CHURCHES

Jefferson argued against the state requiring money to be paid to churches.
The result would be a decline in "freedom of religion." The Quakers, he pointed
out, considered mandatory payments to be against their religious principles.

He believed strongly that civil government should only recognize people's
right to free exercise of religion and should not make appropriations nor laws
regarding the practice of religion. To make his point, Jefferson compiled a "List
of Acts of Parliament and of Virginia Assembly, 1661-1759, concerning
Religion."[39] The first laws established a Protestant Church, inducting the ministers,
appointing the vestries, maintaining holy relics and declaring holy days and times
of fasting.

In the first half of the 18th century, a series of laws established punishments
for "blasphemous, wicked and dissolute persons . . . preventing incestuous mar-
riages and copulations." Laws against "blasphemy," swearing against God or the
Church, limited the freedom of speech and suppressed religious reform. Laws
against "wickedness," punished people for committing sins, as interpreted from
the Bible. Laws against dissolution, punished acts deemed immoral. Laws against
incest prevented brothers and sisters or parents and their children from marrying.
Laws against copulation made it a crime to engage in sexual relations outside of
marriage blessed by the Church. The charge of heresy was used to suppress
religious reform or dissent. One law prevented dissenters from being vestrymen
in the Church. Other laws made by Protestants were intended to "disarm" and
limit the rights of Catholics to the point of prohibiting "a papist from keeping
horse above £5.3."

JEFFERSON'S DEFENSE FOR
A SEPARATION BETWEEN CHURCH AND STATE

Jefferson's research on religious laws in Great Britain and colonial Virginia
provided evidence in defense of his case for the separation of Church and State.[40]
He cited these examples of outrageous British and Colonial laws:

- "Failure to attend Sunday Church services was against the law.
- Speaking against the sacrament was punishable by fines and imprisonment.
- Religious courts were to be established to prosecute religious crimes.
- Any prayers uttered other that those in the "Book of Common Prayer" was punishable first by six months imprisonment. The third instance of illegal praying would result in life imprisonment.
- Acts of heresy were punishable by burning at the stake, administered by the religious leaders.
- Ministers who varied from the established ceremonies associated with communion would result in imprisonment from one year to life.
- Anyone who composes a play, song, poem or prose considered against the "Book of Common Prayers" would be imprisoned for six months to life, forfeiting all personal property.
- Any schoolmaster who did not attend church would no longer be allowed to teach and would be imprisoned for a year.
- Anyone who did not recognize the King and Queen of England as the head of the Church, or who spoke, wrote or published materials challenging their royal supremacy would be imprisoned until they conformed and made a public recantation. If they refuse to cooperate, they may be banished from the country. If they refuse to leave, they shall be put to death without receiving the last sacraments, thus condemned to hell.
- Anyone who speaks profanely or uses the name of God, Jesus Christ, the Holy Ghost or the Trinity, shall be fined £10. for every offense.
- No minister may preach in America without being ordained by a bishop in England.
- No minister may teach anything other than the Church Catechism.
- No one may deny the existence of one God, punishable by being denied any public office and imprisonment for up to three years.
- No one may deny the Christian religion, punishable by being denied any public office and imprisonment for up to three years.
- No one may deny that the Bible is of divine authority, punishable by being denied any public office and imprisonment for up to three years."[41]

Jefferson pointed a finger at the more outrageous religious laws as clear examples of why the civil government should not become involved in legislating matters of religion. Like James Madison, Jefferson believed lawmakers should stay out of religious affairs.

To further defend his position for the separation of Church and State, Jefferson brought forth the writings of two English philosophers: John Locke (1632-1704)[42] and the Earl of Shaftesbury (1671-1713).[43] Locke championed the cause of religious freedom. Locke believed that people should not be punished for having different religious views. In his 1689 "Letter on Toleration," he advocated the separation of Church and State. Shaftesbury advocated "natural religion," and criticized "institutional religion." He embraced a form of global spirituality.

Jefferson drew from both philosophers in posing a fundamental question: "Why persecute [people] for differences in religious opinion?" Jefferson was amazed how some people were capable of persecuting members of their own families and closest loved ones. He asked the legislators to question whether adulterers should be put to death. One may presume that some in his audience were guilty of this offense, thus making a strong point against enactment of severe civil laws for such offenses. While he acknowledged that such moral vices were "diametrically against Christianity & obstructive of salvation of souls," he advanced his personal belief that "our Saviour chose not to propagate his religion by temporal punishments or civil incapacitation."

The purpose of civil government, Jefferson asserted, was to be "a society of men constituted for preserving their civil rights' interests." Those interests were "life, health, indolency of body, liberty, property." He argued that they should not give authority over religion to civil government officials: "The magistrate has no power but what we the people give him." He added that one should not abandon the care of his salvation to another person. Furthermore, no one should force religious beliefs on others.

As an intellectual, Jefferson internalized religion and considered religious worship best when kept free:

> . . . the life & essence of religion consists in the internal persuasion or belief of the mind . . . external forms of worship, when against our belief, are hypocrisy and impiety.[44]

Jefferson was too free-spirited to submit to the impositions of a State religion. He embraced a strong belief in God as a Supreme Being, while advocating acceptance of religious diversity in America.

JEFFERSON AGAINST STATE RELIGION

Jefferson quoted the Bible to support his position against state religions. He selected from the Book of Romans regarding how religious faith should be sincere, strong without doubt.

> He that doubteth is damned, if he eat, because he eateth not of faith: for whatsoever is not of faith is sin.[45]

Chapter 14 in the Book of Romans states that one should not doubt the existence of God and one should not judge one another. The scriptures state that only God should be the true judge. Humans are fallible; therefore their judgments might be in error. Everyone should have the freedom to develop their own opinions, as stated in Romans, Chapter 14, verse 5: "Let every man be fully persuaded in his own mind."

Each person should have faith, Jefferson concurred. One should not judge a brother, as stated in verse 20: "Let us not therefore judge one another any more: but judge this rather, that no man put a stumbling block or an occasion to fall in his brother's way." Thus Jefferson advocated that no one, including civil government, should judge their fellow man regarding religion, because only God could be the ultimate judge in such matters.

The Church should be a "voluntary society," Jefferson asserted. It is "*voluntary* because no man is *by nature* bound to any church." When one enters a church, "hopes of salvation" are before them. However, if one may "find anything wrong in it, he should be as free to go out as he was to come in."

Jefferson then questioned, "What is the power of that church?" The laws of a church should only extend "to its own members." God's definition of society, he contended, could consist of only two or three people, gathered together in his name. No other governance is required. Religious liberty need only "reciprocity" in allowing others the freedom of choice, just as we would wish such liberty for ourselves.

Jefferson challenged the practice of excommunication, a religious leader claiming authority to cut the relationship between God and an individual person, preventing the excommunicated from going to heaven. He believed that human beings could have a direct relationship with God.

"How far does the duty of toleration extend?" Jefferson asked.

Churches, he argued, may choose for themselves who may be their members. However, no church should have right to oppress individuals or other churches that may differ from them.

Jefferson concluded, "Each church being free, no one can have jurisdiction over another; no not even when the civil magistrate joins it." Thus, the officials of Church and State, even when working together, still should not have jurisdiction over the free exercise of religion as practiced by members of any church.

"THE CARE OF EVERY MAN'S SOUL"

Everyone, Jefferson advanced, should recognize, "The care of every man's soul belongs to himself." Furthermore, no one should discriminate against someone because of religion, physical appearance, or any other reason: "Why am I beaten & ill used by others because my hair is not of the right cut?" In America, people were to be free to be different. It should be acceptable to have an exotic hairstyle, to wear different clothes, or be nonconformist in other ways. Even if one was traveling on the road "straight to Jerusalem," one should not be concerned with the "frivolous things which keep Christians at war."

Jefferson simply did not trust the ability of civil magistrates to guide him on matters of salvation:

> I cannot give up my guidance to the magistrate; because he knows no more of the way to heaven than I do & is less concerned to direct me right than I am to go right, if the Jews had followed their kings, amongst so many, what number would have led them to idolatry? Consider the vicissitudes among the emperors, Arians, Athans. Or among our princes.[46]

Jefferson trusted more in the people than he did any king, queen, emperor or other civil leaders. He didn't believe that he could be "saved" and sent to Heaven by some state religion, "a worship I disbelieve & abhor."

Jefferson had faith that a free people would be able to find a path true for themselves. He personified "Truth," as a classic feminine spirit:

[Tr]uth will do well enough if left to shift for herself. She seldom has
received much aid from the power of great men to whom she is rarely
known & seldom welcome. She has no need of force to procure entrance
into the minds of men, error indeed has often prevailed by the assistance
of power or force. Truth is the proper & sufficient antagonist to error.[47]

He pondered the philosopher's proverbial pursuit of the truth. He had enough
political experience to know that one could not always believe everything a
politician said.

As much as Jefferson championed religious and civil liberties, he still
expressed concern over acts of sedition and conspiracies against the State. He did
not support a church being a place of sanctuary for such activities:

[If] any thing pass in a religious meeting seditiously & contrary to the
public peace, let it be punished in the same manner & no otherwise than
as if it had happened in a fair or market. These meetings ought not to be
sanctuaries for faction & flagitiousness.[48]

He was referring to disgraceful crimes considered heinous, wicked, or atrocious.
With this exception, he strongly believed that toleration should be shown to all
religions.

JEFFERSON AND JOHN LOCKE:
RELIGIOUS AND CIVIL RIGHTS FOR ALL

Jefferson returned to the writings of English philosopher John Locke to
explain the principle of "toleration" in society. Locke stated in part:

Neither Pagan nor Mohammedan nor Jew ought to be excluded from the
civil rights of the Commonwealth because of his religion. Shall we suffer
a Pagan to deal with us and not suffer him to pray to his god?[49]

This was a bold statement, even for Jefferson. It was one thing to support freedom of religion for Christians. It was quite another matter to recognize religious
freedom for Pagans, Moslems, and Jews. The term "Pagan" in 18th century
America also referred to American Indians. This may be the first statement by a
U.S. Congressman recognizing American Indian rights to religious freedom.

In the summer of 1776, chiefs of the Iroquois and Algonquian Indian
nations met with the Continental Congress at Independence Hall in
Philadelphia. At the dawn of the Revolutionary War, Indian leaders were concerned about the future of their people. For almost two hundred years, their
history with the European settlers was marked by cycles of war and peace.
Catholic and Protestant missionaries had competed for their souls. After being
told that Christianity was the one true religion and the Bible was the one true
book of the Lord, a chief asked why then were the Christians always fighting
against one another?[50]

Thomas Jefferson viewed this type of question to be fair. He recognized that

European and Colonial American history was fraught with war and religious intolerance. Greater tolerance would have averted many wars. Intolerance led to persecution and oppression. Jefferson asked bluntly:

> Why have Christians been distinguished — above all people who have ever lived — for persecutions? Is it because it is the genius of their religion? No, its genius is the reverse. It is the refusing *toleration* to those of a different opinion which has produced all the hustles & wars on account of religion . . .[51]

More people are said to have been killed in the name of religion than any other cause. Jefferson studied the history of the Crusades, a time when Kings and Popes joined forces to carry on holy wars against the Moslems and other religious groups. The Reformation and Counter-Reformation periods of European history in the 16th and 17th Centuries, Jefferson read, were times of war between Catholics and Protestants. Hundreds of different Christian denominations emerged because of schisms between conflicting religious viewpoints.

Jefferson's historical research taught him to beware of the dangers surrounding matters of Church and State. As long as religious and civil leaders were determined to force others to conform to their will, violent conflicts were inevitable:

> It was the misfortune of mankind that during the darker centuries the Christian priests following their ambition & avarice & combining with the magistrates to divide the spoils of the people, could establish the notion that schismatics might be ousted of their possessions & destroyed, this notion we have not yet cleared ourselves from.[52]

The only hope for the United States to avoid the cycles of religious warfare was to keep the Church and State separated. Religious groups with armies would create so-called Holy Wars.

AN UNHOLY ALLIANCE

Jefferson viewed the relationship between the King of England and the Church of England to be an "unholy alliance." The King used the Church to help him control the people. The Church used the King to help them control competition from opposing religious groups. The result was oppression, persecution and intolerance. These were some of the reasons why Jefferson and other Americans felt compelled to rebel against British authority:

> In this case no wonder the oppressed should rebel, & they will continue to rebel & raise disturbance until their civil rights are fully restored to them & all partial distinctions, exclusions & incapacitations removed.[53]

Jefferson's powerful statement explained why oppressed people around the world rebelled, but more particularly why he and the American Revolutionaries were rebelling. Furthermore, he revealed what it would take for the revolution to end. The American Revolutionaries demanded the full restoration of their civil and religious rights.

Jefferson then turned to the writings of the Earl of Shaftesbury. His vision was to inspire tolerance of different religions and to embrace a form of global spirituality. Drawing lessons from ancient Greek history, the teachings of Plato, Pythagoras, and Epicurius were reviewed. Jefferson concluded that when philosophers and teachers were free, science and the arts flourished. When they weren't free, bloodshed and persecution followed.

Before the 15th century in the Middle Ages of European history, freedom of speech often was squashed by both religious and civil officials who sought conformity of opinion. Jefferson pointed out:

> . . . the consequence was, Christianity became loaded with all the Romish follies. Nothing but free argument, raillery, & even ridicule will preserve the purity of religion.[54]

Jefferson believed that freedom of speech and freedom of religion must go hand-in-hand. Once freedom of expression is lost, oppression is close behind.

Jefferson returned to the writings of the English philosopher, John Locke, to study his "system of Christianity." In his interpretation of the Book of Genesis:

> Adam was created happy & immortal: but his happiness was to have been *Earthly,* and *earthly* immortality, by *sin* he lost this, so that he became subject to total death (like that of brutes) & to the crosses & unhappinesses of this life . . . At the intercession however of the son of God this sentence was in part remitted. A life conformable to the law was to restore them again to immortality, and moreover to those who *believed* their *faith* was to be counted for righteousness. Not that faith without works was to save them.[55]

Salvation did not come by faith alone for Locke and Jefferson. One's good works on earth also counted on the road to heaven.

In search of the fundamental pillars of Christianity, St. James focused on faith and repentance. Faith in God would make up for their defects. Repentance of one's sins was the key to salvation. The goal was the "reformation of life."

"FUNDAMENTALS OF CHRISTIANITY"

In collecting information on the "fundamentals of Christianity," Jefferson studied the Gospels, the stories of the life of Jesus and his teachings. In November of 1776, Jefferson wrote in his notes:

> 1. Faith. 2. Repentance. That faith is everywhere explained to be a belief that Jesus was the Messiah who had been promised. Repentance was to be proved sincere by good works, the advantages accruing to mankind from our Savior's mission are these:
>
> > 1. The knowledge of one God only.
> > 2. A clear knowledge of their duty, or system of morality, delivered

on such authority as to give it sanction.

    3. The outward forms of religious worship wanted to be purged of that farcical pomp & nonsense with which they were loaded.

    4. An inducement to a pious life, by revealing clearly a future existence in bliss, & that it was to be the reward of the virtuous.[56]

Jefferson acknowledged the prophesies of the coming of the Messiah. He recognized Christian teachings identifying Jesus as the Messiah, the Hebrew name for the "deliverer of mankind" and the liberator of the people. The followers of Jesus Christ accepted his moral teachings as their Christian duty, Jefferson observed. His study of early Christians revealed their preference of praying humbly without elaborate ceremony. To live a simple and pious life was considered a virtue, and the reward for a virtuous life was eternal bliss.

    Jefferson then studied the Epistles, letters written by St. Paul and others on the teachings of the Church. In the Episcopal Church, the Epistles included the "Book of Common Prayer." Jefferson noted:

> The Epistles were written *[occasionally]* to persons *already Christians* . . . The fundamentals of Christianity were to be found in the preaching of our Savior, which is related in the Gospels. These fundamentals are to be found in the Epistles . . . explaining to us matters in worship & morality . . . The Apostles' creed was by them taken to contain all things necessary to salvation, & consequently to a communion.[57]

Jefferson learned of the life of Jesus Christ by reading the Gospels. He studied manners of worship and morality through the Epistles. He searched through the Apostles' Creed, a confession of faith that dates from A.D. 500. Jefferson became more personally involved in religion through his own research.

JEFFERSON'S "NOTES ON EPISCOPACY"

    Since Jefferson was raised in the Episcopal Church, he made a detailed study of his own family's religious denomination. His "Notes on Episcopacy" involved the teachings of the Bishops who comprised the governing body of these Anglican Protestants, a branch of the Church of England. He read the letters of St. Paul to Timothy and Titus, the basis upon which the Bishops form their Apostolic institution.

    Jefferson defined the essence of Protestantism:

> As to tradition, if we are Protestants we reject all tradition, & rely on the scripture alone, for that is the essence & common principle of all the Protestant churches.[58]

The Protestant Reformation commenced in 1517, when a German priest named Martin Luther nailed his "95 Theses" to the door of the Wittenberg Church. In the document, he challenged the supremacy of the Pope and sought to reform the Catholic Church. He advocated that the Bible be translated from Latin into German and that it be printed by the Gutenberg Press. This made it possible for the common people to read and study the scriptures with their own copy of the Bible. Martin Luther also challenged "indulgences," the practice of paying money to the Church to be absolved of sins. Nowhere in the Bible could he find evidence to support "indulgences." His theses set off a religious revolution.[59]

To determine the qualifications for religious leadership according to the Bible, Jefferson turned to 1 Timothy, Chapter 3, verse 2, "A bishop then must be blameless, the husband of one wife, vigilant, sober, of good behaviour, given to hospitality, apt to teach . . . Let the deacons be the husbands of one wife, ruling their children and their own houses well."

He then turned to 2 Timothy, Chapter 1, verse 6, "Wherefore I put thee in remembrance, that thou stir up the gift of God, which is in thee by the putting on of my hands." The custom of "laying on of hands" spread through efforts of spiritual healing, with the power of the Lord said to be flowing through the hands of the healer. Jefferson commented:

> This imposition of hands then was some ceremony or custom frequent-
> ly repeated, & certainly is as good a proof that Timothy was ordained by the
> elders (& consequently that they might ordain) as that it was by Paul.[60]

Jefferson searched for who had the power to ordain priests, bishops and other religious leaders. The Apostles originally exerted this authority, but then the power transferred to the elders of the Church.

Church elders also exerted the divine power through spiritual healing performed by laying on the hands and using sacred oils to anoint the bodies of the sick. Jefferson turned to the Book of James, Chapter 5, verse 14:

> Is any sick among you? Let him call for the elders of the church, & let
> them pray over him, anointing him with oil in the name of the lord.[61]

Jefferson emphasized that a government based on the authority of the "Elders" or the people "resembles republican government." However the government of the Episcopal Church was modeled after the political system in England. He didn't want the Church of England and the recognized Episcopal Church to dominate spiritual and political life in America. Jefferson reasoned that the "bishops were always mere tools of the crown."

More liberal Presbyterians, Protestants of Scottish origins, generally embraced the cause of the American Revolution more than most other religious denominations. Jefferson noted:

> The Presbyterian spirit is known to be so congenial with friendly liberty,
> that the patriots after the restoration finding that the humour of people
> was running too strongly to exalt the prerogative of the crown, promoted
> the dissenting interest as a check and balance, & thus was produced the
> Toleration Act.[62]

The Toleration Act, 1689, was "An Act for Exempting their Majesties Protestant Subjects, Dissenting from the Church of England, from the Penalties of certain laws." In 1689, the Church of England, or Anglican Church, reigned supreme.

Church officials tried to oppress those "whose thoughts, deeds, and/or religious loyalties suggested dissent from official Church doctrine." People remained subject to existing religious laws and tithes of money for the Church. However, some other religious groups were to be "tolerated." Protestant Christians who were willing to sign loyalty oaths and belief in the Holy Trinity could be "certified."[63]

Jefferson was quick to point out that the Bible did not make such requirements. These were acts of the King and his ministers:

> St. Peter gave the title of *Clergy* to all God's people till pope
> Higinus and ye. succeeding prelates took it from them & appropriated it
> to priests only.[64]

Jefferson bolstered his position by citing instances in which the rights of "God's people" were acknowledged. This reinforced his political philosophy of the power resting with the people. The people had the right to choose their civil and religious leaders, not the King.

JEFFERSON'S NOTES ON THE HISTORY OF HERESY

Jefferson developed detailed notes on heresy, the act of dissenting from the established Church. Since his bill before Congress was clearly an act of dissent, he surely recognized that he was vulnerable to such a charge. Jefferson searched for a better understanding of the charge of heresy. He concluded that the label "heretic" was hung on someone who questioned the "fundamentals," meaning doctrines of the "Holy Scriptures." Jefferson was not violating biblical law, so a charge of heresy against him would not be justified under the original meaning of the word. He crafted his defense carefully bringing Protestant opinion forward, "The Protestants will say those doctrines . . . are clearly & precisely delivered in the holy scriptures."[65]

Jefferson was searching for his own vindication regarding his revolutionary activities. He considered himself immune to a charge of heresy. He based his innocence on the writings of Dr. Daniel Waterland (1683-1740), who wrote "A Vindication of Christ's Divinity." Waterland believed a charge of heresy would require a violation against the Trinity [Father, Son and Holy Spirit]:

> Dr. Waterland would say the Trinity. But how far this character [of being clearly delivered?] will suit the doctrine of the Trinity I leave others to determine, it is no where expressly declared by any of the earliest fathers, & was never affirmed or taught by the church before the council of Nice [Chillingw. Pref. §18.33.][66]

The first ecumenical Council of Nice in 325 A.D. tried to identify the original teachings of the scriptures and to make a uniform doctrine of Christianity, sanctioned by Emperor Constantine for the Holy Roman Empire. Jefferson was pointing out that the authority of the people was recognized as part of the pre-325 A.D. teachings of Christianity. This gave legitimacy to his position. The Bishops originally had not been given as much authority or power over the people as they now were attempting to assert.

Jefferson's historical research taught him that one of the earliest disputes among early Christians was over the Trinity (God, Jesus and the Holy Spirit). Religious groups - including the Sabellians and Socinians — that embraced God, but not the Trinity, were charged with heresy. The Sabellians were an Indo-European group from south of Rome who spoke an Italic dialect and practiced ancient Italian traditions. The Socinians were a 16th century secret society connected with Faustus and Laelius who also believed in God, but not the Trinity. Jefferson considered Sabellians and Socinians as examples of groups charged with heresy:

> Sabellians. Christian heretics, that there is but one person in the godhead. That the 'Word' & 'holy spirit' are only virtues, emanations, or functions of the deity.
> Socinians. Christian. Heretics, that the Father is the one only God; that the Word is no more than an expression of ye . Godhead & had not existed from all eternity, that Jesus Christ was God no otherwise than by his superiority above all creatures who were put in subjection to him by the father, that he was not a Mediator, but sent to be a pattern of conduct to men. That the punishments of hell are not Eternal.[67]

Jefferson focused on the differences in ideology that provoked the established Roman Catholic Church to brand dissenters "heretics." Groups that did not fully recognize Jesus Christ and the Holy Spirit were targeted.

Jefferson next focused on groups who were harmonious with the Roman Catholic Church, but were at odds with the Calvinists. He looked at the case of the Armenians, Baptist followers of the Dutch Protestant theologian Jacobus Arminius (1560-1609):

> Arminians. They think with the Romish church (against the Calvinists) that there is an universal grace given to all men, & that man is always *free* & at liberty to receive or reject grace. That God creates men free, that his justice would not permit him to punish men for crimes they are predestinated to commit, they admit the prescience of god, but distinguish between fore-knowing & predestinating. All the fathers, before St. Austin were of this opinion.[68]

Armenian Baptists did not believe in predestination, the concept that everything that happens has been predetermined by God. In contrast, they believed that people are in control of their own destinies, and they embraced the idea of free will. St. Austin advocated the concept of predestination. Church of England officials did not want people to believe that they had free will. Therefore, the Armenian Baptists were labeled heretics and were subject to persecution.

Jefferson pointed out that the Arians, followers of the Alexandrian priest Arius (ca. 250 - 336), believed in God, but not the Trinity. They denied the divinity of Christ:

> Arians. Christian. Heretics. They avow there was a time when the Son was not, that he was created in time, mutable in nature, & like the

> Angels liable to sin, they deny the three persons in the trinity to be of the
> same essence. Erasmus & Grotius were Arians.[69]

The Arians were defeated in 330 B.C. by Alexander the Great. Although most of their people were killed or enslaved, their philosophy survived. Erasmus (1469-1536), the Dutch Renaissance scholar, sought to reform the Church to become more humane. Hugo Grotius (1583-1645), the Dutch jurist and humanist, has been called the "founder of international law." He was condemned to life imprisonment but made a daring escape in 1621 and continued to advocate natural law and restraint in war.

Jefferson took note of the philosophy of a 4th century bishop, Apollinaris the Younger, who believed that Christ had a human body and a human sensitive soul, but no human rational mind:

> Apollinarians. Christian heretics. They affirm there was but one nature in
> Christ, that his body as well as soul was impassive & immortal, & that his
> birth, death & resurrection was only in appearance.[70]

Apollinaris was condemned by the Church Councils and killed for his beliefs. His followers also were persecuted until the sect ceased to exist.

Jefferson lastly considered the case of the Macedonians, a culture of people who spread from northern to southern Greece. Their history has been traced back to 2,500 B.C. and reached a pinnacle during the age of Alexander the Great:

> Macedonians. Christian heretics. They teach that the Holy ghost was a
> mere creature but superior in excellence to the Angels.[71]

As a tribal people, the Macedonians were persecuted for centuries, but held onto their traditional culture. After almost three millennia, the established Christian Church challenged their religious beliefs. Jefferson pointed to a specific example of their beliefs regarding the character of the Holy Spirit in relationship to angels.

Just as the Macedonians spread in ancient times from north to south, European colonists of the 18th century increasingly spread from east to west into the heartland of the America frontier. A main difference was that Macedonians established small kingdoms, instead of colonies or states. A central throne at Aegea sought to unite the kingdoms behind a main federal government. Like the Americans, the Macedonians also battled against a dominant society, in this case a larger Greek government, and moved to other lands in search of independence.[72]

Jefferson thus concluded his overview of the history of dissident groups who were branded "heretics" by the established Church.[73] The importance of the topic to him is reflected in the fact that he devoted so much time to it after drafting the Declaration of Independence. He then focused on the history of religion in America.

"MISCELLANEOUS NOTES ON RELIGION"

Under the title "Miscellaneous Notes on Religion," Jefferson compiled a chronology of religious persecution during the 17th century in America. He noted British laws against people who "refuse to have their children baptized." The Act of March 13, 1659 targeted American Quakers who were to be rounded up and interrogated by British officials. Quakers were "imprisoned without bail" until they swore a loyalty oath to the King of England. Quaker Church meetings were prohibited under penalty of £100 sterling. In an attack against freedom of the press, no one was allowed to publish or to possess Quaker books of worship.[74]

On October 4, 1776, Jefferson appealed to the Continental Congress for a redress of British laws that suppressed religious freedom and oppressed foreign immigrants who practiced different religions. He was nominated on October 24 to head a Congressional committee to revise the entire legal system of the United States. At the age of 33, Jefferson took on one of the most difficult assignments in the Congress.[75]

He collaborated with Edmund Pendleton (1721-1803), a senior attorney and fellow Virginia Congressman, on a proposed "Bill for the Naturalization of Foreigners." The change in the law would have given immigrants the same rights as native-born citizens. To encourage immigration, Jefferson added a clause that offered $20 and 50 acres of land to every new foreign settler. Although the bill died in committee, his debate notes survived. They reveal how strongly he felt about extending the rights of citizenship to all the people, including Catholics, Jews and Protestants.[76]

Recorded in his debate notes, Jefferson defended religious freedom as being good for the country in many ways. "Physical Advantages" included increases in productivity, consumption, labor, and procreation. "Moral Advantages" featured honesty and veracity. He challenged members of Congress to accept that other religions were not "less moral." Everyone should be extended full rights to religious freedom, because "all who have not full rights are secret enemies." He concluded by recognizing the contributions of members of the Jewish faith to be "advantageous" to American society.[77]

On Christmas Day, 1776, the Virginia Association of Baptists submitted a "Declaration" supporting Jefferson and Madison in their campaign against an "Established Religion" dominating Americans:

> We believe that Preachers should be supported only by *voluntary Contributions* from the People, and that a general Assesment (however harmless, yea useful some may conceive it to be) is pregnant with various Evils destructive to the Rights and Priveleges of religious Society.[78]

If state or federal money went to the churches, the Baptists contended that the preachers then would "act as Officers of the State." The government then would try to "regulate and dictate to" preachers regarding "what they must preach." The Virginia Association of Baptists warned against the government ever being given this power:

> Yea, farewell to the last Article of the Bill of Rights! Farewell to "the free
> exercise of Religion," if civil Rulers go so far out of their Sphere as to take
> the Care and Management of *religious Affairs* upon them![79]

Society would suffer from the "Seeds of Oppression sown by the Hand of Power;" therefore, the Baptists declared it "our Duty" to prevent the Government "in a legal Way" from ever limiting religious freedom.

From 1776 through 1786, Jefferson devoted himself to revising and establishing federal and Virginia state laws. He composed and co-authored over a hundred bills in Congress. He prepared detailed notes on English statutes, and sought to either abolish or reform laws that affected Americans. James Madison and others joined him in this Herculean feat.[80]

THE ESTABLISHMENT OF
AN AMERICAN LEGAL SYSTEM

Jefferson declined a mission to France, and in October of 1776, he became determined to change the fundamental laws for all Americans. The purpose of reforming the laws was to erase the statutes of the King and replace them with new laws for the American republic. Jefferson sought to create within the United States, "a system by which every [fiber] would be eradicated of ancient or future aristocracy; and a foundation laid for a government truly republican. The repeal of the laws of entail would prevent the accumulation and perpetuation of wealth in select families."[81]

Jefferson struck his metaphorical ax at the base of the American colonial aristocratic system. He led a campaign to end the feudal system under which the eldest son inherited the entire family estate:

> The abolition of primogeniture, and equal partition of inheritances
> removed the feudal and unnatural distinctions which made one member
> of every family rich, and all the rest poor, substituting equal partition, the
> best of all Agrarian laws.[82]

Even though Jefferson himself benefited from the laws of primogeniture, he made the self-sacrifice for the greater good of the republic.

He further defended the rights of the American people not to be subjected to taxation for the support of an established religion:

> The restoration of the rights of conscience relieved the people from taxa-
> tion for the support of a religion not theirs; for the establishment was truly
> of the religion of the rich, the dissenting sects being entirely composed of
> the less wealthy people; and these, by the bill for a general education,
> would be qualified to understand their rights, to maintain them, and to
> exercise with intelligence their parts in self-government, and all this would
> be effected without the violation of a single natural right of any one
> individual citizen.[83]

Jefferson's summation revealed the core of his philosophy which advocated the establishment of the United States as a free republic. He abhorred the thought of the rich controlling the government. The United States government was not to be for sale to the highest bidder. The rich were not to be given favors over the general American citizen. Even the poorest of the poor were to have equal rights comparable to the richest of the rich. Every American citizen, he envisioned, would enjoy the right to "public education." Schools would help teach people to understand their rights. Citizens would assume responsibility to maintain their rights. In this way, true "self-government" would be achieved without violating anyone's "natural rights."

On January 13, 1777, Jefferson chaired a meeting of the Congressional committee to revise the laws of the United States. Congressmen Edmund Pendleton, George Wythe, George Mason, and Thomas Ludwell Lee joined him. The purpose of the meeting was "to settle the plan of operation and to distribute the work."[84] The committee had "full power and authority to revise, alter, amend, repeal, or introduce all or any of the laws of the state, though the work of the Committee would not have the force of law, in any of its parts, until duly passed by the General Assembly."[85]

The scope of the committee went far beyond merely compiling the laws. From 1777-1779, they drafted 126 resolutions to change the law. They stopped short of repealing all previous laws. The task of writing the revised and new laws fell largely upon the shoulders of three men - Jefferson, Pendleton, and Wythe.[86] In February 1779, the committee met to review their work. A report delivered on June 18 to Congress was later published in 1784.[87] In time, parts of their recommendations were passed into law.

Jefferson explained his intentions in his autobiography:

> I knew that our legislation under the regal government had many very vicious points which urgently required reformation, and I thought I could be of more use in forwarding that work. I therefore retired from my seat in Congress on the 2d. of Sep. [1779], resigned it, and took my place in the legislature of my state.[88]

Jefferson, along with his colleague James Madison, was one of the most influential members of Congress regarding the establishment of the American legal system. Their writings help to provide legal precedence for many cases. Their hands touched a multitude of laws and founding principles in America.

Jefferson and Madison also were committed to public education. In March of 1779, Samuel Stanhope Smith presented Jefferson with a state plan for education. Jefferson's greatest concern for the successful implementation of this education plan had to do with conflicting rivalries between Presbyterians and Episcopalians.[89]

"A Bill for Establishing Religious Freedom"

Amidst the mountain of bills, the star jewel from Jefferson's pen was "A Bill for Establishing Religious Freedom." In 1777, he wrote the first draft of his call for religious liberty. When he became Governor of Virginia in 1779, he introduced a draft of the bill on June 12 in the Virginia legislature. Patrick Henry led the opposition of the Anglican old guard who sought to establish an official State religion. Jefferson believed all religions should be freely accepted, instead of having just one official religion. His act found support among Baptists, Presbyterians, Jews, and freethinkers.

The matter was tabled through the tumultuous years of the Revolutionary War. The text was changed many times. In 1785, a dramatic speech by James Madison to the Virginia General Assembly won support for Jefferson's bill.[90] Madison maneuvered the bill through the Virginia State Assembly until it was finally passed on January 16, 1786 with some amendments. What follows is Jefferson's original full text of what many consider the most important document in American religious history:

> "A Bill for Establishing Religious Freedom"
>
> Well aware that the opinions and belief of men depend not on their own will, but follow involuntarily the evidence proposed to their minds; that Almighty God hath created the mind free, and manifested his supreme will that free it shall remain by making it altogether insusceptible of restraint . . .[91]

Freedom of Religion was considered by Jefferson to be a divine right of humanity. Because "Almighty God" created our minds to be free, citizens were to enjoy religious liberty. Jefferson intended to make religion "insusceptible of restraint," meaning resistant or incapable of being influenced. In the final draft, the legislature condensed the opening paragraph to read: "Well aware that Almighty God hath created the mind free . . ."

No civil laws were to limit the religious freedom, because government intrusions would lead to "hypocrisy and meanness:"

> . . . that all attempts to influence it by temporal punishments, or burthens [burdens], or by civil incapacitations, tend only to beget habits of hypocrisy and meanness, and are a departure from the plan of the holy author of our religion, who being lord both of body and mind, yet chose not to propagate it by coercions on either, as was in his Almighty power to do . . .[92]

Government intrusion upon religion was considered to be against God's "plan."

Jefferson commented on this passage in his autobiography. He explained that the original intent of the "Bill for Establishing Religious Freedom" was to extend its protections not only to Christians, but also to citizens of other religions as well.

> Where the preamble declares that coercion is a departure from the plan of the holy author of our religion, an amendment was proposed, by inserting the word 'Jesus Christ,' so that it should read, 'a departure from the plan of Jesus Christ, the holy author of our religion' the insertion was rejected by a great majority, in proof that they meant to comprehend, within the mantle of its protection, the Jew and the Gentile, the Christian and Mahometan [Moslem], the Hindoo [Hindu], and infidel of every denomination.[93]

Jefferson clarified their intent to extend religious freedom to "every denomination." Religious freedom was not just for Christians, but also for Jews, Moslems, and other denominations. This was a bold and courageous stand for the right of "every denomination" to exist in the United States. Therefore, citizens may enjoy religious freedom, even if some people consider a person to be an "infidel," meaning a "non-believer."

Regarding religion, the legislators recognized that the government and citizens were not to "propagate it by coercions," meaning no force, moral or physical, could be used to make citizens do something related to religion. God had this power, but chose not to use it to force people to follow His plan. God chose not to limit religious freedom:

> . . . but to extend [exalt] it by its influence on reason alone; that the impious presumption of legislators and rulers, civil as well as ecclesiastical, who, being themselves but fallible and uninspired men, have assumed dominion over the faith of others, setting up their own opinions and modes of thinking as the only true and infallible, and as such endeavoring to impose them on others, hath established and maintained false religions over the greatest part of the world and through all time.[94]

No one was to assume "dominion over the faith of others." To do so would lead to lording over someone, a role best fulfilled by God, not by man. Jefferson challenged the concept of "infallibility," a presumption claimed by both civil and religious leaders throughout history. The idea is that someone was above making a mistake. The purpose is to assert absolute authority, the object of numerous rulers over the ages. The legislature chose only to include the first phrase of the preceding quote.

Absolute rulers often forced people to be taxed to support an established Church, something Jefferson and Congress were squarely against:

> That to compel a man to furnish contributions of money for the propagation of opinions which he disbelieves and abhors, is sinful and tyrannical; that even the forcing him to support this or that teacher of his own religious persuasion, is depriving him of the comfortable liberty of giving his contributions to the particular pastor whose morals he would make his pattern, and whose powers he feels most persuasive to righteousness; and is withdrawing from the ministry those [temporal] rewards, which proceeding from an approbation of their personal conduct, are an additional incitement to earnest and unremitting labours for the instruction of mankind . . .[95]

Jefferson used most powerful words — "sinful and tyrannical" — to describe the practice of giving tax money to churches. Some members of Congress considered the words too harsh and sought the tone to be tempered.

However, Jefferson and his supporters believed that an American citizen's "civil rights" should not be limited by one's "religious opinions."

> . . . that our civil rights have no dependence on our religious opinions, any more than our opinions in physics or geometry; that therefore the proscribing any citizen as unworthy the public confidence by laying upon him an incapacity of being called to offices of trust and emolument, unless he profess or renounce this or that religious opinion, is depriving him injuriously of those privileges and advantages to which, in common with his fellow citizens, he has a natural right . . .[96]

Although the legislature deleted this phrase, Jefferson intended to outlaw the practice of making citizens take oaths of religious and civil obedience. This was a tool of oppression. Violators of the oaths were threatened with civil or criminal penalties and sometimes outright torture. Jefferson wrote strongly against oaths of religious and civil obedience:

> . . . that it tends also to corrupt the principles of that [very] religion it is meant to encourage, by bribing, with a monopoly of worldly honours and emoluments, those who will externally profess and conform to it; that though indeed these are criminal who do not withstand such temptation, yet neither are those innocent who lay the bait in their way; that the opinions of men are not the object of civil government, nor under its jurisdiction . . .[97]

Jefferson placed religion outside of the "jurisdiction" or legal authority of the State. Civil government officials clearly were being instructed to assume a "hands-off" policy regarding matters of religion. The legislature retained only the last phrase in the preceding quote.

Civil government intrusions into matters of religion would tend to destroy civil and religious freedom. The result would be civil leaders who would be tempted to rule as judge and jury over dissenting citizens:

> . . . that to suffer the civil magistrate to intrude his powers into the field of opinion and to restrain the profession or propagation of principles on supposition of their ill tendency is a dangerous [fallacy], which at once destroys all religious liberty, because he being of course judge of that tendency will make his opinions the rule of judgment, and approve or condemn the sentiments of others only as they shall square with or differ from his own . . .[98]

Jefferson sought to protect American citizens from overzealous civil government officials who would make their personal religious opinions the rule of law. Without a clear separation between Church and State, politics would invade religion and change spiritual pursuits into political advantage. The legislature deleted the preceding quote.

Only in the extreme case of a religious war, Jefferson argued, should civil governments seek to restore the peace. And once peace is restored, civil officials should still remain outside the resumption of religious practices:

> . . . that it is time enough for the rightful purposes of civil government for its officers to interfere when principles break out into overt acts against peace and good order; and finally, that truth is great and will prevail if left to herself; that she is the proper and sufficient antagonist to error, and has nothing to fear from the conflict unless by human interposition disarmed of her natural weapons, free argument and debate; errors ceasing to be dangerous when it is permitted freely to contradict them.[99]

Truth, personified as feminine in gender, would prevail in society if left untouched by human intervention. Freedom of speech and right of assembly were essential to allow truth and freedom to flourish. Jefferson and Congress abided by the old biblical adage, "The truth will set you free."[100] The legislature deleted the preceding quote.

With the preamble concluded, they defined the specifics of the law. Madison strongly advocated to the legislature that Jefferson's wording of the enacting clause should not be changed. Only a minor addition was made to the opening, "Be it therefore enacted by the General Assembly . . . ":

> We the General Assembly of Virginia do enact that no man shall be compelled to frequent or support any religious worship, place, or ministry whatsoever, nor shall be enforced, restrained, molested, or burthened [burdened] in his body or goods, nor shall otherwise suffer, on account of his religious opinions or belief; but that all men shall be free to profess, and by argument to maintain, their opinions in matters of religion, and that the same shall in no wise diminish, enlarge, or affect their civil capacities.[101]

The main points of the Religious Freedom law are the following:

- No one will be forced to attend a particular church.
- No one will be forced to give money to a particular church.
- No one will be forced to support a particular minister.
- No illegal search and seizures, restraining orders, fines, etc.
- Freedom of speech and right of assembly insured.
- One may express any religious opinions and beliefs freely.

The power of the Religious Freedom law derives from its directness. All those subject to this law then enjoyed greater religious freedom than perhaps anyone in Western Civilization. Citizens could no longer be forced to support any religion not of their own choosing. No citizen could be restricted in their religion by civil government. Religious persecution was hereby outlawed.

Jefferson felt so strongly about religion as a "natural right," he wrote a warning to future assemblies not to repeal, nor limit religious freedom:

> And though we well know that this Assembly, elected by the people for the ordinary purposes of legislation only, have no power to restrain the

acts of succeeding Assemblies, constituted with powers equal to our own, and that therefore to declare this act irrevocable would be of no effect in law; yet we are free to declare, and do declare, that the rights hereby asserted are of the natural rights of mankind, and that if any act shall be hereafter passed to repeal the present or to narrow its operation, such act will be an infringement of natural right.[102]

Any act against religious freedom would forever be considered "an infringement of natural right." His concluding flurry reflected a man of reason in the Age of Enlightenment.

Jefferson expressed strong feelings regarding popular sovereignty. Only the people could guarantee their own freedom. On January 4, 1786, Jefferson wrote to George Washington:

It is an axiom in my mind that our liberty can never be safe but in the hands of the people themselves, and that, too, of the people with a certain degree of instruction. That is the business of the state to effect, and on a general plan.[103]

The responsibility of the government was to help facilitate the transfer of power and liberty into the capable hands of the people. Here we see evidence that Jefferson, like James Madison, strongly supported popular sovereignty. The American people were deemed more trustworthy than politicians when it came to fundamental protections of religious and civil liberties.

On January 22, 1786, James Madison wrote to Jefferson to tell him the good news that his "Bill for Establishing Religious Freedom" had passed:

. . . The enacting clauses [passed] without a single alteration, and I flatter myself have in this country extinguished for ever the ambitious hope of making laws for the human mind.[104]

News of Jefferson's success in protecting religious freedom was reported far and wide. The text of the law was printed widely in American and European newspapers. The law was translated into scores of foreign languages. Reviews were offered. Debates were inspired.[105]

JEFFERSON IN PARIS

At the time of the passage of the law in 1786, Jefferson was serving as the American ambassador in France. He acted as resident minister at the Court of Versailles. The immediate response of the Court was one of admiration for his bold act of religious and intellectual freedom.

On August 13, 1786, Jefferson wrote to Virginia Congressman George Wythe:

Our act for freedom of religion is extremely applauded. The ambassadors and ministers of the several nations of Europe resident at this court have asked of me copies of it to send to their sovereigns, and it is inserted at full length in several books now in the press; among others, in the new

> Encyclopedia. I think it will produce considerable good even in these countries, where ignorance, superstition, poverty, and oppression of body and mind in every form, are so firmly settled on the mass of the people, that their redemption from them can never be hoped.[106]

The good news helped bolster the American image and reverse the tide of negative press. He presented the United States as a new form of government that was on the vanguard of progressive change.

JEFFERSON & THE INTERNATIONAL CALL FOR RELIGIOUS FREEDOM

Jefferson championed the cause of religious freedom. He viewed this as part of a larger vision to defend the civil rights of one and all. He saw American citizens as sitting above their European counterparts in enjoying the blessings of liberty:

> If all the sovereigns of Europe were to set themselves to work to emancipate the minds of their subjects from their present ignorance and prejudices, and that as zealously as they now endeavor the contrary, a thousand years would not place them on that high ground on which our common people are now setting out.[107]

Jefferson's "Bill for Establishing Religious Freedom" became a model for countless governments around the world. Some embraced religious freedom, while others continued to suppress popular liberties. Those nations that enacted laws for religious freedom provided greater security to protect fundamental religious rights.

Jefferson believed that the separation of Americans from Europeans by the Atlantic Ocean allowed his countrymen a fertile environment for freedom to grow. He trusted the commonsense of the American people to preserve and protect their new liberties:

> Ours could not have been so fairly put into the hands of their own common sense had they not been separated from their parent stock and kept from contamination, either from them or the other people of the old world, by the intervention of so wide an ocean. To know the worth of this, one must see the want of it here.[108]

Jefferson ranked the importance of his "Bill for Establishing Religious Freedom" equal to the Declaration of Independence. The right of the American people to choose their religion now was on parity with their right to choose their own government. Both were considered by Jefferson to be fundamental "natural rights."

JEFFERSON TO JAMES MADISON:
"THE RIGHT OF INTELLECTUAL FREEDOM"

On December 16, 1786, Jefferson penned a letter to James Madison. Jefferson had not been able to write for three months because he had sprained his hand and dislocated a bone. Before departing for French mineral springs for therapy, he wrote in pain to Madison. Jefferson reflected on the European history of oppression, and lauded Americans who raised a banner for religious freedom:

> In fact it is comfortable to see the standard of reason at length erected, after so many ages during which the human mind has been held in vassalage by kings, priests and nobles . . .[109]

After centuries of oppression, Americans had successfully broken the cycle of domination by civil and religious leaders. The State was separated from the Church and the power was entrusted to the people.

Jefferson expressed his pride in the ways in which the United States was taking form. He penned in his letter of that date to James Madison:

> It is honorable for us to have produced the first legislature who has had the courage to declare that the reason of man may be trusted with the formation of his own opinions.[110]

The power of the people was a profound and revolutionary idea. For perhaps the first time in history, citizens enjoyed the right to develop and express their own opinions freely. Jefferson and his supporters placed their faith in the ability of the common man to act with reason. In contrast to having the power resting with a king or queen, placing the power in the hands of the people reflects a true "leap of faith."

Jefferson's influence on world history is found in constitutions and statutes from nations who applied his model to their own country, state and municipality. The separation of Church and State, religious toleration, and complete intellectual freedom were his goals. Although the call for religious freedom has not been heeded in every corner of the earth, the impact of Jeffersonian civil and religious ethics continues to be felt every day.

JEFFERSON'S ADVICE TO
A YOUNG MAN REGARDING RELIGION

Jefferson sought to personally influence the life of his favorite nephew, Peter Carr (1770-1815). Peter wanted very much to join his uncle and cousins in Paris, but Jefferson discouraged the idea because he thought that a young man could not resist the temptations of beautiful Parisian women. On August 10, 1787, Jefferson wrote to his seventeen-year-old nephew, encouraging him to read the classics and the Bible:

> You will naturally examine first the religion of your own country. Read the

Bible then, as you would read Livy [Roman historian, ca. 59 B.C. - 17 A.D.] or Tacitus [Roman historian, ca. 55 - 117 A.D.]. The facts which are within the ordinary course of nature you will believe on the authority of the writer, as you do those of the same kind in Livy and Tacitus. The testimony of the writer weighs in their favor in one scale, and their not being against the laws of nature does not weigh against them. But those facts in the Bible which contradict the laws of nature, must be examined with more care, and under a variety of faces. Here you must recur to the pretensions of the writer to inspiration from God.[111]

Thus, Jefferson revealed how he reconciled religion and science. Anything that could not be explained by science could be reasoned as an inspiration from God:

For example in the book of Joshua we are told the sun stood still several hours. Were we to read that fact in Livy or Tacitus we should class it with their showers of blood, speaking of statues, beasts &c., but it is said that the writer of that book was inspired. Examine therefore candidly what evidence there is of his having been inspired. The pretension is entitled to your enquiry, because millions believe it. On the other hand you are Astronomer enough to know how contrary it is to the law of nature that a body revolving on its axis, as the earth does, should have stopped, should not by that sudden stoppage have prostrated animals, trees, buildings, and should after a certain time have resumed its revolution, and that without a second general prostration. Is this arrest of the earth's motion, or the evidence which affirms it, most within the law of probabilities?[112]

Jefferson explained Joshua's claim that the "sun stood still several hours" as an example of a man "inspired" by God. Joshua was believed to be divinely inspired in his writings, therefore the passage could be presumed to have a deeper meaning.

Jefferson encouraged his nephew to read the New Testament of the Bible. He explained to him two main interpretations of Jesus:

You will next read the New Testament. It is the history of a personage called Jesus. Keep in your eye the opposite pretensions. 1. Of those who say he was begotten by God, born of a virgin, suspended and reversed the laws of nature at will, and ascended bodily into heaven; and 2. Of those who say he was a man, of illegitimate birth, of a benevolent heart, enthusiastic mind, who set out without pretensions to divinity, ended in believing them, and was punished capitally for sedition by being gibbeted according to the Roman law which punished the first commission of that offence by whipping, and the second by exile or death *in furcâ*.[113]

For the benefit of his teenage nephew, Jefferson simplified the story of Christianity. He did not try to force him to believe in God, but rather presented his logic in a reasonable way:

If you find reason to believe there is a God, a consciousness that you are acting under his eye, and that he approves you, will be a vast additional incitement.[114]

Jefferson believed that faith in God could have a powerful effect on people. He felt God was watching over us. Furthermore, if people strongly believed they were acting with God's approval, the realization would be truly inspiring.

Jefferson encouraged his nephew to consider the existence of Heaven in hopes that a belief in the afterlife and the divine existence of Jesus might inspire him to live a better life:

> If that there be a future state, the hope of a happy existence in that increases the appetite to deserve it; if that Jesus was also a God, you will be comforted by a belief of his aid and love.[115]

Jefferson explained how the love of Jesus and His divine aid may touch one's life in profound ways. He described Heaven as a "future state" of "happy existence."

Jefferson advocated a personal relationship with God. He trusted in the human ability to reason right from wrong. If people could trust their own judgment and not be overly swayed by others, Jefferson reasoned, the approach would lead to "uprightness of the decision":

> In [conclusion], I repeat that you must lay aside all prejudice on both sides, and neither believe nor reject any thing because any other person, or description of persons have rejected or believed it. Your own reason is the only oracle given you by heaven, and you are answerable not for the rightness but uprightness of the decision.[116]

Jefferson did not dictate to his nephew. He did not demand that the teenager accept religion under fear of Hell and Damnation. Quite the contrary, he encouraged him to use his own mental abilities and use reason to reach his own opinions. Belief in God and religion, Jefferson concluded, may be freely reached as a personal decision. Jefferson sent the letter along with a trunk load of books on religion, morals, philosophy, history, and poetry, as well as books on mathematics, science, chemistry, botany, medicine, agriculture, politics, and law. He also sent texts in French and Spanish, emphasizing that learning foreign languages was important to future international relations. The Virginia statesman comforted the young man to "be assured of the interest I take in your success."

JEFFERSON TO JAMES MADISON:
PROS VS. CONS OF THE U.S. CONSTITUTION

On December 20, 1787, Jefferson requested a personal performance review as a diplomat and statesman from his friend, James Madison. In this letter, one of his most famous, Jefferson explained exactly what he liked and disliked regarding the U.S. Constitution:

> I like much the general idea of framing a government which should go on of itself peaceably, without needing continual recurrence to the state legislatures. I like the organization of the government into Legislative, Judiciary and Executive.[117]

Jefferson liked how the U.S. Constitution would promote a smooth-running government. He liked the tripartite separation of powers as a system of checks and balances. He explained his support of a citizen's right to elect those who would have the power of taxation, "preserving inviolate the fundamental principle that the people are not to be taxed but by representatives chosen immediately by themselves."[118]

Jefferson further liked the balance of power between small states and big states. He supported the power of the people to vote in elections. He also liked the ways in which the power of the government could be limited, so one branch did not become too powerful.

Jefferson then critically analyzed the shortcomings of the U.S. Constitution:

> I will now add what I do not like. First the omission of a bill of rights providing clearly and without the aid of sophisms for freedom of religion, freedom of the press, protection against standing armies, restriction against monopolies, the eternal and unremitting force of the habeas corpus laws, and trials, by jury in all matters of fact triable by the laws of the land and not by the law of Nations.[119]

Jefferson foresaw the necessity of the First Amendment of the Constitution. At the top of his list, "freedom of religion" needed to be protected under a citizen's Bill of Rights. Second, "freedom of the press" must be guaranteed. Without this right, a democratic republic could not flourish. Third, "protection against standing armies," was needed, so the republic might never be overthrown by a military dictatorship. Fourth, "restrictions against monopolies" were necessary, so a free market might keep the American economy healthy. The right to a speedy trial by a jury of one's peers also needed to be protected. Jefferson underscored his call for a Bill of Rights:

> Let me add that a bill of rights is what the people are entitled to against every government on earth, general or particular, and what no just government should refuse, or rest on inference.[120]

Jefferson believed strongly that the fundamental rights of the people needed to be protected from intrusions by government officials. He wanted to restrain the tendency of government officials to be overzealous in claiming power and authority over the people.

Jefferson next expressed the need for term limits on how many times a politician might serve in office. The advantages to an incumbent were too great, so steps needed to be taken to prevent individual politicians from holding an office for life. The political pot needed to be stirred. He especially was concerned about the office of the Presidency in which a job for life could become comparable to dictatorship. It was imperative, Jefferson asserted, that the Presidency be up for a vote every four years and that the number of terms be limited.

He admitted that he preferred a more limited government, "I own I am not a friend to a very energetic government. It is always oppressive."[121] Government could best be kept limited by keeping an ear to the full and active voices of the people. The right of the people to protest certain actions by government officials was to be accepted.

Jefferson offered his constructive criticism of the Constitution to his dear friend, James Madison, in a good spirit:

> After all, it is my principle that the will of the Majority should always prevail. If they approve the proposed Convention in all it's parts, I shall concur in it cheerfully, in hopes that they will amend it . . .[122]

Jefferson viewed the Constitution as a dynamic document, not something chiseled in granite. It could be changed when necessary.

He expressed confidence that the United States of America would "remain virtuous for centuries." He envisioned a process by which the country would experience bountiful westward expansion followed by overpopulation of certain cities. He thought it was unhealthy for people to "get piled upon one another in large cities." Here corruption would breed, as it had in Europe.

Jefferson placed the need for public education as a top priority. He placed great faith in the American people. The better they were educated, the better citizens they might become. Education in Europe and other parts of the world was kept private, often only for members of the aristocratic class. Jefferson lobbied strongly in support of public education:

> Above all things I hope the education of the common people will be attended to; convinced that on their good sense we may rely with the most security for the preservation of a due degree of liberty.[123]

Contrary to some portrayals of Jefferson as an elitist, he believed passionately in the "good sense" of American citizens. He placed the security of American liberty in the hands of the people rather than in some security agency of the federal government. The Constitution was like a treaty between the people and their government. Its purpose was to define the system of government and to limit the powers of government officials and agencies. Therefore, the religious and civil liberties of "We, the People" must be protected, Jefferson concluded, by the Constitution, Bill of Rights, "laws of the land" and the common man.[124]

JEFFERSON ON THE DOCTRINES OF JESUS

Jefferson served as Minister to France from 1785 to 1789. He then served until 1793 as President George Washington's Secretary of State. He resigned in protest of Alexander Hamilton's fiscal and centralizing policies. From 1797 to 1801, Jefferson served as Vice President under John Adams, his political rival. When Adams advocated the Alien and Sedition Acts, Jefferson and Madison joined forces in opposition and formed the Virginia and Kentucky Resolutions of 1798. They championed personal freedom and states' rights.

During his Presidency, Jefferson often contemplated the subject of religion. On April 19, 1803, he wrote about the moral principles of Jesus Christ in a letter to the Massachusetts Congressman Edward Dowse (1756-1828):

> I concur with the author in considering the moral precepts of Jesus as

more pure, correct, and sublime than those of the ancient philosophers, yet I do not concur with him in the mode of proving it. He thinks it necessary to libel and decry the doctrines of the philosophers; but a man must be blinded, indeed, by prejudice, who can deny them a great degree of merit. I give them their just due, and yet maintain that the morality of Jesus, as taught by himself, and freed from the corruptions of latter times, is far superior. Their philosophy went chiefly to the government of our passions, so far as respected ourselves, and the procuring our own tranquility. In our duties to others they were short and deficient. They extended their cares scarcely beyond our kindred and friends individually, and our country in the abstract. Jesus embraced with charity and philanthropy our neighbors, our countrymen, and the whole family of mankind. They confined themselves to actions; he pressed his sentiments into the region of our thoughts, and called for purity at the fountain head.[125]

Jefferson encouraged comparative analysis between Christianity, other religions, the classics, and other philosophies. He found an open dialogue to be healthy. An open mind could better receive an education.

He recommended the writings of Unitarian Dr. Joseph Priestley (1733-1804) who engaged in comparative analysis of the teachings of Jesus Christ and Socrates:

In a pamphlet lately published in Philadelphia by Dr. Priestley, he has treated, with more justice and skill than Mr. Bennet, a small portion of this subject. His is a comparative view of Socrates only with Jesus. I have urged him to take up the subject on a broader scale.[126]

Jefferson encouraged scholars to expand the scope of comparative analysis of religions and philosophies.

On April 21, 1803, he wrote a letter to Dr. Benjamin Rush, Universalist physician and fellow signer of the Declaration of Independence.[127] Jefferson attached to the letter a copy of his treatise entitled, "A Syllabus of an Estimate of the Merit of the Doctrines of Jesus" (ca. 1803).[128] He stated that he was fulfilling an earlier promise to record some of his views on the Christian religion, "the result of a life of inquiry and reflection." Jefferson chided his critics who knew nothing of his true religious beliefs, and then clarified that he was a Christian:

To the corruptions of Christianity I am indeed opposed, but not to the genuine precepts of Jesus himself. I am a Christian, in the only sense in which he wished anyone to be: sincerely attached to his doctrines in preference to all others, ascribing to himself every human excellence, and believing he never claimed any other.[129]

After having reviewed scores of religions from the past five millennia, Jefferson chose to follow Christianity. He considered his religious views to be personal and asked Dr. Rush to hold them in confidence:

I am moreover averse to the communication of my religious tenets to the public, because it would countenance the presumption of those who have endeavored to draw them before that tribunal, and to seduce public opinion to erect itself into that inquisition over the rights of conscience which the laws have so justly proscribed.[130]

Jefferson was concerned that his criticism of certain religious leaders and corruptions might be misconstrued as criticism of those religions as a whole. For example, his criticism of corrupt Jewish officials during the time of Jesus Christ might be misconstrued as anti-semitic.[131]

Jefferson didn't want his personal religious sentiments to be politicized by his political rivals. Jefferson and Madison had established that religious inquisitions were illegal in the United States. However, much could be hidden under the guise of political campaign speeches.

Jefferson attached to the letter his treatise on religion. His comparative analysis of Christianity and other religions reveals much about his personal religious views. Regarding Jesus Christ, Jefferson wrote in his "Syllabus of an Estimate of the Merit of the Doctrines of Jesus, Compared with Those of Others":

> In this state of things [when reform was needed] among the Jews, Jesus appeared. His parentage was obscure; his condition poor; his education null; his natural endowments great; his life correct and innocent: he was meek, benevolent, patient, firm, disinterested, and of the sublimest eloquence. The disadvantages under which his doctrines appear are remarkable.[132]

Jefferson was awed by the fundamental beginnings of Jesus Christ. From those humble roots, one of the world's largest religions grew.

Jefferson noted that Jesus did not personally write the Bible. He did not write about his life. Not one letter or manuscript in the hand of Jesus is known to exist.

> Like Socrates and Epictetus, he wrote nothing himself . . . all the learned of his country, entrenched in its power and riches, were opposed to him, lest his labors should undermine their advantages . . .[133]

Without taking up the pen, Jesus mounted a formidable challenge to those in power. Local officials viewed him as a threat.

Some religious and civil officials joined forces against Jesus. This exemplified what could be called an "unholy alliance" between Church and State:

> According to the ordinary fate of those who attempt to enlighten and reform mankind, he fell an early victim to the jealousy and combination of the altar and the throne, at about thirty-three years of age, his reason having not yet attained the maximum of its energy, nor the course of his preaching, which was but of three years at most, presented occasions for developing a complete system of morals.[134]

Jefferson, then sixty years of age, was amazed by the achievements of Jesus Christ when only in his thirties.

Jefferson respected Jesus for developing such a remarkable moral system:

> Notwithstanding these disadvantages, a system of morals is presented to us
> which, if filled up in the style and spirit of the rich fragments he left us,
> would be the most perfect and sublime that has ever been taught by man.[135]

In fact, Jefferson appraised the Christian moral system as the greatest in human
history.

What made Christian moral teachings so powerful, Jefferson concluded, was
their universal nature that embraced all humanity:

> His moral doctrines, relating to kindred and friends, were more pure and
> perfect . . . not only to kindred and friends, to neighbors and countrymen,
> but to all mankind, gathering all into one family under the bonds of love,
> charity, peace, common wants and common aids.[136]

Jefferson learned from the teachings of Jesus that people could be united not by
force or threat of revolution, but by peaceful means.

Jefferson compared the moral teachings of Jesus with the teachings of classic philosophy and the "Hebrew code":

> The precepts of philosophy, and of the Hebrew code, laid hold of actions
> only. He pushed his scrutinies into the heart of man; erected his tribunal
> in the region of his thoughts, and purified the waters at the fountain
> head.[137]

While the classics and Judaic Law restrained man's actions, Jefferson concluded
that the teachings of Jesus influenced people through reason and inspiration.
This approach appealed greatly to Jefferson and inspired him to be a good
Christian.

JEFFERSON'S PRESIDENCY

From 1801 to 1809, Jefferson served as the third President of the United
States. At the time of his inauguration, the population of the United States had
grown to over five million. Two-thirds of the people lived along the Atlantic
seaboard, while one-third were settling farther and farther westward toward the
Mississippi River.

Jefferson's administration was marked by reason and economy. From the
office of the Presidency, he defended the Constitution and protected the Bill of
Rights. However, the most famous achievement during his Presidency was the
Louisiana Purchase. On April 30, 1803, the United States representatives signed
a treaty agreeing to pay $12 million to Napoleon and France for the Louisiana
Territory, 827,000 square miles extending far west of the Mississippi. At 3
cents/acre, some consider the purchase to be one of the greatest real estate
bargains in history. The geographic size of the United States doubled. Jefferson
bought the land sight unseen. No American was known to have ever traveled that
far west in the American frontier. Jefferson won a Congressional appropriation to

send his secretary, Meriwether Lewis, and friend William Clark on an historic expedition to explore and map the uncharted Western lands.

President Jefferson recorded his views regarding the potential impact of the Louisiana Purchase on the future of America:

> This little event, of France's possessing herself of Louisiana is the embryo of a tornado which will burst on the countries on both sides of the Atlantic and involve in it's effects their highest destinies.[138]

On May 14, the expedition embarked from St. Louis, traveled up the Missouri River, arriving on October 26 at the Mandan and Hidatsa villages in North Dakota. About the same time, half way around the world, the Pope was crowning Napoleon as Emperor of France. Unlike the United States, European monarchs and leaders of the established Church demonstrated no intention of separating Church and State.

Back in the Louisiana Territory, Lewis and Clark were trekking across the Rocky Mountains and the Plateau region, with the help of a Shoshone woman named Sacagawea. They struggled onward for a year. Finally, on November 7, 1805, after traveling thousands of miles, they sighted the Pacific Ocean in Oregon Country. Captain Clark recorded in his journal, "Ocian [Ocean] in view! O! the joy."[139]

On January 4, 1806, President Jefferson met with a delegation of Missouri, Oto, Arikara, and Yankton Sioux chiefs. He thanked them for helping Lewis and Clark's expedition and expressed his hope "that we may all live together as one household." Jefferson later told a Mandan Chief:

> I thank the Great Spirit that he has protected you through the journey and brought you safely to the residence of your friends, and I hope He will have you constantly in his safe keeping, and restore you in good health to your nations and families . . . we are descended from the old nations which live beyond the great water, but we and our forefathers have been so long here that we seem like you to have grown out of this land. We consider ourselves no longer of the old nations beyond the great water, but as united in one family with our red brethren here . . . I wish you to live in peace and friendship with one another as brethren of the same family ought to do. How much better is it for neighbors to help than to hurt one another; how much happier must it make them . . . I have now opened my heart to you, let my words sink into your hearts and never be forgotten.[140]

Jefferson promised the Indians that any disturbance of their peace and friendship in the future would be addressed and resolved:

> If ever lying people or bad spirits should raise up clouds between us, call to mind what I have said, and what you have seen yourselves. Be sure there are some lying spirits between us; let us come together as friends and explain to each other what is misrepresented or misunderstood, the clouds will fly away like morning fog, and the sun of friendship appear and shine forever bright and clear between us.[141]

Although Jefferson's Indian policies were better than most, his promises to Native Americans were not well kept by successive presidents and other government officials. Jefferson's Northwest Ordinance set up a chain of federal trading posts and extended credit to Indians for food and vital trade goods.

Over a period of two and a half years, Lewis and Clark traveled thousands of miles. They met with American Indians of many nations. On September 23, 1806, the Corps of Discovery returned to St. Louis. Soon thereafter, they received a hero's welcome. Reportedly, spontaneous celebrations and parties were held in the towns along their way to Washington, D.C.

While Americans were celebrating their discoveries and freedoms, the old European monarchies and the established Church were teetering in their unholy alliance. Only a month earlier, Emperor Francis I abdicated his throne and the old Holy Roman Empire ceased to exist. Great Britain, Russia, Austria, and Sweden joined in an alliance against France. War was raging in Europe as Napoleon's armies marched into battles against their enemies.

While the maps of Europe were being redrawn, so too were the maps of the United States. The world was changing. The fact that the United States could be created as a free republic excited hopes in oppressed peoples everywhere. The powerful dreams for freedom and liberty being realized in America encouraged the common people of Europe to take up arms to liberate themselves. The French Revolution was the first of many revolts. The struggle for human rights took on international proportions. The impact of the American Revolution was being felt — and is still being felt — around the world.

In the last year of his Presidency, Jefferson took time to write a letter on religious freedom to Rev. Samuel Miller:

> I consider the government of the U S. as interdicted by the Constitution from intermeddling with religious institutions, their doctrines, discipline, or exercises. This results not only from the provision that no law shall be made respecting the establishment, or free exercise, of religion, but from that also which reserves to the states the powers not delegated to the U.S. Certainly no power to prescribe any religious exercise, or to assume authority in religious discipline, has been delegated to the general government. It must then rest with the states, as far as it can be in any human authority.[142]

More important, President Jefferson clarified his interpretation of the Constitution and Bill of Rights regarding the relationship between Church and State. In perhaps his most direct statement on the subject, he explained that regarding religion and religious practices, the federal government had no jurisdiction, because the federal government was "interdicted by the Constitution from intermeddling." "Interdicted" is defined as "prohibited" or "restrained authoritatively." Jefferson stated that the federal government had "no power" regarding "religious institutions, their doctrines, discipline or exercises." This sweeping statement makes Jefferson's position clear that the federal government should keep their hands off religious matters. The separation between Church and State was to remain far apart.

JEFFERSON'S RETIREMENT

In 1809, Jefferson retired from the Presidency. He returned to Monticello, his Virginian estate, but kept up a lively correspondence with his friends and associates. He wrote his old friend, the Polish Revolutionary War patriot, Thaddeus Kosciusko (1746-1817):

> I am retired to Monticello, where, in the bosom of my family, and sur-
> rounded by my books, I enjoy a repose to which I have been long a
> stranger. My mornings are devoted to correspondence. From breakfast to
> dinner, I am in my shops, my garden, or on horseback among my farms;
> from dinner to dark, I give to society and recreation with my neighbors
> and friends; and from candle light to early bed-time, I read. My health is
> perfect.[143]

After having reviewed and analyzed countless religions and systems of morality, Jefferson came to the conclusion that he personally preferred the teachings of Jesus Christ. On September 18, 1813, Jefferson wrote a letter on moral principles and religion to William Canby:

> An eloquent preacher of your religious society, Richard Motte, in a dis-
> course of much emotion and pathos, is said to have exclaimed aloud to his
> congregation, that he did not believe there was a Quaker, Presbyterian,
> Methodist or Baptist in heaven, having paused to give his hearers time to
> stare and to wonder. He added, that in heaven, God knew no distinctions,
> but considered all good men as his children, and as brethren of the same
> family. I believe, with the Quaker preacher, that he who steadily observes
> those moral precepts [at the] gates of heaven, as to the dogmas in which
> they all differ. That on entering there, all these are left behind us, and the
> Aristides and Gatos, the Penns and Tillotsons, Presbyterians and Baptists,
> will find themselves united in all principles which are in concert with the
> reason of the supreme mind.[144]

Jefferson was making the point that he believed one's salvation was not determined by one's religious denomination. Jefferson was born into the Episcopal Church, but he found it difficult to embrace their Trinitarian theology. He attended the church of Dr. Joseph Priestley when in Pennsylvania and became associated with Unitarianism.

Jefferson suggested to Canby that they shared the "same religion." Jefferson had studied the history of moral teachings and found the teachings of Jesus to be "pure." However, Jefferson questioned the presumptions of men who dismissed the logic of Euclidean geometry and claimed that they alone had the authority to deliver divine judgments:

> Of all the systems of morality, ancient or modern, which have come under
> my observation, none appear to me so pure as that of Jesus. He who follows
> this steadily need not, I think, be uneasy, although he cannot comprehend
> the subtleties and mysteries erected on his doctrines by those who, calling
> themselves his special followers and favorites, would make him come into

the world to lay snares for all understandings but theirs. These metaphys-ical heads, usurping the judgment seat of God, denounce as his enemies all who cannot perceive the Geometrical logic of Euclid in the demonstra-tions of St. Athanasius, that three are one, and one is three; and yet that the one is not three nor the three one. In all essential points you and I are of the same religion; and I am too old to go into inquiries and changes as to the unessential.[145]

On October 12, 1813, Jefferson wrote to John Adams regarding Jesus Christ. Jefferson revealed his pursuit to identify and focus on the true teachings of Jesus:

> We must reduce our volume to the simple evangelists, select, even from them, the very words only of Jesus, paring off the Amphibologisms into which they have been led by forgetting often, or not understanding, what had fallen from him, by giving their own misconceptions as his dicta, and expressing unintelligibly for others what they had not understood themselves.
> There will be found remaining the most sublime and benevolent code of morals which has ever been offered to man.[146]

Jefferson actually took two copies of the Bible and began to compile a scrap-book of those passages he deemed the "very words only of Jesus." This original project began in 1804, entitled "The Philosophy of Jesus." In later years, he refined and greatly expanded his Biblical scrapbook. The final product, completed in 1820, he called the "Life and Morals of Jesus of Nazareth," which was the ver-sion Congress published. The final compilation was published in the early 20th century under the title "Jefferson Bible," 46 pages of "pure doctrines" from apostles, the "Apostolic fathers, and the Christians of the 1st. century."[147]

Jefferson referred to his compilation in a later letter to his friend of half a century, Charles Thomson, the retired Secretary of the Continental Congress:

> A more beautiful or precious morsel of ethics I have never seen; it is a doc-ument in proof that I am a real Christian, that is to say, a disciple of the doc-trines of Jesus, very different from the Platonists, who call me infidel . . .[148]

To anyone who questioned whether or not Thomas Jefferson was a Christian, his own words should lay the matter to rest.

Jefferson further recommended the benefits of comparing the teachings of Jesus Christ with Socrates and the classics. He read the controversial writings of philosopher Dr. Joseph Priestley (1733-1804) and reform theologian William Enfield (1747-1791).[149] Jefferson's appetite for books was fed by his determina-tion to keep current on philosophic and religious publications.

Almost a decade earlier, Jefferson had written a letter to Dr. Priestley regarding their mutual interest in comparative theology and philosophy. Jefferson was attracted to Dr. Priestley's belief that "Jesus' moral teaching was entirely compatible with natural law." Jefferson commended Dr. Priestley and offered the following suggestions:

> I rejoice that you have undertaken the task of comparing the moral doc-
> trines of Jesus with those of the ancient Philosophers . . . I think you can-
> not avoid giving, as preliminary to the comparison, a digest of his moral
> doctrines, extracted in his own words from the Evangelists, and leaving
> out everything relative to his personal history and character. It would be
> short and precious. With a view to do this for my own satisfaction, I had
> sent to Philadelphia to get two testaments Greek of the same edition, &
> two English, with a design to cut out the morsels of morality, and paste
> them on the leaves of a book, in the manner you describe as having been
> pursued in forming your Harmony.[150]

Dr. Priestley's books caused a firestorm of controversy. However, he never completed his comparative analysis of Jesus Christ and the classics. Priestley passed
away shortly after receiving Jefferson's letter.[151]

On April 19, 1814, Jefferson expressed shock and dismay at news that a
bookseller had been arrested for selling Jefferson a copy of a book by M. de
Becourt, *Sur la Creation du Monde, Un Systeme d'Organisation Primitive* ["On
the Creation of the World, A System of Primitive Organization"]. Censorship of
the book was being attempted as "an offence against religion." Jefferson
expounded against book censorship in a letter to N. G. Dufief, the middleman
who purchased the book for him:

> I am really mortified to be told that, in the United States of America, a
> fact like this can become a subject of inquiry, and of criminal inquiry too,
> as an offence against religion; that a question about the sale of a book can
> be carried before the civil magistrate. Is this then our freedom of religion?
> And are we to have a censor whose imprimatur shall say what books may
> be sold, and what we may buy? And who is thus to dogmatize religious
> opinions for our citizens? Whose foot is to be the measure to which ours
> are all to be cut or stretched?[152]

The issue of Creationism has been a hotbed of controversy throughout history.
In this case, a Pennsylvania magistrate attempted to assert authority to ban or
censor books considered contrary to his views on religion. Jefferson challenged
his actions:

> Is a priest to be our inquisitor, or shall a layman, simple as ourselves, set
> up his reason as the rule for what we are to read, and what we must
> believe? It is an insult to our citizens to question whether they are ration-
> al beings or not, and blasphemy against religion to suppose it cannot stand
> the test of truth and reason.[153]

Religion, Jefferson asserted, was strong enough to withstand the "test of truth
and reason." Censorship of books would violate freedom of the press.
Censorship of religious books also would violate the "free exercise of religion."

Jefferson contended that the proper approach was to allow books to be
subjected to debate. The public had a right to hear this debate so everyone may
form their own opinions:

> If M. de Becourt's book be false in its facts, disprove them; if false in its reasoning, refute it. But, for God's sake, let us freely hear both sides, if we choose. I know little of its contents, having barely glanced over here and there a passage, and over the table of contents. From this, the Newtonian philosophy seemed the chief object of attack; the issue of which might be trusted to the strength of the two combatants; Newton certainly not needing the auxiliary arm of the government, and still less the holy Author of our religion, as to what in it concerns Him. I thought the work would be, very innocent, and one which might be confided to the reason of any man; no? Likely to be much read if let alone, but, if persecuted, it will be generally read. Every man in the United States will think it a duty to buy a copy, in vindication of his right to buy, and to read what he pleases.[154]

The debate between science and religion seemed at issue. Government officials need not interfere with Sir Isaac Newton or Jesus Christ. Jefferson acted as referee in advocating a free and healthy debate. He warned the perpetrators of repression to consider that any book censored surely would become a bestseller.

On September 26, 1814, Jefferson wrote another letter, also on the topic of moral principles and religion, to Miles King, a friend of twenty-five years:

> I must ever believe that religion substantially good which produces an honest life, and we have been authorized by One whom you and I equally respect, to judge of the tree by its fruit. Our particular principles of religion are a subject of accountability to our God alone. I inquire after no man's, and trouble none with mine; nor is it given to us in this life to know whether yours or mine, our friends or our foes, are exactly the right. Nay, we have heard it said that there is not a Quaker or a Baptist, a Presbyterian or an Episcopalian, a Catholic or a Protestant in heaven; that, on entering that gate, we leave those badges of schism behind, and find ourselves united in those principles only in which God has united us all. Let us not be uneasy then about the different roads we may pursue, as believing them the shortest, to that our last abode; but, following the guidance of a good conscience, let us be happy in the hope that by these different paths we shall all meet in the end.[155]

On January 29, 1815, Jefferson wrote on the subject of moral principles and religious hierarchies in a letter to Charles Clay:

> I should as soon think of writing for the reformation of Bedlam, as of the world of religious sects. Of these there must be, at least, ten thousand, every individual of every one of which believes all wrong but his own. To under take to bring them all right, would be like undertaking, single-handed, to fell the forests of America.[156]

The multitude of different religious denominations — all claiming to know the truth — confounded Jefferson. To reconcile them all was impossible.

Jefferson made no bones about the fact that he felt free to criticize corrupt priests and other religious leaders. He disdained as sacrilege corrupt acts done in the name of religion:

. . . I abuse the priests, indeed, who have so much abused the pure and holy doctrines of their Master, and who have laid me under no obligations of reticence as to the tricks of their trade. The genuine system of Jesus, and the artificial structures they have erected, to make them the instruments of wealth, power, and preeminence to themselves, are as distinct things in my view as light and darkness; and while I have classed them with soothsayers and necromancers, I place Him [Jesus Christ] among the greatest reformers of morals, and scourges of priest-craft that have ever existed. They felt Him as such, and never rested until they had silenced Him by death.[157]

Jefferson viewed Jesus Christ as a great "reformer of morals." Morality stood as one of Jefferson's preeminent fields of study.

Jefferson admired Jesus for chasing the moneychangers out of the temple. The act emboldened Jefferson to stand up and speak out against corruption in Church and State:

Government, as well as religion, has furnished its schisms, its persecutions, and its devices for fattening idleness on the earnings of the people. It has its hierarchy of emperors, kings, princes, and nobles, as that has of popes, cardinals, archbishops, bishops, and priests. In short, cannibals are not to be found in the wilds of America only, but are reveling on the blood of every living people.[158]

Jefferson's graphic language reflected his dramatic flair and passion over the issue of corruption in Church and State. By likening greedy Church and State officials to "cannibals" who were "reveling on the blood" of the people, he could not have been more critical.

Four month later, on May 5, 1817, Jefferson wrote to John Adams, continuing their dialogue on the topic of religion.

. . . If by religion we are to understand sectarian dogmas, in which no two of them agree, then your exclamation on that hypothesis is just, 'that this would be the best of all possible worlds, if there were no religion [religious denominations] in it.' But if the moral precepts, innate in man, and made a part of his physical constitution, as necessary for a social being, if the sublime doctrines of philanthropism and deism taught us by Jesus of Nazareth, in which all agree, constitute true religion, then, without it, this would be, as you again say, 'something not fit to be named even, indeed, a hell.'[159]

Jefferson clarified that the word "religion" could refer to "religious denominations." Thus, their criticism of "religion" really referred to their criticism of corrupt practices by conflicting religious denominations, not criticism of religion as a theology. Jefferson further clarified that he recognized that "deism," the teaching of there being one God, finds its source in Jesus Christ. Jesus said there was one God. Jefferson searched, but found no direct source in the Bible where Jesus claimed himself to be a God. This led Jefferson to refer to the "humanity of Jesus." Regarding the Holy Spirit, the third part of the Trinity, Jefferson searched for its origins in ancient traditions three thousand years before the lifetime of Jesus Christ. Thus, Jefferson expressed concern for the many thousands of people who had been persecuted as heretics over the centuries simply because their beliefs regarding the Trinity did not conform to shifting views of the established Church of the day.

On March 21, 1819, at the age of seventy-six, Jefferson described his personal habits to Dr. Vine Utley. Jefferson admitted to a temperate lifestyle. He drank a little "weak" wine, a little coffee or tea, but preferred apple cider for breakfast. He ate little meat, preferring vegetables, and was proud to still have all his teeth. He exercised by riding on horseback six to eight miles a day. Before falling asleep, he read "something moral" for an hour or longer. Each morning he rose "with the sun." From childhood to retirement, Jefferson remained an avid reader and an enthusiastic student, especially in science, philosophy, and religion.[160]

Jefferson continued to be attracted to the most tolerant and least doctrinarian denomination, the Unitarians, who believed in one God and accepted people of varying viewpoints. On June 26, 1822, Jefferson explained his summation of the teachings of Jesus Christ to Unitarian Benjamin Waterhouse:

> The doctrines of Jesus are simple, and tend all to the happiness of man.
>
> 1. That there is only one God, and he all perfect.
> 2. That there is a future state of rewards and punishments.
> 3. That to love God with all thy heart and thy neighbor as thyself, is the sum of religion.[161]

Jefferson could not have described his belief in Jesus and Christianity more simply. Word of Jefferson's views on religion spread among Unitarians. In time, he became viewed as a central figure within Unitarian places of worship. The Unitarian Church, however, was not officially organized until after Jefferson's death.

Toward the end of Jefferson's life, he continued to attend the local Episcopal Church. However, he was known to have contributed financially, in fair proportion, to every denomination in his area. He increasingly embraced his own personal relationship with God:

> Had the doctrines of Jesus been preached always as pure as have been Christian. I rejoice that in this blessed country of free inquiry and belief, which has surrendered its creed and conscience to neither kings nor priests, the genuine doctrine of one only God is reviving, and I trust that there is not a young man now living in the United States who will not die an Unitarian...Be this the wisdom of Unitarians, this the holy mantle which shall cover within its charitable circumference all who believe in one God, and who love their neighbor![162]

Although not yet formally organized, Unitarianism was spreading in the United States and Europe. The word "Unitarian" historically refers to the "oneness of God," in contrast with Trinitarianism, the theology of the Father, Son, and Holy Ghost. Jefferson, along with Thomas Paine and Benjamin Franklin were closely associated with Unitarians. It has been said, "Unitarians can tolerate anything except intolerance." Unitarians generally accept people of many different ways of thinking. Jefferson also has been called a deist, because he believed that "God made the world but now leaves it alone." It was up to "we, the People" to perform good works for the benefit of the world.

Jefferson's good works and genius reflect a "Renaissance man" with a passion for knowledge. His main fields of study included science, philosophy, history, political theory, agriculture, and religion. He was a self-professed Christian who believed in God and emphasized the moral teachings of Jesus Christ. However, he studied and incorporated into his theology the moral teachings of a multitude of religious and philosophical teachings, believing that everyone would be united without divisions in Heaven.

However, just because Jefferson embraced Christian teachings, he did not turn a blind eye to corruption among Church officials. He spoke out strongly against collusion between Church officials and government officers. This violated his strong principles for a clear separation between Church and State. Jefferson's political rivals used his criticism of corrupt Church officials against him. Some accused him of not believing in God, but this was not true. Up to the end of his life, Jefferson remained a powerful voice in support of religious freedom, while he privately prayed to God.

In a November 2, 1822 letter, Jefferson defended his beloved University of Virginia. They had decided not to have a single professorship of religion, but rather encouraged different denominations to sponsor their teachers:

> In our university you know there is no Professorship of Divinity . . . after stating the constitutional reasons against a public establishment of any religious instruction, we suggest the expediency of encouraging the different religious sects to establish, each for itself, a professorship of their own tenets . . . And by bringing the sects together, and mixing them with the mass of other students, we shall soften their asperities, liberalize and neutralize their prejudices, and make the general religion a religion of peace, reason, and morality.[163]

Thus, Jefferson dealt with the university's critics by opening the door for different denominations to express their views.

On February 17, 1826, Jefferson wrote a personal letter to his dear friend, James Madison. Jefferson confided his hopes and problems to Madison, whose friendship had "subsisted between us, now half a century, and the harmony of our political principles and pursuits, have been sources of constant happiness to me through that long period." Jefferson concluded:

> . . . To myself you have been a pillar of support thro' life. Take care of me when dead, and be assured that I shall leave with you my last affections.[164]

As Jefferson was tying up his affairs, he left Madison with the task of defending Jefferson's name and honor for history.

On June 24, 1826, he wrote his last letter, a response to Roger C. Weightman, declining an invitation to attend the 50th Anniversary of the Declaration of Independence:

> RESPECTED SIR, — The kind invitation I receive from you on the part
> of the citizens of the city of Washington, to be present with them at their
> celebration on the fiftieth anniversary of American Independence as one
> of the surviving signers of an instrument pregnant with our own, and the
> fate of the world, is most flattering to myself . . . our fellow citizens, after
> half a century of experience and prosperity, continue to approve the choice
> we made. May it be to the world . . . the signal of arousing men to burst
> the chains under which monkish ignorance and superstition had persuaded
> them to bind themselves, and to assume the blessings and security of self-
> government.[165]

Jefferson was determined to live to the day of the 50th Independence Day, but
he did not have the energy to travel to the nation's capital for the celebration.

The establishment of an independent republic replaced despotism with a
state of liberty in America, Jefferson explained:

> That form which we have substituted restores the free right to the
> unbounded exercise of reason and freedom of opinion. All eyes are
> opened, or opening, to the rights of man. The general spread of the light
> of science has already laid open to every view the palpable truth that the
> mass of mankind has not been born with saddles on their backs, nor a
> favored few booted and spurred, ready to ride them legitimately by the
> grace of God. These are grounds of hope for others. For ourselves, let the
> annual return of this day forever refresh our recollections of these rights,
> and an undiminished devotion to them.[166]

The freedoms guaranteed to all Americans under the Constitution liberated the
pursuit of knowledge, science, and religion. He hoped the annual celebration of
Independence Day would inspire a continued appreciation for the rights of
Americans.

Jefferson regretted that he did not feel strong enough to attend the celebration. He longed to visit the nation's capitol once again, a place filled with so
many memories:

> I will ask permission here to express the pleasure with which I should have
> met my ancient neighbors of the city of Washington and its vicinities, with
> whom I passed so many years of a pleasing social intercourse; an inter-
> course which so much relieved the anxieties of the public cares and left
> impressions so deeply engraved in my affections as never to be forgotten.
> With my regret that ill health forbids me the gratification of an acceptance,
> be pleased to receive for yourself and those for whom you write, the assur-
> ance of my highest respect and friendly attachments.[167]

Jefferson reflected on his life, counting the days, trying to hold on at least until
Independence Day. As the end drew near, he reportedly said, "Well, Doctor, a few
hours more and the struggle will be over." One-by-one, he spoke to his family
members. He gave his daughter a small Morocco case. He asked her to open it
"immediately after his decease." She soon learned that it contained an "elegant and
affectionate" poem "on the virtues of his dutiful and incomparable daughter."[168]

With less than 24 hours remaining before Independence Day, Jefferson grew determined to live a little longer, "that he might breathe the air of the Fiftieth Anniversary, when he would joyfully sing with old Simeon, Nunc dimittis, Domine." Through the day and into the night, the elder statesman experienced flashes of his life. He relived parts of the American Revolution. At one point, he rose from bed and ordered, "Warn the committee to be on their guard."

On the morning of July 4, 1826, Jefferson breathed the "air of the Fiftieth Anniversary" of Independence Day. He greeted his physician, "Well Doctor, you see I am here yet . . . Do you think I fear to die?"

Shortly after noon, Jefferson calmly delivered directions for his funeral, "forbidding all pomp and parade." He called for his family and friends to gather around him, proclaiming, "I have done for my country and for all mankind all that I could do, and I now resign my soul without fear to my God, my daughter to my country."

He began repeating softly, "Nunc Dimittis, Domine — Nunc Dimittis, Domine," then drifted gently away.[169] These words are part of a prayer found in St. Luke's Gospel. A man in Jerusalem named Simeon who was told that he would not die before he had seen the Lord delivered the prayer. When baby Jesus was presented in the Temple, Simeon prayed:

> Sovereign Lord, as you have promised, you now dismiss your servant in peace. For my eyes have seen your salvation, which you have prepared in the sight of all people, a light for revelation to the Gentiles and for glory to your people Israel.[170]

Thomas Jefferson passed away at the age of eighty-three. The time was ten minutes before one o'clock. Five hours later, John Adams, his friend and fellow signer of the "Declaration of Independence, passed away after uttering, "Independence forever," and "Thomas Jefferson still survives."[171]

In a private note found among Jefferson's papers, he suggested that in case any memorial of him should ever be thought of, a small granite obelisk should be erected with the following inscription:

HERE WAS BURIED

THOMAS JEFFERSON

AUTHOR OF THE DECLARATION OF AMERICAN INDEPENDENCE,

OF THE STATUTE OF VIRGINIA FOR RELIGIOUS FREEDOM

AND FATHER OF THE UNIVERSITY OF VIRGINIA.[172]

James Madison, "A Memorial & Remonstrance" (June 1785), Library of Congress.

Chapter Three

"JAMES MADISON ON RELIGION AND THE STATE"

This chapter traces the fascinating life and times of James Madison (1751-1836), "father of the United States Constitution." As the principal author of the Constitution and Bill of Rights, what Madison wrote directly affects the lives of every American citizen. His democratic model has also inspired others who seek human rights and civil liberties from their own governments around the world. Madison was the champion of the separation of Church and State. Because he penned the phrase "free exercise of religion" in the First Amendment, a better understanding of his "original intent" is most relevant. When the U.S. Supreme Court interprets the Constitution, justices often consider the original intent of the law. In this chapter, we will look closely at Madison's personal history and writings to help understand the original ideas behind his words.

THE ROOTS OF JAMES MADISON

James Madison's English ancestry can be traced back to 1653, when his Great-great-grandfather John Madison (or Maddison), a ship's carpenter, arrived in Virginia. As a reward for his payment of passage for eleven other immigrants, John Madison was granted 600 acres of land on the Mattapony River. He became a neighbor of the Mattapony Indians, an Algonquian-speaking tribe related to the Powhatans of Pocahontas fame. These Indians were a devoutly spiritual people who believed strongly in religious freedom, as articulated later by one of their Algonquian cousins:

> Trouble no one about their religion; respect others in their view, and demand that they respect yours. Love your life, perfect your life, [and] beautify all things in your life. Seek to make your life long and its purpose in the service of your people. (Tecumseh - Shawnee Chief)[1]

Perhaps it was more than a coincidence that Madison's religious philosophy mirrored that of the local Native Americans whose tribal government provided a model for participatory democracy.

James Madison's great-grandfather, John Madison, Jr., served as justice of the peace and sheriff. He patented 2,000 acres on the upper Mattapony River, where he and his wife, Isabella, raised three sons, including Ambrose Madison, the grandfather of President Madison. In 1732, Ambrose, his wife Frances Taylor, and their three sons moved to Mount Pleasant, Virginia. Six months later, Grandfather Ambrose mysteriously died from poisoning. Frances Taylor buried her husband nearby and never remarried. She developed their 2,337 acres into a plantation, growing local native tobacco and food crops with the help of twenty-nine African American slaves, fourteen of whom were children. She was a strong woman who succeeded as an exporter of tobacco to England.

In 1741, at the age of eighteen, Madison's father, James, Sr., received title to the estate. He was good farmer and gradually assumed responsibility for running the family business. He became the leading planter in Orange County, started a blacksmith shop, and offered building services. At the age of 26, he met and married Nelly Conway, daughter of his business associate on the Rappahannock River. They raised twelve children at Mount Pleasant, the eldest being James Madison, Jr., who was to become the fourth President of the United States.[2]

MADISON'S CHILDHOOD IN VIRGINIA

As the birth of her first child neared, Nellie Madison returned to her parents' home at Port Conway, King George County, Virginia. On March 16, 1751, James Madison, Jr. was born. When the baby was strong enough to travel, mother and child returned to the Mount Pleasant plantation. As a boy, he must have found arrowheads and other Indian relics, since archeologists later discovered over 80 Indian sites on the property. Collecting arrowheads was a hobby of local boys, including Thomas Jefferson, who later was dubbed America's first archeologist.

In 1760, the family completed construction of a larger home on the estate that became known as Montpelier. James, Jr. was nine years old when his family moved into the eight-room brick house. Fifty years later, Madison expanded the house into a mansion befitting him and his wife Dolly for their retirement.

In his childhood, young James and his parents attended religious services at the local Episcopalian Church of the established Anglican Protestant faith. His father, James, Sr., served as a vestryman who helped maintain the sacred vessels and garments of the minister, and also ran the temporal affairs of the local church. Based in Great Britain, the Episcopalian Church was governed by a religious organization of Bishops. In Virginia in the 1760s, the Episcopalians were considered the "established Church." Young James never entered full communion and did not identify himself as an Episcopalian in later life.

In 1762, at the age of eleven, Madison attended his first school. He perhaps was unaware that the seeds of the American Revolution were brewing then with Patrick Henry's revolt against the Stamp Act. Young Madison's first teacher, Donald Robertson, was a Presbyterian minister. The Presbyterians were religious moralists rooted in Scotland. They studied the teachings of the French Protestant reformer John Calvin (ca. 1509-64), who emphasized doctrines of predestination and salvation solely by God's grace. Young Madison was attracted to their more democratic organization governed by the church elders called "presbyters." Their ecclesiastical court and governing body were made up of all the ministers and a number of elders from churches in a district. Here young Madison found a model for a congress that more represented the people, in contrast with the controls of British colonial governance by an elite hierarchy of noblemen.

Because Robertson's tidewater boarding school was located in distant King and Queen County, young James lived at the school, returning home for holidays. He learned foreign languages, including Latin and Greek to study the classics. His attendance continued for five years, after which he returned to Montpelier at the age of sixteen. During the next two years, Madison was educated by a tutor, Rev. Thomas Martin, a prominent Episcopalian religious teacher.

Young Madison's early education thus was a mixture of established teachings of Episcopalians and the "Scottish moral-sense philosophy" of Presbyterians. At the age of eighteen he was ready to go to college. However, his health was not good. His mind was strong and brilliant, but his body was frail and weak.[3]

MADISON'S COLLEGE EDUCATION
AT PRINCETON UNIVERSITY

In 1769, James Madison began his higher education at the College of New Jersey, which became known later as Princeton University. The choice of schools is notable, since he traveled out of state. Princeton originally was a Presbyterian college in the north. President John Witherspoon was noted for his orations on moralistic toleration. His teachings would have a profound influence on Madison.

Madison attended college dressed in black homespun suits. The style was uniquely American, perhaps a statement of choice over British imports. However, he further developed his foreign language skills and studied the classics in the libertarian tradition.

On August 10, 1769, Madison wrote his earliest surviving letter to Rev. Thomas Martin, his former tutor. Madison enclosed a publication supporting John Wilkes, a pro-American radical living in London, who proclaimed, ". . . from our attachment to 'peace and good order' we wait for a constitutional redress." Madison grew impassioned with the rise of American revolutionary thought. Letters to his father reveal an inquisitive mind with which he began questioning what was happening with current political affairs in America.

When the British enacted the repressive Townsend Acts to tax Americans for imported English goods such as paper, glass and tea, Madison and his friends staged student protest demonstrations. They were angered by the British establishment of an American Board of Commissioners of Customs designed to raise money from the Americans to pay the salaries of British governors and judges who supported British colonial controls over Americans. British taxes were harsh and extracted from the Americans a total 257,000 British pounds sterling in ten years. Madison and his fellow protestors rang the school bell and burned copies of the official British documents. They reportedly urged local American businessmen to join in their protests against British oppression.

Madison's revolutionary passions were ignited while at college. On the eve the American Revolution, Princeton became known as "fiercely patriotic." Madison worked at a feverish pace. He completed his undergraduate work in two years. However, his health suffered to the point that he did not feel strong enough to return home.

Through the early months of 1772, Madison pursued his postgraduate studies of foreign languages and theology, learning Hebrew and reading the Old Testament. While President Witherspoon was his tutor, Madison considered a career as a Protestant minister. He also focused on the study of government and law critical to his political future.[4]

MADISON'S EARLY STAND FOR SEPARATION OF CHURCH AND STATE

In mid-1772, Madison returned home from college in near total exhaustion. So severe was his general health, he didn't think that he was going to live long. At the young age of twenty-one, he contemplated death.

In the late fall of 1772, Madison wrote to William Bradford, Jr.:

> As for myself, I am too dull and infirm now to look out for any extraordinary things in this world, for I think my sensations for many months past have intimated to me not to expect a long and healthy life.[5]

Madison's near-death experience brought him closer to God. He felt that his name would soon be added to the "annals of Heaven." Had Madison died at this early age, the history of the United States would have changed in ways unimaginable. Who would have written the U.S. Constitution and Bill of Rights? Without Madison's reasoned thinking and powerful advocacy for civil liberties, our fundamental rights might not have been secured.

Madison's revolutionary spirit and will to live were provoked by news from Boston's Sons of Liberty and the struggle of Americans to throw off the yoke of British imperialism. In December, 1773, Samuel Adams called a meeting at the Old South Meeting House and organized the famous Boston Tea Party. To protest the Townsend Duties on tea, the patriots dumped 342 chests of tea into Boston Harbor. It is noteworthy that the patriots dressed up as "Mohawk Indians," one of the Six Nations of the Iroquois Confederacy. The Indians symbolized "liberty and freedom" for some American patriots, because the Iroquois Confederacy in upstate New York maintained the oldest participatory democracy in the world. Benjamin Franklin recognized their united government as a model for the United States.[6]

In response to the Boston Tea Party and emergence of the Continental Congress in Philadelphia, Madison penned a letter to his Pennsylvania classmate and close friend, William Bradford, Jr., on January 24, 1774:

> My WORTHY FRIEND . . .
>
> I congratulate you on your heroic proceedings in Philadelphia with regard to the tea. I wish Boston may conduct matters with as much discretion as they seem to do with boldness. They seem to have great trials and difficulties by reason of the obduracy and ministerialism of their Governor. However, political contests are necessary sometimes, as well as military, to afford exercise and practice, and to instruct in the art of defending liberty and property. I verily believe the frequent assaults that

have been made on America (Boston especially) will in the end prove of real advantage.[7]

Madison recognized that public protests such as the Boston Tea Party would incite American patriots to action. He objected to the involvement of the Church of England in trying to influence people to be loyal to the British Crown. He disapproved of one denomination being the official religion of the State, as the Church of England was asserting in the southern colonies. British institutional support for slavery further incited Madison. His feelings against slavery were growing stronger, even though his own family still had slaves. He expressed his opinion that the British and the Church of England were trying to make all Americans slaves of the British Empire.

Madison wrote fervently in support of a clear separation of Church and State:

> If the Church of England had been the established and general religion in all the northern colonies as it has been among us here, and uninterrupted tranquility had prevailed throughout the continent, it is clear to me that slavery and subjugation might and would have been gradually insinuated among us. Union of religious sentiments begets a surprising confidence, and ecclesiastical establishments tend to great ignorance and corruption; all of which facilitate the execution of mischievous projects.[8]

Madison became so enraged over collusions between the British colonial officials and the leaders of the established Church, that he became frustrated in writing of the subject.

The young Virginian grew impatient with politics and politicians who tried to mediate with British officials. The thought of British tyrannies evoked his anger. One side of Madison's sentiments longed for more libertarian pursuits:

> But away with politics! Let me address you as a student and philosopher, and not as a patriot, now. I am pleased that you are going to converse with the Edwards and Henrys and Charleses . . . who have swayed the British sceptre, though I believe you will find some of them dirty and unprofitable companions, unless you will glean instruction from their follies, and fall more in love with liberty by beholding such detestable pictures of tyranny and cruelty.[9]

Madison was torn between his love for liberal arts vs. his need to study politics and law. He made an analogy about processing the sour grapes of politics into the refined wine of true law and philosophy:

> I was afraid you would not easily have loosened your affection from the belles lettres. A delicate taste and warm imagination like yours must find it hard to give up such refined and exquisite enjoyments for the coarse and dry study of the law. It is like leaving a pleasant flourishing field for a barren desert; perhaps I should not say barren either, because the law does bear fruit, but it is sour fruit, that must be gathered and pressed and distilled before it can bring pleasure or profit. I perceive I have made a very

> awkward comparison; but I got the thought by the end, and had gone too far to quit it before I perceived that it was too much entangled in my brain to run it through; and so you must forgive it. I myself used to have too great a hankering after those amusing studies. Poetry, wit, and criticism, romances, plays, &c., captivated me much; but I began to discover that they deserve but a small portion of a mortal's time, and that something more substantial, more durable, and more profitable, befits a riper age. It would be exceedingly improper for a laboring man to have nothing but flowers in his gardens or to determine to eat nothing but sweet meats and confections. Equally absurd would it be for a scholar and a man of business to make up his whole library with books of fancy, and feed his mind with nothing but such luscious performances.[10]

While Madison was recouping his strength to travel in the spring, he was enjoying the peace and tranquility of his home. He knew that war and agitation were brewing throughout the colonies. Something deep inside him would not allow him to sit back and enjoy the benefits of the leisure class.

Madison was provoked by the thought of British officials and Church of England priests conspiring to persecute the American people:

> I want again to breathe your free air. I expect it will mend my constitution and confirm my principles. I have indeed as good an atmosphere at home as the climate will allow; but have nothing to brag of as to the state and liberty of my country. Poverty and luxury prevail among all sorts; pride, ignorance, and knavery among the priesthood, and vice and wickedness among the laity. This is bad enough, but it is not the worst I have to tell you. That diabolical, hell-conceived principle of persecution rages among some; and to their eternal infamy, the clergy can furnish their quota of imps for such business. This vexes me the worst of anything whatever.[11]

Madison further wrote passionately about the importance of freedom of speech and freedom of the press. He believed everyone should have "liberty of conscience," the freedom to determine right from wrong within oneself. However, he knew from his reading that many intellectuals throughout history had been condemned to prison. The very thought of government officials intruding on his personal freedoms enraged him.

Madison himself, as an intellectual, was in danger of being subjected to such oppression should he speak out and publish his views:

> There are at this time in the adjacent country not less than five or six well-meaning men in close jail for publishing their religious sentiments, which in the main are very orthodox. I have neither patience to hear, talk, or think of anything relative to this matter; for I have squabbled and scolded, abused and ridiculed, so long about it to little purpose, that I am without common patience. So I must beg you to pity me, and pray for liberty of conscience to all . . . Till I see you, Adieu![12]

Madison obviously was concerned about people being jailed for publishing their religious views. He believed strongly that government officials should not become involved in trying to control people's religious practices and writings. On such matters of separation of Church and State, Madison did speak out and clearly lost his patience.

MADISON'S EARLY STAND FOR RELIGIOUS AND CIVIL LIBERTY

On April 1, 1774, James Madison wrote again to his friend, William Bradford, Jr., expressing strong convictions in support of religious freedom. As the seeds of revolution were sprouting across America, British officials worked through their Church of England priests to repress rebellion. Madison reported that the Virginia Assembly was making plans to defend local Baptists, Presbyterians, and others who were dissenting against British authority:

> Our Assembly is to meet the first of May, when it is expected something will be done in behalf of the dissenters. Petitions, I hear, are already forming among the persecuted Baptists, and I fancy it is in the thoughts of the Presbyterians also, to intercede for greater liberty in matters of religion.[13]

Madison was skeptical about the effectiveness of their petitions. He thought it prudent that they should state their case accurately without telling "extravagant stories" that might lose them credibility. However, he believed strongly that the dissenters should be extended "toleration." He further warned against those who sided with the established Church of England against the American patriots.

Madison acknowledged that Virginia social structure was hierarchical in comparison with the more egalitarian structure in the North. The South had slavery, while the northern colonies did not. Madison himself came from a wealthy and powerful southern family, but he was not blinded to the rights of the common man. He would not compromise when it came to the "rights of conscience," which he considered essential to the freedom of all citizens:

> The sentiments of our people of fortune and fashion on this subject are vastly different from what you have been used to. That liberal, catholic, and equitable way of thinking, as to the rights of conscience, which is one of the characteristics of a free people, and so strongly marks the people of your province, is but little known among the zealous adherents to our hierarchy. We have, it is true, some persons in the Legislature of generous principles both in Religion and Politics; but number, not merit, you know, is necessary to carry points there. Besides, the clergy are a numerous and powerful body, have great influence at home by reason of their connection with and dependence on the Bishops and Crown, and will naturally employ all their art and interest to depress their rising adversaries; for such they must consider dissenters who rob them of the good will of the people, and may, in time, endanger their livings and security.[14]

Madison observed that American clergy of the Church of England were dependent upon and received their orders from the Bishops in England, who in turn received their orders from the British Crown. If the British Crown felt threatened, they would send directives to the Bishops to order the clergy to control the Americans. Here was clear justification for him to take a strong stand for the separation of Church and State.

Madison did not want to see religious groups become tools of oppression employed by the State. Conversely, he didn't want the State interfering with the private religious practices of the people. Madison expressed to this friend how Americans in the North enjoyed greater liberties compared to Americans in the South:

> You are happy in dwelling in a land where those inestimable privileges are fully enjoyed; and the public has long felt the good effects of this religious as well as civil liberty. Foreigners have been encouraged to settle among you. Industry and virtue have been promoted by mutual emulation and mutual inspection; commerce and the arts have flourished; and I cannot help attributing those continual exertions of genius which appear among you to the inspiration of liberty, and that love of fame and knowledge which always accompany it. Religious bondage shackles and debilitates the mind, and unfits it for every noble enterprise, every expanded prospect. How far this is the case with Virginia will more clearly appear when the ensuing trial is made.[15]

For a young man at the age of twenty-three, Madison's dialogue reflects how deeply he was thinking about the current state of American society on the eve of the Revolution.

Madison's logical reasoning told him that religious and civil liberty would create a healthy and creative society. "Religious bondage," in contrast, would weaken society because creativity would be stifled. Protections of religious and civil rights, he concluded, were the keys to achieving public liberty.

MADISON'S EARLY STAND FOR CIVIL LIBERTIES

In the summer of 1774, Madison's quest for public liberty was dealt a serious blow when British authorities enacted the Coercive or Intolerable Acts. This was a series of colonial laws designed to crack down on the Americans. The first law was the Boston Port Act that ordered a blockade of the Boston port until the Americans paid for losses from the Boston Tea Party. The second law, the Quartering Act, gave royal governors and British commanders authority to move troops into any American's private home. British soldiers simply could show up at anyone's front door, walk in, and expect free room and board. Imagine the horror of the parents of young daughters when brash British soldiers came barging in demanding their food, their drinks, and their beds! This was a bald show of British force and authority that the Americans dubbed "intolerable."

When word of the Intolerable Acts reached Virginia, young Madison mustered his strength and marched around with the local militia. He was still physically prone to illness. His mother also was weak, having given birth to her twelfth child. She wanted to keep her children close to her.

Madison's sheer will to stand up against the British somehow gave him the strength to go outside and join the Orange County Militia. His commanding presence and family stature earned him a rank of Colonel. However, his career was not to be in the military, but rather in civil service.

On September 5, 1774, the First Continental Congress met at Independence Hall in Philadelphia. During the next month and a half, fifty-six delegates from twelve colonies met. (Georgia was not in attendance.) Virginia delegate Peyton Randolph was elected President. They discussed problems between Great Britain vs. the Americans and debated possible solutions. One of their early acts was to declare that the Coercive or Intolerable Acts were "not constitutional." They agreed to stop trade with Great Britain, thus boycotting British goods and refusing to export American goods. They further agreed to stop the slave trade by signing an agreement known as the "Continental Association."

In December 1774, Madison was appointed to the Orange County Committee of Safety. He began organizing on a local level. Before the year was out, word arrived that a group of American patriots in New Hampshire captured the British Fort William and Mary, confiscating their guns and a hundred pounds of gunpowder.

On March 23, 1775 at the Virginia Convention in Williamsburg, a resolution was introduced to establish a Virginia Militia to defend against British aggression. The author of the bill, Patrick Henry, made his famous speech and concluded:

> There is a just God who presides over the destiny of nations . . . The battle, sir, is not to the strong alone; it is to the vigilant, the active, the brave . . . Is life so dear, or peace so sweet, as to be purchased at the price of chains and slavery? Forbid it, Almighty God! I know not what course others may take; but as for me, give me liberty or give me death![16]

Henry grabbed his ivory letter opener and swung it toward his heart to get his point across!

THE DAWN OF THE AMERICAN REVOLUTION

A month later, when General Thomas Gage ordered British troops against the American Revolutionaries, Paul Revere made his famous ride to warn, "The British are coming! The British are coming!" His friend Dr. Joseph Warren, an eyewitness of the Battles of Lexington and Concord, wrote in part:

> . . . on the night preceding the 19th of April [1775], a body of the King's troops under the command of Colonel Smith, were secretly landed at Cambridge, with an apparent design to take or destroy the military and other stores provided for the colony . . . the regulars rushed on with great violence and first began hostilities by firing on said Lexington company, where they killed eight, and wounded several others . . . a great number of houses on the road were plundered . . . several were burned, women in childbed were driven by the soldiery naked into the streets, old men

peaceably in their houses were shot dead, and such scenes exhibited as
would disgrace the annals of the most uncivilized nation . . .

Nevertheless, to the persecution and tyranny of his cruel Ministry we
will not tamely submit—-appealing to Heaven for the justice of our cause,
we determine to die or be free.[17]

Less than two months later General Gage proclaimed martial law in Boston, and
Dr. Warren volunteered to fight British forces in the Battle of Bunker [Breed's]
Hill. On June 17, 1775, he was killed along with a thousand other men, the first
casualties of the Revolutionary War.

About the same time at the Second Continental Congress in Philadelphia,
John Adams nominated George Washington to be the Commander-in Chief of
the Continental Army. Washington was a Virginia planter and a veteran of the
French and Indian War. His reputation was well known to young Madison. On
July 2, General Washington took control of his troops consisting of several
thousand armed farmers with limited supplies. They reportedly only had nine
cartridges per man. Washington's task was formidable.

On August 23, 1775, King George III proclaimed that the American
colonists were in a "state of rebellion." Lord Dartmouth soon summoned
General Thomas Gage back to England. Sir William Howe took command of
British forces in the colonies, while Sir Guy Carleton commanded British troops
in Canada. Benedict Arnold and 1,100 American troops set out to do battle in
the North. General Richard Montgomery joined in the northern campaign and
lost his life on December 31 in a battle at Quebec. General Washington contemplated how to drive the British out of Boston. On New Year's day in 1776,
Washington raised a new American flag with 13 red and white strips as a symbol
of American unity. The following day, British ships with a hundred cannons
bombed Norfolk, Virginia. A month later, General Howe and the Virginia forces
had to abandon Norfolk. The war moved to within 100 miles from the Madison
family estate of Montpelier.

In January 1776, Thomas Paine's revolutionary pamphlet, "Common
Sense," appeared and sold 120,000 copies as America's new bestseller. He drew
from "simple fact, plain argument and common sense" to justify an American
Revolution. In response to British atrocities and oppression, Paine proclaimed,
"The last cord now is broken."[18]

MADISON AND THE VIRGINIA STATE CONSTITUTION

In 1776 James Madison was elected as a representative of Orange County
to the Virginia Convention in Williamsburg. He won his seat with strong support from local Baptists who were grateful for his involvement in defending them
against false imprisonment and religious persecution. In his autobiography,
Madison recalled his actions in defense of religious freedom as "mere duty pre-
scribed by his conscience . . ."[19]

In May, Madison arrived in Williamsburg for the Virginia Convention which
was attended by 112 representatives. He was chosen to be on the committee that

drafted Virginia's first state Constitution and a "Declaration of Rights."[20] George Mason, the wealthy Virginia jurist, wrote an initial draft that called for a revolutionary break with England and protections of civil rights. Regarding religious freedom, Mason wrote:

> That Religion, or the duty which we owe to our CREATOR, and the manner of discharging it, can be directed only by reason and conviction, not by force or violence: and therefore, that all men should enjoy the fullest toleration in the exercise of religion, according to the dictates of conscience, unpunished, and unrestrained by the magistrate, unless under colour of religion, any man disturb the peace, the happiness, or safety of Society. And that it is the mutual duty of all to practice Christian forbearance, love, and charity, towards each other.[21]

Banning and other scholars have recognized that Mason's text was influenced by John Locke, especially his "Letter Concerning Toleration" on separation of Church and State.[22]

Young Madison asserted that the phrase "all men should enjoy the fullest toleration," did not go far enough. He penned an amendment to Mason's draft and garnered the support of Patrick Henry who proposed the change in wording:

> All men are equally entitled to the full and free exercise of [their religion] according to the dictates of conscience; and therefore that no man or class of men ought, on account of religion, to be invested with peculiar emoluments or privileges; nor subject to any penalties or disabilities unless, under color of religion, any man disturb the peace, the happiness, or the safety of society.[23]

When Patrick Henry was asked if he intended to "disestablish the Anglican Church," he backed off and the amendment failed.

Not to be thwarted, Madison again picked up his pen and wrote a new amendment that changed Mason's "All men should enjoy the fullest toleration . . . unpunished and unrestrained by the magistrate" to the following:

> All men are equally entitled to enjoy the free exercise of religion unless the preservation of equal liberty and the existence of the state are manifestly endangered.[24]

The convention approved the change. Madison successfully "raised the bar" to protect "the free exercise of religion."

More than freedom of thought and prayer, Madison advanced the cause that citizens should be allowed *freedom of religious practices*. Though the differences may seem small at first, the implications are huge. "Toleration" implied that the "State" had power *over* the "People," rather than the power resting *with* the "People." "Free exercise of religion" was not a privilege permitted by the "State," but rather a natural and unalienable right of the "People."

Madison sought to protect citizens from government intrusions. The only exception was in a case where the very "existence of the state" or the "equal liberty" of others would be "manifestly endangered." Madison thus made a bold step far beyond Mason's standard that religious practices not "disturb the peace, the happiness, or safety of Society." Now government agents would have to prove that the government would cease to exist if they did not act. Madison hoped this would put an end to religious persecution by overzealous government agents and officers of competing religious denominations.

MADISON IN THE VIRGINIA HOUSE OF DELEGATES

During the next two years, 1776-77, Madison served in the Virginia House of Delegates. They functioned not under British rule, but in accordance with their new Virginia State Constitution. Here we find a model for Madison's later U.S. Constitution, as well as the roots of many of the ideas that would inspire Thomas Jefferson to write the "Declaration of Independence." The Virginia Constitution proclaimed in part:

> That all men are by nature equally free and independent, and have certain inherent rights, of which, when they enter into a state of society, they can not by any compact, deprive or divest their posterity: namely, the enjoyment of life and liberty, with the means of acquiring & possessing property, and preserving and obtaining happiness and safety.[25]

In the "Declaration of Independence" Jefferson wrote in comparison, "We hold these truths to be self-evident, that all men are created equal, that they are endowed by their Creator with certain unalienable rights, that among these are life, liberty and the pursuit of happiness."[26] In the original draft, Jefferson first wrote, " . . . life, liberty and property." Then in an afterthought, he crossed out "property" and inserted "in the pursuit of happiness." In the "Virginia State Constitution, human rights came from "nature," but in Jefferson's "Declaration of Independence," our unalienable rights came from the "Creator."

Jefferson made a distinction that the rights of Americans came divinely from God. This interpretation rose above the Natural Rights espoused by philosophers of the Enlightenment.

In 1777, Madison suffered defeat in his re-election bid to the Virginia State Assembly. However, the Virginia legislature soon chose him as a member of the Council of State. During the next three years, 1778-80, he served Governor Patrick Henry, followed by Governor Thomas Jefferson.

In 1780, Madison was chosen to represent Virginia in the Continental Congress. He was the youngest delegate and served two terms (1780-83 and 1786-88). During the interim years (1784-86) he returned to his seat in the Virginia House of Delegates.

MADISON'S SUPPORT FOR
SEPARATION OF CHURCH AND STATE

In the summer of 1784, the issue of religious rights and the relationship of Church and State surfaced in Virginia. The old Anglican leaders advocated tax-supported Churches.[27] The Baptists protested the proposed State incorporation of favored Churches. The two main issues were as follows:

1. Should official State recognition be granted to favored churches, giving Church leaders authority to amass unlimited property?
2. Should tax money be given to favored churches?

Madison and Jefferson would oppose both points.

On June 21, the president of Hampden-Sydney College, John B. Smith, wrote to Madison regarding the proposed "General Assessment" of taxes to give state money to favored churches. Several churches began lobbying the legislature in hopes of becoming the official State religion. The Episcopal clergy, Smith wrote critically, was attempting "to draw the State into an [illicit] connection and commerce with them." This would give the state legislature legal jurisdiction, and essentially make the state the "head of the church."[28]

On July 3, 1784, Madison penned the following letter to Thomas Jefferson:

> Several Petitions came forward in behalf of a [General] Assessment which was reported by the Council of Religion to be reasonable. The friends of the measure did not [choose] to try their strength in the House. The Episcopal Clergy introduced a notable project for reestablishing their independence of the laity. The foundation of it was that the whole body should be legally incorporated, invested with the present property of the Church, made capable of acquiring indefinitely — empowered to make canons & bye-laws not contrary to the laws of the land, and incumbents when once chosen by vestries, to be immovable otherwise than by sentence of the Convocation. Extraordinary as such a project was, it was preserved from a dishonorable death by the talents of Mr. [Patrick] Henry. It lies over for another Session . . . Adieu My dear friend.[29]

Various churches lobbied the Virginia State Legislature for official "State Recognition." They presented petitions to a legislative committee in charge of "all matters relating to religion and morality." The Baptists and Presbyterians asked for an end to the favored status of the Episcopal Church, so that "religious freedom be established upon the broad basis of perfect political equality." For two days a bill for the Episcopal Church was debated. The matter was so controversial that the Assembly tabled the issue until autumn.[30]

Religious issues heated up over the summer of 1784. Madison traveled during that time, attending an American Indian gathering above the Potomac River and visiting friends in Philadelphia. By late autumn, he prepared to speak out against tax money being given to favored churches. In November, he penned his "Notes of Speech Against Assessments for Support of Religion."[31] Madison began by stating his position that religion should not be under the control or "purview of civil authority." He did not want the government to make laws that inevitably would result in convictions and punishments by the government. He reinforced the importance of keeping a separation between Church and State. Addressing the bureaucracies of religious organizations, Madison asked if religious establishments were necessary for religions. He said no. A person could be religious without being a member of an official religion.

Madison advanced the "propensity of man to Religion." He warned that involvement by the State could result in religions being "corrupted by Establishments." Conversely, such a path could lead to the "Downfall of States."

Madison argued strongly against tax dollars going to favored Churches. He first made a legal argument, citing cases in Pennsylvania and New Jersey that led to "factions." He then drew from the annals of history, invoking the era of "primitive Christianity." He recounted the Protestant Reformation of 16th century Europe, pointing out what happened to people who dissented from the official Church. The result was religious oppression and persecution. To encourage the assembly, Madison sang the praise of the great "progress of religious liberty" found in America.

Many people did not want their hard earned tax dollars going to support religions other than their own. If the government approved "General Assessments," Madison warned that some people would leave the country. Furthermore, such a policy might discourage immigration. The nation should rather be an "asylum" for people seeking the free exercise of religion.

MADISON AGAINST STATE RECOGNIZED RELIGIONS

Madison further warned against the establishment of State-recognized religions. He pointed to religious wars, "bad laws," and using the issue as "pretext from taxes." These points and more are like the "true causes of disease" within society. The "remedies" Madison suggested for a healthy society included "being out of war." As an alternative, he suggested that they make "laws to cherish virtue," and he counseled the wise "administration of justice." He said their time might be better spent focusing on the "education of youth."

Madison challenged the assembly with a thought-provoking question, "What is Christianity?" Did they want the Courts of the State to be interpreting this question?

Which edition of the Bible would the civil courts use, Madison asked. "What copy, what translation? Hebrew, Septuagint, or Vulgate?" While in college, Madison had studied different versions of the Bible, including the Hebrew translation, the Septuagint of the Old Testament in Greek, and the Latin version of the Vulgate used by Catholic priests. He demonstrated his scholarship in religious studies.

Madison further explained the pitfalls of creating State-recognized religions. The courts would be forced to choose which religious texts would be as canon law, like the "papists" of the Roman Catholics. Would the law be based on the Old Testament or the New Testament? Viewpoints differed between the Catholics and the Protestants. Different denominations of Protestants formed because people's opinions differed over key issues.

Madison questioned the assembly. Would the Bible be interpreted literally, "as dictated every letter by inspiration, or the essential parts only?" Or, would the Bible be interpreted "in general not the words?"

From the simple to the complex, Madison mounted his arguments against State-recognized religions. How would the State deal with a society of people representing so many different religions? Madison noted differences between various religious philosophies. "Trinitarianism" was based on the Trinity, the union between the "Father, Son and the Holy Spirit." "Arianism" followed the doctrines of Arius, who taught that Jesus was not the same substance as God, but a "created being" exalted above all other creatures. "Socinianism" was the doctrine of Faustus Socinus, denying the divinity of Jesus, the Trinity and explaining sin and salvation rationally. Madison further sketched out his arguments in his notes: "Is it salvation by faith or works also, by free grace or by will?"

Madison asked the lawmakers to ponder, "What clue is to guide [a] Judge [through] this labyrinth when ye question comes before them whether any particular society is a Christian society?" Civil judges of the State thus would be forced to determine what is "orthodoxy" and what is "heresy." Here Madison conjured images of the "Grand Inquisition," the horrors of which the assemblymen dare not re-create. He warned against passing the proposed legislation, because it "Dishonors Christianity." To preserve a clear separation of Church and State, he concluded, would bring praise and honor upon those who supported the position.[32] He won the support of young progressives who expressed that he "displayed great Learning & Ingenuity, with all the Powers of a close reasoner."[33]

Despite Madison's strong arguments against tax dollars going to State-recognized Churches, Patrick Henry supported the resolution encouraged by various clergy who were lobbying for State recognition and State money. Henry argued that "the people of the commonwealth, according to their respective abilities, ought to pay a moderate tax or contribution for the support of the Christian religion, or of some Christian church, denomination, or communion of Christians, or of some form of Christian worship."[34]

On November 14, 1784, Madison wrote a letter to James Monroe, in which he reported his struggle in trying to prevent the legislature from distributing tax dollars to State-recognized churches. Did the State have a right to tax its citizens in support of a religious establishment? Madison said no. He pointed out that the bill "excludes all but Christian Sects." He had learned from his religious studies that the world engendered many more diverse religions. The Presbyterian clergy protested "against any narrow principles," but the Episcopalian clergy demonstrated their power in lobbying the legislature. Madison predicted that "a trial will be made of the practicability of the project."[35]

On November 26, Richard Henry Lee responded to Madison: "Refiners may weave as fine a web of reason as they please, but the experience of all times shews Religion to be the guardian of morals." The following morning, Madison reported to James Monroe that the political climate was heating up over the "Bill for a Religious Assessment." Madison called the author of the bill, Patrick Henry, the "father of the scheme." Henry argued that State support of religion was needed because of the "decline in morals during the war."[36] Tensions grew so hot over the issue that Henry gave up his seat in the House of Delegates. Those who wanted State taxes for recognized churches lost their champion with

Henry's withdrawal. Madison characterized Henry's move as a "circumstance very inauspicious to his offspring."[37]

On December 22, Madison decided to vote for incorporation of churches, but remained strongly against religious taxation. The incorporation bill was modified to his liking. Rather than incorporating the clergy alone, which Madison opposed, the successful bill made each parish, their vestry and clergyman a corporate body. Thus church lands were to be held on the local level, rather than by the higher church officials. The vote was 47 to 38. Madison justified his vote by acknowledging that the act was necessary to allow churches to legally hold and manage church properties. However, a cap was placed on the amount of incorporated lands not to exceed £800 per year. Today, church lands may be incorporated and remain tax exempt.[38]

On Christmas Eve of 1784, Madison took time to write to James Monroe. He addressed matters of criminal jurisdiction within the State, as well as relations with foreign sovereigns. He then reported that the Assembly now was split over the issue of tax-supported Churches. The most recent vote was 44 to 42 in favor. Because the vote was so close, the Assembly decided to give the matter more time for public debate and "consideration of the people."[39]

On January 9, 1785, Madison wrote a long letter to Thomas Jefferson first summarizing the winter session of the Virginia Assembly. Madison reported that Patrick Henry had been elected Governor, a move that took him out of the Assembly. An act was passed establishing county courts. Madison viewed it as "a means of reconciling to our [government], the discontented extremities of the State."[40] Second, he reported that General George Washington appeared before the Assembly to voice support of "An Act for opening and extending the navigation of [the] Potomac River . . . and [the] James River." Also proposed was construction of better roadways. General Washington was rewarded with shares in the companies that would do the work. Today, such an act would be illegal and considered a kickback. Third, Madison reported that taxes were being cut thanks to the increased productivity of corn and tobacco that provided greater revenues. Fourth, the inventor of a revolutionary new boat requested a ten-year monopoly. Fifth, the question of extraditing felons to foreign countries was addressed.

The sixth matter Madison reported to Jefferson focused on the issue of separation of Church and State. The Protestant Episcopal Church continued their campaign to be a State-recognized church:

> This act declares the Ministers & vestries who are to be triennially chosen in each parish a body corporate, enables them to hold property not exceeding the value of £800 per annum, and gives sanction to a Convention which is to be composed of the Clergy and a lay deputy from each parish, and is to regulate the affairs of the Church.[41]

Serious flaws were pointed out that made the proposed act unacceptable to both sides.

Madison was especially against tax-supported Churches and tax dollars going to the salaries of the clergy:

> A negative of the bill too would have doubled the eagerness and the pre-texts for a much greater evil, a general [tax] Assessment, which, there is good ground to believe was parried by this partial gratification of its warmest votaries. A Resolution for a legal provision for the "teachers of the Christian Religion" had early in the Session been proposed by Mr. Henry, and in spite of all the opposition that could be mustered, carried by 47 against 32 votes.[42]

Madison characterized the idea of State taxes being given to recognized churches as dangerous, tending toward religious "discrimination," and "chiefly obnoxious on account of its dishonorable principle and dangerous tendency."[43]

On April 12, 1785, he wrote a letter to James Monroe in which he expressed his support for Thomas Jefferson's diplomatic mission to France and for a resolution to Western land claims. Furthermore, Madison updated Monroe on the issue of State taxes for churches:

> The only proceeding of the late Session of Assembly which makes a noise thro' the Country is that which relates to a [General Tax] Assessment. The Episcopal people are generally for it, [though] I think the zeal of some of them has cooled. The laity of the other sects are equally unanimous on the other side. So are all the Clergy except the Presbyterian who seem as ready to set up an establishment which is to take them in as they were to pull down that which shut them out. I do not know a more shameful contrast than might be found between their memorials on the latter & former occasion.[44]

It took Madison by surprise when some of the Presbyterian clergy switched sides. They were against the tax when they thought that they would be excluded. However, they decided to support it when it looked like they would be included in the benefits. When the majority opinion of the Presbyterian Church members against the religious tax was strongly voiced, the Presbyterian clergy soon retracted their support of the measure, following the wishes of their people.

Two weeks later, Madison penned another letter to Monroe in which he discussed the political fallout over the religious tax or General Assessment bill:

> In some counties they are influenced by the Bill for a [General] Assessment. In Culpeper [County] Mr. [Edmund] Pendleton a worthy man & acceptable in his general character to the people was laid aside in consequence of his vote for the Bill, in favor of an Adversary to it.[45]

Madison was supported by a majority of people who did not want their tax dollars going to select churches. They preferred supporting their personal churches directly through the collection plate. This position demonstrated advocacy for a clear separation between Church and State.

Over a month later, on May 29, 1785, Madison wrote again to Monroe expressing his glee that Congress recently had squashed a proposal to give a parcel of land to each township for the majority religion:

> It gives me much pleasure . . . [that] Congress had expunged a clause
> . . . for setting apart a district of land in each Township for supporting the
> Religion of the majority of inhabitants. How a regulation so unjust in
> itself, so foreign to the Authority of [Congress], so hurtful to the sale of
> the public land, and smelling so strongly of an antiquated Bigotry,
> could have received the countenance of a Committee is truly matter of
> astonishment.[46]

This proposal, like the proposed church tax, was considered by Madison to be
"encroachments on Religious Liberty . . . " Furthermore, he observed that some
supporters of such measures were "laid aside for voting for the Bill . . ."[47]

Madison reported that the Presbyterian clergy recently re-joined the majority of their followers against religious taxes. Their change in viewpoint, Madison
speculated, " . . . [was] either compelled by the laity of that sect, or alarmed at
the probability of further interferences of the Legislature, if they once begin to
dictate in matters of Religion."[48] Madison was clearly against giving the State
authority over the Church. Government officials inevitably would "interfere"
with religious groups, a thought that made many Church leaders think twice and
then pull back. The proverbial carrot looked attractive, but the potential price
was too great to pay. With Federal or State funds would come government over-
sight and audits. The result would be government agents meddling in Church
affairs.

MADISON'S MOST FAMOUS RELIGIOUS MEMORIAL

Madison succeeded in setting the stage for public participation over the
issue of tax dollars going to favored Churches. The process for public input
involved petitions being written and circulated to collect signatures from citizens.
Over 80 petitions were written against the religious tax vs. 11 petitions for the
tax. A total of 10,929 citizens signed at least one of the anti-tax petitions.[49]

Madison was inspired and encouraged to write an anti-tax petition, "A
Memorial and Remonstrance Against Religious Assessments," which was printed
June 20, 1785. The document has been called a "cornerstone in the American
tradition of religious freedom."[50]

Madison first warned that a religious tax would "be a dangerous abuse of
power." As citizens of a free State, they had a right to protest or "remonstrate
against it." Madison listed fifteen reasons why they were against State-sponsored
religion and religious taxation:

> 1. Because we hold it for a fundamental and undeniable truth, 'that
> Religion or the duty which we owe to our Creator and the manner of dis-
> charging it, can be directed only by reason and conviction, not by force or
> violence.[51]

Here Madison quoted from Article 16 of the Virginia State Constitution. He
contributed to the re-drafting of this article on religious freedom from the original text written by the Virginia statesman, George Mason.

Religion, Madison argued, was a fundamental human right. It was outside the scope of civil government:

> The Religion then of every man must be left to the conviction and conscience of every man; and it is the right of every man to exercise it as these may dictate. This right is in its nature an unalienable right. It is unalienable, because the opinions of men, depending only on the evidence contemplated by their own minds cannot follow the dictates of other men.[52]

Religion was a right that everyone possesses, Madison asserted. Religious freedom was an "unalienable right," so government officials should not try to dictate to citizens how they should practice their religion. Everyone should be free to exercise their religion without government interference. Madison continued:

> It is unalienable also, because what is here a right towards men, is a duty towards the Creator. It is the duty of every man to render to the Creator such homage and such only as he believes to be acceptable to him. This duty is precedent, both in order of time and in degree of obligation, to the claims of Civil Society.[53]

One's religious duty to God, Madison reasoned, was greater than one's obligation to a civil government. People should be free to choose for themselves what is an acceptable homage to express their personal reverence for God. Government agents, simply put, should not order citizens to pay religious taxes or to exercise their religions in any particular way.

One's first duty in life, according to Madison's religious philosophy, was a personal relationship with God:

> Before any man can be considered as a member of Civil Society, he must be considered as a subject of the Governour of the Universe: And if a member of Civil Society, who enters into any subordinate Association must always do it with a reservation of his duty to the General Authority; much more must every man who becomes a member of any particular Civil Society, do it with a saving of his allegiance to the Universal Sovereign.[54]

The "Governour of the Universe" — God — was greater in authority when compared with a governor of a State. Even when a person becomes a government employee or official, their first allegiance is still to God, the "Universal Sovereign."

Madison did not quibble or make exceptions to the rule. He was straightforward in his conclusion that the Church and the State must remain separated:

> We maintain therefore that in matters of Religion, no man's right is abridged by the institution of Civil Society and that Religion is wholly exempt from its cognizance.[55]

Government officials should not even think about getting involved in the religious affairs of society. And just because one is a citizen of a nation, it does not mean one has to give up any religious rights.

Madison acknowledged that in a democracy the majority generally ruled. In matters of religious freedom the rights of the minority are most often in need of protection. Therefore, the majority needed to restrain itself from trampling the rights of the religious minority:

> True it is, that no other rule exists, by which any question which may divide a Society, can be ultimately determined, but the will of the majority; but it is also true that the majority may trespass on the rights of the minority.[56]

Madison was concerned that minority groups might suffer from discrimination and oppression from a majority group. Laws were needed to protect minority groups, not laws that would empower and enrich the majority.

In his second major point, Madison warned the legislative branch of government to restrain itself from treading on the religious liberties of its citizens:

> 2. Because if Religion be exempt from the authority of the Society at large, still less can it be subject to that of the Legislative Body. The latter are but the creatures and vicegerents of the former. Their jurisdiction is both derivative and limited: it is limited with regard to the co-ordinate departments, more necessarily is it limited with regard to the constituents.[57]

Madison made the point that government officials in a democracy were not dictators, but rather "vicegerents" or representatives of the people. The power and legal authority of democratic government officials came from the people and was limited.

Madison asserted that there were limits in governmental powers. The government was divided into "departments of power." Not only should these lines of power be honored internally, but moreover, government officials should never overstep the external bounds protecting religious and civil rights of the people:

> The preservation of a free Government requires not merely, that the metes and bounds which separate each department of power be invariably maintained; but more especially that neither of them be suffered to overleap the great Barrier which defends the rights of the people.[58]

Using the terms of a land surveyor to define boundaries — "metes and bounds" — Madison defined the separation of Church and State. His terminology recalls the writings of the 17th Century English philosopher, John Locke, who delineated "the true bounds between the church and the commonwealth."[59]

Madison got tough with government officials who crossed the line and tried to limit a citizen's free exercise of religion:

> The Rulers who are guilty of such an encroachment, exceed the commission from which they derive their authority, and are *Tyrants*.[60]

The word "tyrant," Madison knew well, derived from the ancient Greek term, "tyrannos," referring to a cruel master or evil and oppressive despot. This was the term some American patriots used to criticize the King of England during the American Revolution.

Madison acknowledged that along with religious rights came equal responsibilities for citizens to stand up against government encroachments:

> The People who submit to it are governed by laws made neither by them-
> selves nor by an authority derived from them, and are *slaves.*[61]

Religious freedom was something for which people had to remain ever vigilant.
One lapse in diligence by the people could result in corrupt government officials
doing away with the rights of the people. Madison advocated a "participatory"
form of democracy in which citizens kept a close eye and were ready to jump in
to protest against any government wrongdoings.

Protesting against the government, from Madison's perspective, was more
than a right. It was everyone's responsibility to take a stand in defense of religious
and civil liberties, as he defined in his third major point:

> 3. Because it is proper to take alarm at the first experiment on our liberties.
> We hold this prudent jealousy to be the first duty of Citizens, and one of
> the noblest characteristics of the late Revolution. The free men of
> America did not wait till usurped power had strengthened itself by exer-
> cise, and entangled the question in precedents. They saw all the conse-
> quences in the principle, and they avoided the consequences by denying
> the principle.[62]

Madison underscored that the "first duty of Citizens" was to "take alarm" at
the earliest threat to religious freedom and civil liberties. No one should wait
until our freedoms are lost. For example, in 1775 when the British claimed a
"right of unbounded legislation over the colonies of America," Thomas
Jefferson responded promptly by writing a "Declaration of the Causes and
Necessity for Taking Up Arms."[63]

The American patriots learned the importance of defending their freedoms
with all their might. If they had failed to do so, the United States would never
have come into being. Madison pointed out:

> We revere this lesson too much soon to forget it. Who does not see that
> the same authority which can establish Christianity, in exclusion of all
> other Religions, may establish with the same ease any particular sect of
> Christians, in exclusion of all other Sects? That the same authority which
> can force a citizen to contribute three pence only of his property for the
> support of any one establishment, may force him to conform to any other
> establishment in all cases whatsoever?[64]

Madison took a bold step in defending all religions, not only those of the
Christian faith. He was against Christianity being established as the "State
Religion." If the government could create a religious tax, they could also force
citizens to "conform" to any religion of their choosing. This would be wrong,
Madison argued. Acceptance of all religions was the key to true religious freedom.
There could be no exceptions.

"Equality" was paramount in Madison's philosophy. Anything that chipped
away at our "equal rights" should be viewed as a red flag. This was one of the

fundamental flaws he identified in the "General Assessment," as he illuminated in his fourth major point, which was against the religious tax bill:

> 4. Because the Bill *violates that equality* which ought to be the basis of every law, and which is more indispensable, in proportion as the validity or expediency of any law is more liable to be impeached. If "all men are by nature equally free and independent," all men are to be considered as entering into Society on equal conditions; as relinquishing no more, and therefore retaining no less, one than another, of their natural rights.[65]

Madison cited in the margin the source of his quote which was from Article I of the "Virginia Declaration of Rights." He further interpreted the quote to mean that every citizen should enjoy equal rights. This position challenged the old aristocracy and hierarchal class system of Europe. Rigid social structure crept into colonial America, as Madison observed growing up in Virginia. His philosophy of equal rights also would be found in his writings advocating the abolition of slavery. Regardless of one's "race, creed or national origin," a citizen of the United States should retain equal rights, Madison argued:

> Above all are they to be considered as retaining an '*equal* title to the free exercise of Religion according to the dictates of Conscience'.[66]

Here Madison penned into the margin that the source of his quote was also from Article I of the "Virginia Declaration of Rights."

So there would be no confusion of Madison's intent, he clearly defined the extent of our religious freedoms:

> Whilst we assert for ourselves a freedom to embrace, to profess and to observe the Religion which we believe to be of divine origin, we cannot deny an equal freedom to those whose minds have not yet yielded to the evidence which has convinced us. If this freedom be abused, it is an offence against God, not against man: To God, therefore, not to man, must an account of it be rendered.[67]

Here Madison espoused the teachings of religious toleration that he learned from Rev. Witherspoon at Princeton. While he was a Christian, he urged fellow Christians to be tolerant of those who were not. Religious intoleration, he said, was an "offense against God." Violators would have to atone before God. Because the battle for religious toleration was won, America is today a place where people can freely practice Judaism, Islam, Buddhism, and Native American religions to name but a few.

Madison continued his direct attack against the "General Assessment" bill to create a religious tax:

> As the Bill violates equality by subjecting some to peculiar burdens, so it violates the same principle, by granting to others peculiar exemptions. Are the Quakers and Menonists the only sects who think a compulsive support of their Religions unnecessary and unwarrantable?[68]

The answer was no. There were followers of many religions who did not want a

State-sponsored Church. Madison selected only two examples. The Quakers or Society of Friends were and still are a religion of Protestant pacifists. In the 17th and 18th centuries, many settled in Pennsylvania and participated in their "holy experiment." Their meetings are characterized by long periods of silence. The Menonists or Mennonites were founded in the 16th century in Friesland, a province in Holland. These evangelical Protestants oppose serving in the government or the military. They do not baptize babies, preferring to wait until children mature to an age when they can freely choose whether to join the Church. They forbid taking oaths to anyone but God. Both Quakers and Mennonites would never compel someone to join their church or to give their church money.

Madison continued his case against religious taxes. He asked if people could really trust the government to be loyal in administering state jurisdiction over religious practices:

> Can their piety alone be entrusted with the care of public worship?[69]

No was the answer Madison sought. No, government officials should not be entrusted with legal powers to meddle in the free exercise of religion. This would create an "unholy alliance" between Church and State.

Church historians knew full well what happened when one Church claimed supremacy over others. The result was often religious wars, which filled the pages of European history books. Madison spoke against the proposed State-sponsored religions:

> Ought their Religions to be endowed above all others with extraordinary privileges by which proselytes may be enticed from all others? We think too favorably of the justice and good sense of these denominations to believe that they either covet pre-eminences over their fellow citizens or that they will be seduced by them from the common opposition to the measure.[70]

A favored church enriched with State money would create unfair competition between religions. No, religious groups in America would not be corrupted by the lure of money, Madison hoped. He praised religious groups for having the "good sense" not to seek superiority over their neighbors. They should not be "seduced" by the State money being dangled before them by Madison's opponents.

It would be unreasonable to force a civil judge to become a "Judge of Religious Truth." This would be an unfair burden to place upon a civil judge. They could not be expected to know all divine truths and the details of all religious history required to be a fair judge of divine justice. This was a seat reserved for God. Madison proclaimed in his fifth major point against the proposed legislation:

> 5. Because the Bill implies either that the Civil Magistrate is a competent Judge of Religious Truth; or that he may employ Religion as an - engine of Civil policy. The first is an arrogant pretension falsified by the contradictory opinions of Rulers in all ages, and throughout the world: the second an unhallowed perversion of the means of salvation.[71]

Madison warned against government officials using religion as a tool for advancing political gains. Politicians should not offer public tax money to favored religious groups as a reward for their political support. Corrupt politicians should not think that this could be their ticket to Heaven. Madison criticized such an act to be an "unhallowed perversion."

The Virginia gentleman may have been influenced in his reasoning by the writings of the philosopher John Locke, who stated:

> The commonwealth seems to me to be a society of men constituted only for preserving and advancing their civil goods. What I call civil goods are life, liberty, bodily health and freedom from pain, and the possession of outward things, such as lands, money, furniture, and the like. It is the duty of the civil magistrate, by impartially enacted equal laws, to preserve and secure for all the people . . . these things that belong to this life . . . The whole jurisdiction of the magistrate is concerned only with these civil goods.[72]

While Locke gave some exceptions to the rule separating Church and State, Madison was more staunch in limiting the powers of the government.

Madison asserted that religious groups did not need government aid. They could support their religion through voluntary support from their followers. Madison stated his position clearly in his sixth major point:

> 6. Because the establishment proposed by the Bill is not requisite for the support of the Christian Religion. To say that it is, is a contradiction to the Christian Religion itself, for every page of it disavows a dependence on the powers of this world: it is a contradiction to fact; for it is known that this Religion both existed and flourished, not only without the support of human laws, but in spite of every opposition from them, and not only during the period of miraculous aid, but long after it had been left to its own evidence and the ordinary care of Providence.[73]

Christianity, Madison concluded, was dependent upon God's divine power, not on the power of the State. The lessons of history taught that many religious groups escaped persecution from civil laws to seek sanctuary for religious freedom in America. Civil governments largely had been their main opposition in Europe. The fact that some oppressed minority religious groups had survived and prospered in America was like a miracle created by the care and benevolent guidance of God.

Madison questioned the validity of a State-sponsored religion. Such a religion would be an invention of the State. It would not have the historic roots that were nurtured through time. Madison continued:

> Nay, it is a contradiction in terms; for a Religion not invented by human policy, must have pre-existed and been supported, before it was established by human policy. It is moreover to weaken in those who profess this Religion a pious confidence in its innate excellence and the patronage of its Author; and to foster in those who still reject it, a suspicion that its friends are too conscious of its fallacies to trust it to its own merits.[74]

Madison warned that State-sponsored religious groups would develop a false belief that they were superior to other religions. Deep down, a sense of insecurity inevitably would grow in their hearts over unjustified professions of superiority. The divine trust relationship therefore would be in jeopardy.

Madison then unleashed his most bold statement regarding religious history. In its purist form, religion had the power to produce the most laudable effects on society. However, some religious leaders in the past defamed this purity through their lust for power and control. The very legality of Christianity was questioned and challenged throughout history:

> 7. Because experience witnesseth that ecclesiastical establishments, instead of maintaining the purity and efficacy of Religion, have had a contrary operation. During almost fifteen centuries has the legal establishment of Christianity been on trial. What have been its fruits? More or less in all places, pride and indolence in the Clergy, ignorance and servility in the laity, in both, superstition, bigotry and persecution.[75]

Madison wanted to put an end to religious persecution. A free American society offered a precious opportunity to that end. In place of "pride and indolence," American religious leaders should demonstrate humility and resourcefulness. In place of "ignorance and servility," American people should have the opportunity to receive public education and to be free citizens.

Madison appealed for all to look back to the early beginnings of Christianity. Here one would find the greatest teachers. They did not depend on the State for handouts. To the contrary, they relied on voluntary donations received through passing the collection plate. Madison challenged his readers:

> Enquire of the Teachers of Christianity for the ages in which it appeared in its greatest lustre; those of every sect, point to the ages prior to its incorporation with Civil policy. Propose a restoration of this primitive State in which its Teachers depended on the voluntary rewards of their flocks, many of them predict its downfall. On which Side ought their testimony to have greatest weight, when for or when against their interest?[76]

Madison chided the supporters of the religious tax who claimed that Christian morality would suffer without State funding. The defeat of this bill would not result in the "downfall" of society. To the contrary, Madison continued:

> 8. Because the establishment in question is not necessary for the support of Civil Government. If it be urged as necessary for the support of Civil Government only as it is a means of supporting Religion, and it be not necessary for the latter purpose, it cannot be necessary for the former. If Religion be not within the cognizance of Civil Government how can its legal establishment be necessary to Civil Government?[77]

The response Madison sought was that State sponsorship of religion was not needed. Civil government officials should not even be thinking about controlling religious groups. Religion should be outside government purview and beyond the scope of State jurisdiction.

Madison further warned what could happen if the Church and State were not kept separate. The outcome could be a "holy war" resulting in "spiritual tyranny." Some kings proclaimed in the past that they ruled by "divine right." Such dictators never protected the rights of the people, as Madison pointed out:

> What influence in fact have ecclesiastical establishments had on Civil Society? In some instances they have been seen to erect a spiritual tyranny on the ruins of the Civil authority; in many instances they have been seen upholding the thrones of political tyranny: in no instance have they been seen the guardians of the liberties of the people.[78]

The general citizenry often suffered terrible oppression under kings who justified their actions by "divine right."

Madison warned that societies suffered when the Church and State were not kept apart. Civil and religious officials sometimes were guilty of collusion, conspiring for their own selfish gains. The only governmental act Madison viewed as justifiable in this case was official recognition of religious freedom:

> Rulers who wished to subvert the public liberty, may have found an established Clergy convenient auxiliaries. A just Government instituted to secure & perpetuate it needs them not. Such a Government will be best supported by *protecting every Citizen in the enjoyment of his Religion* with the same equal hand which protects his person and his property; by neither invading the equal rights of any Sect, nor suffering any Sect to invade those of another.[79]

Government officials needed to restrain themselves from "invading" the equal rights of each religious group. Such restraint needed to be equal to a citizen's rights against invasion of privacy and private property.

Madison then made his ninth major point against religious persecution:

> 9. Because the proposed establishment is a departure from that generous policy, which, *offering an Asylum to the persecuted and oppressed of every Nation and Religion,* promised a lustre to our country, and an accession to the number of its citizens."[80] What a melancholy mark is the Bill of sudden degeneracy? "Instead of holding forth an Asylum to the persecuted, it is itself a signal of persecution. It degrades from the equal rank of Citizens all those whose opinions in Religion do not bend to those of the Legislative authority. Distant as it may be in its present form from the Inquisition, it differs from it only in degree. The one is the first step, the other the last in the career of intolerance.[81]

America was intended to be a sanctuary for people who escaped foreign persecution and immigrated to this land to enjoy the blessings of freedom. This precious religious freedom would be lost, Madison argued, if this bill of "General Assessment" passed. It would mark the beginning of State-sponsored religious persecution in America. This might lead to an American "Inquisition."

Madison believed that if Americans lost their religious freedom, other people around the world would be discouraged from immigrating to this country. He was a strong supporter of immigration and generally welcomed immigrants from foreign lands. He believed cultural diversity helped make America great. It was especially important, Madison argued, for the most oppressed people in the world to feel with confidence that their lives would improve if only they could reach our freedom-loving country:

> The magnanimous sufferer under this cruel scourge in foreign Regions, must view the Bill as a Beacon on our Coast, warning him to seek some other haven, where liberty and philanthropy in their due extent, may offer a more certain repose from his Troubles.[82]

Some Americans developed a prejudice against foreign immigrants and too quickly forgot that most of their own ancestors were once immigrants. Instead of welcoming immigrants and helping them get established in this country, some bigots called them derogatory names and attempted to limit their freedoms. Madison thought such bigotry was clearly wrong.

If American freedoms were lost, Madison feared, people may decide to leave this country. He warned that State-sponsored religion could drive away minority groups:

> 10. Because it will have a like tendency *to banish* our Citizens. The allurements presented by other situations are every day thinning their number. To superadd a fresh motive to emigration by revoking the liberty which they now enjoy, would be the same species of folly which has dishonoured and depopulated flourishing kingdoms.[83]

America needed more citizens, not less. The strength of America was reflected in the strength of its citizenry. If America wanted to grow stronger among the family of nations, then our government must not revoke our religious and civil liberties.

Madison strongly advocated that America should be a nation of just laws. When the civil government demonstrates religious toleration, the model will inspire religious groups to maintain a sense of harmony. However, if the civil government is intolerant, it can result in civil and religious wars. Once religious wars commence, civil government officials may find the conflicts most difficult to quell.

> 11. Because it will destroy that moderation and harmony which the forbearance of our laws to intermeddle with Religion has produced among its several sects. Torrents of blood have been spilt in the old world, by vain attempts of the secular arm, to extinguish Religious discord, by proscribing all difference in Religious opinion.[84]

Madison cautioned civil government officials not to attempt to outlaw the free exercise of religion. They could not simply outlaw religious differences, whenever religious conflicts erupted. Such attempts would be doomed to failure:

> Time has at length revealed the true remedy. Every relaxation of narrow and rigorous policy, wherever it has been tried, has been found to assuage the disease. The American Theatre has exhibited proofs that equal and compleat liberty, if it does not wholly eradicate it, sufficiently destroys its

malignant influence on the health and prosperity of the State.[85]

The right course for civil governments was to stop trying to control people regarding their religions. Full, unrestricted religious liberty was the answer, along with a clear separation between Church and State.

Madison conceded that there wasn't even a word to describe how foolish it would be for the State to try to restrict religious freedom:

> If with the salutary effects of this system under our own eyes, we begin to contract the bounds of Religious freedom, we know no name that will too severely reproach our folly. At least let warning be taken at the first fruits of the threatened innovation. The very appearance of the Bill has transformed "that Christian forbearance, love and charity," which of late mutually prevailed, into animosities and jealousies, which may not soon be appeased. What mischiefs may not be dreaded, should this enemy to the public quiet be armed with the force of a law?[86]

Madison noted in the margin that the quotation came from Article XVI of the Virginia State Constitution. He advocated patient self-control, love for your neighbor and a return to Christian charity. He criticized how this proposed religious tax already was creating jealous discord between different religious groups. This was not good for America. If they thought it bad then, Madison predicted religious strife would become much worse should the religious tax become law.

Madison made his twelfth major point that the proposed religious tax would hurt the spread of religion in America:

> 12. Because the policy of the Bill is adverse to the diffusion of the light of Christianity. The first wish of those who enjoy this precious gift ought to be that it may be imparted to the whole race of mankind. Compare the number of those who have as yet received it with the number still remaining under the dominion of false Religions; and how small is the former![87]

Madison appealed to the personal faith of local Christians. He addressed their desire to increase their followings and assured them this bill would hurt their efforts to spread Christianity:

> Does the policy of the Bill tend to lessen the disproportion? No; it at once discourages those who are strangers to the light of revelation from coming into the Region of it; and countenances by example the nations who continue in darkness, in shutting out those who might convey it to them. Instead of Levelling as far as possible, every obstacle to the victorious progress of Truth, the Bill with an ignoble and unchristian timidity would circumscribe it with a wall of defense against the encroachments of error.[88]

State sponsored religion would be exclusive [excluding those who were not in favored status]. Madison argued that it was better for religious groups to be inclusive — opening their arms to accept new members. He first wrote of "strangers to the light of truth," then changed the last word to read "strangers to the light of revelation." For most Christians, spiritual revelations spoke to God's disclosure to man of His will and very existence. Some Christians also embraced a more personal relationship with a God who might reveal to individuals some divine message.

In his next major point, Madison scorned the proposed law that he predicted would weaken their entire legal system:

> 13. Because attempts to enforce by legal sanctions, acts obnoxious to so great a proportion of Citizens, tend to enervate the laws in general, and to slacken the bands of Society." If it be difficult to execute any law which is not generally deemed necessary or salutary, what must be the case, where it is deemed invalid and dangerous? And what may be the effect of so striking an example of impotency in the Government, on its general authority?[89]

When people recognized that politicians were capable of creating such a bad law, many citizens might lose faith in their government as a whole. Madison appealed to the great diversity of religious groups in America. To those that leaned toward supporting State-sponsored religion, he urged them to reconsider their positions for the greater good of society.

In accordance with the principles of democracy, special interest groups should not dictate over the majority of citizens.

> 14. Because a measure of such singular magnitude and delicacy ought not to be imposed, without the clearest evidence that it is called for by a majority of citizens, and no satisfactory method is yet proposed by which the voice of the majority in this case may be determined, or its influence secured. 'The people of the respective counties are indeed requested to signify their opinion respecting the adoption of the Bill to the next Session of Assembly.'[90]

Here Madison quoted from a resolution passed late in 1784 that called for public input regarding religious taxes. The majority will of the people was to be determined through public responses to various petitions, including Madison's "Memorial."

> But the representation must be made equal, before the voice either of the Representatives or of the Counties will be that of the people. Our hope is that neither of the former will, after due consideration, espouse the dangerous principle of the Bill. Should the event disappoint us, it will still leave us in full confidence, that a fair appeal to the latter will reverse the sentence against our liberties.[91]

Madison hoped state and county politicians would back off from supporting State aid for Churches. He expressed faith that the majority of the citizens would support his viewpoints. He therefore expected that the public representatives would listen to and heed the will of the people.

Madison saved his most powerful argument against State-sponsored religion for last:

> 15. Because finally, "the equal right of every citizen to the free exercise of his Religion according to the dictates of conscience" is held by the same

tenure with all our other rights.[92]

Every American citizen, Madison advanced, presently held the right to "free exercise of Religion." This was greater than just freedom of personal thought. The very practices of each individual religious group were protected as an "unalienable right." Religious freedom was as important as all other essential civil rights.

> If we recur to its origin, it is equally the gift of nature; if we weigh its importance, it cannot be less dear to us; if we consult the "Declaration of those rights which pertain to the good people of Virginia, as the basis and foundation of Government," it is enumerated with equal solemnity, or rather studied emphasis.[93]

Madison once again drew from the Virginia State Constitution. The "free exercise of religion" was then protected under state constitutional law.

> Either then, we must say, that the Will of the Legislature is the only measure of their authority; and that in the plenitude of this authority, they may sweep away all our fundamental rights; or, that they are bound to leave this particular right untouched and sacred.[94]

Madison did not want citizens to sit back and let the legislative branch of government pass laws that would chip away at their religious and civil rights. Even though he himself was one of those legislators, Madison believed that the power of the people should reign preeminent. If this was to be a government "of the people, for the people and by the people," then citizens would have to actively participate in governmental affairs. Politicians would have to be viewed as public servants, and the will of the public would have to be made known and honored.

Madison warned the public of the dangers of not exercising their right to actively participate in their government. If the government was permitted to limit their religious freedom, then the legislature also could take away other fundamental civil rights:

> Either we must say, that they may [control] the freedom of the press, may abolish the Trial by Jury, may swallow up the Executive and Judiciary Powers of the State; nay that they may despoil us of our very right of suffrage, and erect themselves into an independent and hereditary Assembly or, we must say, that they have no authority to enact into law the Bill under consideration.[95]

Was this a government of the people — a democracy — or was this a government of the politicians? If the legislative branch of government became omnipotent, then they might destroy democracy and put in its place a system of hereditary privilege. America offered an opportunity where someone born penniless could succeed through hard work and determination. There remained a chance for upward social mobility.

Did the majority of American citizens want to sacrifice the freedoms of democratic society and replace it with an aristocratic class system? Madison hoped the people would respond, "No! No! Never!"

> We the Subscribers say, that the General Assembly of this Commonwealth have no such authority: And that no effort may be omitted on our part against so dangerous an usurpation, we oppose to it, this remonstrance; earnestly praying, as we are in duty bound, that the Supreme Lawgiver of the Universe, by illuminating those to whom it is addressed, may on the one hand, turn their Councils from every act which would affront his holy prerogative, or violate the trust committed to them: and on the other, guide them into every measure which may be worthy of his blessing, may redound to their own praise, and may establish more firmly the liberties, the prosperity and the happiness of the Commonwealth.[96]

Madison ended with a flourish. Rarely did one see him so passionate on an issue. He more often employed quiet, reserved reasoning. He was said to speak publicly with a soft, gentle tone of voice. Here he spoke with the religious fervor of an impassioned minister. Religious freedom remained an issue that ignited his passions throughout his life.

Madison was victorious. So overwhelming was public outcry against religious taxes, the bill died an inglorious death when no one tried to resurrect the issue. Madison may have privately celebrated his success, but he remained reserved in public.

As an endnote to Madison's "Memorial and Remonstrance Against Religious Assessments," it is significant that he did not reveal himself as the author of document. The "Memorial" originally was published anonymously. He apparently did not state why he wanted to keep his authorship a secret. One may only speculate that he was determined to address the issue unrestrained without suffering any potential political fallout. Madison waited 40 years before acknowledging his authorship of the "Memorial." On July 14, 1826, he wrote a letter to George Mason's grandson. In this letter, he revealed to the young Mason that his grandfather and George Nicholas "thought it advisable, that a Remonstrance against the Bill should be prepared for general circulation & signature, and imposed on me the task of drawing up such a paper."[97]

On June 21, 1785, the day after Madison is believed to have finished the "Memorial," he wrote a letter to James Monroe. Rather than singing a personal victory song, Madison humbly gave the credit for the defeat of religious taxes to the citizens of rural Virginia:

> A very warm opposition will be made to this innovation by the people of the middle and back Counties, particularly the latter. They do not scruple to declare it an alarming usurpation on their fundamental rights and that tho' the Genl. Assembly should give it the form, they will not give it the validity of a law. If there be any limitation to the power of the Legislature, particularly if this limitation is to be sought in our Declaration of Rights or Form of Government, I own the Bill appears to me to warrant this language of the people.[98]

How unusual it was for a politician not to bask in the glory of success. Madison stood as a unique statesman in American history. His abilities would lead him to the national stage.

Forty years later, he wrote a letter to General Lafayette, the French American hero, outlining highlights of the history of religious freedom in America:

> The Anglican hierarchy existing in Virginia prior to the Revolution was abolished by an early act of the Independent Legislature. In the year 1785, a bill was introduced under the auspices of Mr. [Patrick] Henry, imposing a general tax for the support of "Teachers of the Christian Religion." It made a progress, threatening a majority in its favor. As an expedient to defeat it, we proposed that it should be postponed to another session, and printed in the meantime for public consideration. Such an appeal in a case so important and so unforeseen could not be resisted.[99]

Here Madison reveals how the Americans tore down the old hierarchy of colonial power, just as Lafayette had sought to do in France.

Madison then revealed his personal role in the plan to excite the power of the people:

> With a view to arouse the people, it was thought proper that a memorial should be drawn up, the task being assigned to me, to be printed and circulated throughout the State for a general signature. The experiment succeeded. The memorial was so extensively signed by the various religious sects, including a considerable portion of the old hierarchy, that the projected innovation was crushed . . .[100]

Madison learned how important it was in representative government to seek the power of the people. By gaining popular support and trusting in the people's authority, Madison and his circle succeeded in transforming the old aristocracy into a modern democracy.

MADISON'S 1785 PETITION TO REPEAL CHURCH INCORPORATION

With the political tide moving in his favor, Madison penned another petition to repeal an earlier legislative action incorporating the Protestant Episcopal Church. This was to be signed only by members of that religion, which presently consisted of over seventy parishes in Virginia. It is intriguing that Madison would write this document on behalf of the Episcopal Church. He stood on his principles that a religious tax was wrong. Madison took his case to the general membership through a petition entitled, "Protestant Episcopal Church Petition to the General Assembly of Virginia" (ca. July 1785).[101] Herein the members of the Episcopal Church protested the State incorporation of their religion for seven main reasons:

> Because the law admits the power of the Legislative Body to interfere in matters of Religion which we think is not included in their jurisdiction.[102]

Here Madison took a bold stand that the State should not have legal jurisdiction over religious matters. Church and State should be clearly separated.

The second main point charges that the Episcopal clergy had improperly acted without first seeking the opinion of the general members. Therefore, the petitioners called for a repeal of the bill:

> Because the law was passed on the petition of some of the Clergy of the Protestant Episcopal Church without any application from the other members of that Church in whom the law is to operate, and we conceive it to be highly improper that the Legislature should regard as the sense of the whole Church the opinion of a few interested members who were in most instances originally imposed on the people without their consent & who were not authorized by even the smallest part of this community to make such a proposition.[103]

This clause must have caused more than a stir among those clergy who took the lead in the matter. At that time, high officials in the Episcopal religion were making decisions over which clergymen went to particular churches. Madison saw this as hierarchal and preferred that power should rest with the people rather than with the Church or the State.

In the third main point, Madison argued that people should choose their own representatives:

> Because the law constitutes the Clergy members of a Convention who are to legislate for the laity contrary to their fundamental right of Chusing their own Legislators.[104]

Madison was counting on a substantial number of Episcopalians to support his view that the time had come for the people in the Church to stand up for their rights.

Just as Madison had participated in the American Revolution, he now was encouraging a revolt within the Episcopal Church. He presented in his fourth main point:

> Because by that law the most obnoxious & unworthy Clergyman cannot be removed from a parish except by the determination of a body, one half of whom the people have no confidence in & who will always have the same interest with the minister whose conduct they are to judge of.[105]

Madison knew the selection of acceptable ministers was important to Virginia Episcopalians, because in 1785 they needed to hire over thirty ministers. The local people should make decisions over which minister served in their local church.

In his fifth point, Madison pointed out how the power structure was flawed:

> Because by that law power is given to the Convention to regulate matters of faith, & the obsequious Vestries are to engage to change their opinions as often as the Convention shall alter theirs.[106]

Rather than recognizing the power resting with the people, the legislature had empowered the religious hierarchy as decision makers. The signers of the petition asserted that power rested with the general membership of the church as their fundamental right.

In his sixth and final point, Madison condemned the incorporation law as being so unreasonable as to be laughable. He called the law "servile," coming from the Latin word "servilus," meaning "slave-like."

> Because a System so absurd & servile, will drive the members of the Episcopal Church over to other Sects, where there will be more consistency & liberty.
>   We therefore hope that the wisdom & impartiality of the present Assembly will incline them to repeal a law so pregnant with mischief & injustice.[107]

The possibility that the law might "drive" members of the church to other religions was a sobering thought. This concerned the health and well being of the Episcopal Church as a whole. Therefore, Madison and the petitioners called for the incorporation law to be repealed. In a final blow, he called the law "pregnant with mischief and injustice." This implied that the authors and supporters of the measure were up to no good and their supposed allegiance to justice for the people was highly questionable. Madison pulled no punches, while remaining the anonymous author of this petition.

MADISON TO JEFFERSON: A REPORT ON RELIGIOUS ISSUES IN 1785

On August 20, 1785, Madison wrote a letter to Thomas Jefferson in which he reported the opposition was gaining against the proposed religious tax. He acknowledged that he was the author of a petition against the tax and enclosed a copy. It may be assumed that this was "Madison's Memorial of 1785." The petition was sent through a "medium of confidential persons in a number of the upper Counties, and I am told will be pretty extensively signed." Madison then illuminated some of the reasons why the Presbyterians and Episcopalians were at odds with one another:

> The Presbyterian clergy, have at length espoused the side of the opposition [against the religious tax], being moved either by a fear of their laity or a jealousy of the Episcopalians. The mutual hatred of these sects has been much inflamed by the late Act incorporating the latter. I am far from being sorry for it, as a coalition between them could alone endanger our religious rights, and a tendency to such an event had been suspected.[108]

The Presbyterians sided with Madison against the proposed religious tax. Some of the Episcopalians signed his petition against incorporation. Although both groups remained at odds with one another, Madison successfully solicited support from each, a masterful feat of diplomacy. His anonymity as the author of both religious petitions perhaps aided in his success.

THE RELIGIOUS FREEDOM ACT OF 1785

In the autumn of 1785, Madison decided to push forward the revision of the Virginia state legal codes. The effort, commenced a decade earlier by Thomas Jefferson, represented not only a complete revision of old statutes, but also the creation of new ones. The purpose was to "eliminate all vestiges of monarchism and substitute republican tenets."[109]

On October 31, Madison introduced over a hundred bills before the Virginia legislature. Although he was Chairman of the Committee for Courts of Justice, the sheer volume of legislation was so great, they could only get through 43 bills by year's end. Madison selected from the remaining bills, the one he deemed most important, #82 — "An Act for Establishing Religious Freedom."[110] The author of the bill, Thomas Jefferson, was not present, being on a diplomatic mission to France. Before his departure, Jefferson had personally asked Madison if he might help shepherd the passage of the measure. Fighting back a proposed amendment to the preamble, Madison succeeded in securing approval of Jefferson's bill. The political battles to pass the Religious Freedom Act were described by Madison to Jefferson in some detail.

On January 22, 1786, Madison wrote to Thomas Jefferson a long report on the Virginia Convention. The Assembly met during the previous 97 days. Late in the session, Madison was determined to secure passage of the "Religious Freedom Act:"

> The only one of these which was pursued into an Act is the Bill concerning Religious freedom. The steps taken throughout the Country to defeat the [religious tax or] Genl. Assessment, had produced all the effect that could have been wished. The table was loaded with petitions & remonstrances from all parts against the interposition of the Legislature in matters of Religion.[111]

The public petitions protesting religious taxes and State-sponsored religions represented the strong voice of the people. Madison advocated public protest and the petition process as ways for the people to assert their rights and authority in a free society. This represented an example of participatory democracy.

Religious groups, such as the Presbyterians, were among those who united in support of the "Religious Freedom Act:"

> A General convention of the Presbyterian church prayed expressly that the bill in the Revisal might be passed into a law, as the best safeguard short of a constitutional one, for their religious rights.[112]

Madison would conclude that the "free exercise of religion" did require a constitutional safeguard, as later realized in the First Amendment of the U.S. Constitution. In 1785, "The Religious Freedom Act" took a big step in protecting religious rights.

Madison informed Jefferson that some of the legislators edited part of the text of the act:

> The bill was carried thro' the [House] of Delegates, without alteration. The Senate objected to the preamble, and sent down a proposed substitution of the 16th. art: of the [Virginia] Declaration of Rights. The H. of D. disagreed. The Senate insisted and asked a Conference.[113]

Although Madison did not clarify exactly what changes were being requested, Jefferson later revealed that some of the Virginia legislators advocated inserting the name "Jesus Christ" before the phrase "the holy author of our religion."[114] The reason why Madison and others wanted to leave the text alone was because they wanted to welcome to America not only Christians, but also people of other religions. Another factor may have been the spread of deism, a belief in the existence of God from a rational perspective without embracing revelation or authority. Deists believe that God created the world and the Laws of Nature.

Madison identified the legislators who tried to change the preamble: Speaker Benjamin Harrison, John Francis Mercer, Francis Corbin and Carter Henry Harrison. They sought to replace Jefferson's preamble with ideas from Article 16 of the "Virginia Declaration of Rights:"

> The preamble was sent up again from the H. of D. with one or two verbal alterations. As an amendment to these the Senate sent down a few others; which as they did not affect the substance though they somewhat defaced the composition, it was thought better to agree to than to run further risks, especially as it was getting late in the Session and the House growing thin.[115]

Two main protections were preserved in the "Religious Freedom Act." First, citizens were free to exercise their religions as they saw fit. Second, religious taxes were declared illegal.

Madison reported to Jefferson the best news — the essential parts of the text passed unchanged. This must have pleased Jefferson, who actually wrote the text six years earlier in 1779.

> The enacting clauses [passed] without a single alteration, and I flatter myself have in this Country extinguished for ever the ambitious hope of making laws for the human mind.[116]

Madison's disdain for "laws for the human mind" illuminates his position that the government should not try to legislate how people think. Citizens should be encouraged to be part of a "free-thinking society," an issue closely related to "freedom of speech," "freedom of the press," and "right of assembly."

PRELUDE TO THE U.S. CONSTITUTION

Madison's analysis brought his thinking to a logical conclusion — the United States needed a national Constitution. He voted on January 21, 1786, for a national meeting under the auspices of discussing foreign trade. The Annapolis Convention was held in September at the Maryland State House and furthered discussions initiated at the Mount Vernon Convention of 1785. The big question was — should they revise the old Articles of Confederation or establish a new national Constitution?

The question was taken up in greater earnest in May 1787 at the Philadelphia conference endorsed by the Continental Congress. Their resolution stated that they were gathering for the "sole and express purpose of revising the Articles of Confederation and reporting to Congress and the several legislatures such alterations and provisions therein as shall when agreed to in Congress and confirmed by the States render the federal constitution adequate to the exigencies of Government & the preservation of the Union."[117]

On the eve of the Constitutional Convention, Madison feared the United States was on the verge of collapse. He worried about the mountain of problems facing America. The national treasury was dangerously short of funds. The national army was reduced to 700 unpaid soldiers. The Treaty of Paris that ended the American Revolution was being violated, and the British held onto their claims to a string of frontier forts. Thomas Jefferson and John Adams were not present to help him because they were in Europe on diplomatic missions. Conflicts were growing between issues of State rights vs. Federal rights. Madison prayed that the Constitutional Convention would help heal their wounds and unite the American people behind their national government.

When George Washington arrived in Philadelphia at the Constitutional Convention, Madison's optimism was revived. Washington's attendance gave a sense of legitimacy to the proceedings. His commanding presence helped to unite the delegates in this good work at the grand Pennsylvania State House next to Independence Hall. Here in the heart of Philadelphia, where the "Declaration of Independence" was signed in 1776, the United States Constitution would take form in the summer of 1787.

THE CONSTITUTIONAL CONVENTION OF 1787

Beginning on May 17 and ending on September 17, 1787, fifty-five delegates worked on developing, debating, and drafting the U.S. Constitution. Twenty-six of the delegates were college graduates, three were professors, and two were college presidents. Twenty-eight were former congressmen, while most had served in state legislatures. James Madison was then only thirty-five years old and one of the youngest delegates. George Washington was then fifty-five, while Benjamin Franklin was the eldest of the group at the age of eighty-one.[118]

Rather than merely amending the old Articles of Confederation, they proposed to draft a new federal Constitution. During the first several weeks of debate, they agreed on little. However, George Washington was elected President of the convention unanimously. On May 29, the "Virginia Resolves," a plan written by Madison and the Virginia delegation, was introduced for consideration. The hottest issue was how the legislative branch of government would fairly distribute and share power in a representative government.

The delegates to the Constitutional Convention were not paid for their services, nor were they even reimbursed for their travel expenses. When their debates grew very heated, Franklin suggested the need for prayer to reunite their higher purpose. After some debate, they concluded that they had no money to pay a preacher, so the prayer proposal was tabled.

After taking a two-day break to celebrate Independence Day, Madison reported that on July 5th their debate was refocused when Gouverneur Morris of Pennsylvania stated:

> He came here as a representative of America; he flattered himself that he came here in some degree as a Representative of the whole human race; for the whole human race will be affected by the proceedings of the Convention. He wished gentlemen to extend their views beyond the present moment of time; beyond the narrow limits of place . . . Much has been said of the sentiments of the people. They were unknown, they could not be known. All that we can infer is that if the plan we recommend be reasonable and right; all who had reasonable minds and sound intentions will embrace it . . . This country must be united. If persuasion does not unite it, the sword will.[119]

The "Great Compromise" that allowed the Constitutional Convention to move forward was predicated on an agreement that the U.S. House of Representatives would be determined by a formula based on the population within each state. Each state would have an equal number of representatives in the U.S. Senate. Madison opposed the compromise because it lessened the power of larger states like Virginia. However, he and others finally agreed, motivated by the greater need to establish a strong union for the benefit of the whole nation.

Other major features of the Constitution were hammered out after long debates. The Judicial Branch of government with a federal court system was established to address federal legislation and matters of national peace and harmony. The Executive Branch of government had a difficult birth, as delegates disagreed on the powers and terms of the Presidency.

On July 24, 1787, the task of consolidating their collective ideas to create a first draft of the U.S. Constitution was entrusted to five delegates: John Rutledge of South Carolina, Edmund Randolph of Virginia, James Wilson of Pennsylvania, Oliver Ellsworth of Connecticut and Nathaniel Gorham of Massachusetts. Surprisingly, Madison was not among the group. However, they drew from the Virginia Plan that largely came from Madison's pen. By August 1, a preamble and 23 articles were printed and returned for review by the Constitutional Convention that reconvened on August 6th.

Madison's direct influence on the text of the U.S. Constitution was expanded. After five weeks of debate, the draft was turned over to a five-member style committee. The distinguished group of editors included Madison, Alexander Hamilton, Rufus King, William Samuel Johnson and Gouverneur Morris.

On September 17, 1787, the Constitution of the United States of America was approved and signed by the remaining thirty-nine delegates. The document then was printed and distributed for ratification by the states. Four million people from 13 states had the opportunity to read the U.S. Constitution that began:

WE THE PEOPLE of the United States, in Order to form a more perfect Union, establish Justice, insure domestic Tranquility, provide for the common defense, promote the general Welfare, and secure the Blessings of Liberty to ourselves and our Posterity, do ordain and establish this Constitution for the United States of America.[120]

The U.S. Constitution is preserved at the National Archives in Washington, D.C., where one can see the originals. Everyone is free to share in the experience of viewing the seminal documents of our nation. Much of the research for this book was done at the National Archives, and we personally found seeing the original documents with our own eyes to be a moving experience. One also may read the full text of the U.S. Constitution and other major documents by visiting the National Archives website at www.nationalarchives.gov.

The Constitution did not become the law of the land until ratified by the states. Voters from each state elected delegates to a state convention. Once nine states ratified the Constitution, the new government could commence. The supporters of the new government were called the Federalists. The anti-Federalists did not support the document and lobbied against it. George Washington, Benjamin Franklin, Thomas Jefferson, John Jay, Alexander Hamilton and James Madison were among the leading Federalists who supported ratification of the Constitution and the establishment of the new government.

THE FEDERALIST PAPERS & RATIFICATION OF THE U.S. CONSTITUTION

During 1787-88, a series of 85 articles were written in support of the Constitution, known today as the "Federalist Papers." Most of the articles were published in newspapers across the land. Although Hamilton wrote the largest number of articles, Madison wrote twenty-six of them and his writings are the most quoted.

In Federalist No. 10, Madison wrote of the importance of republican, self-government in protecting the rights of minority groups against a majority faction:

> Among the numerous advantages promised by a well-constructed Union, none deserves to be more accurately developed that its tendency to break and control the violence of faction . . . To secure the public good and private rights against the danger of such a faction, and at the same time to preserve the spirit and form of popular government, is then the great object to which our enquiries are directed . . . extend the sphere, and you take in a greater variety of parties and interests; you make it less probable that a majority of the whole will have a common motive to invade the rights of other citizens.[121]

Madison was addressing himself to every citizen or small group who had witnessed or personally felt their rights had been harmed by a majority group. As so many people had been oppressed throughout history, Madison's words found hungry ears and the widespread support that he sought. Small religious groups,

Madison had personally witnessed, often needed protection from abuses committed either by larger religious factions or by government officials who overstepped their bounds. The protection of religious and civil rights for all citizens was paramount in defending the liberty of the nation. Many people feared what might happen when the nation grew much larger.

Madison saw the benefits of encouraging many diverse religions to take root in America. The greater the number of religious groups, the less likely one or two groups could form an oppressive majority. He held a similar belief in the value of encouraging political diversity. He never dreamed that only two main political parties would dominate U.S. politics throughout much of the next two centuries. A by-product of the two party system is the factionalism seen today in Republican-Democrat rivalries.

In Federalist No. 39, Madison wrote in support of a "republican" form of government [referring to a self-governing Republic, not the Republican Party of today]:

> No other form would be reconcilable with the genius of the people of America, with the fundamental principles of the Revolution, or with the honorable determination which animates every votary of freedom to rest all our political experiments on the capacity of mankind for self-government.[122]

Madison offered a persuasive case for the benefits of self-government. Although he proclaimed the potential of the long-term durability of the Constitution, he probably would be surprised to learn that the document has survived over two centuries and continues to serve over 250 million people in the 21st Century. Part of the key to the Constitution's longevity is the way in which it moderates power with checks and balances.

Just as Madison supported a clear separation of Church and State, he advocated separation of State powers by establishing three divisions within the federal government — executive, legislative, and judicial branches. Each would have its own method of checks and balances. In Federalist No. 51, Madison wrote in part:

> To what expedient, then, shall we finally resort for maintaining practice the necessary partition of power among the several departments, as laid down in the Constitution? . . . each department should have a will of its own; and consequently should be so constituted that the members of each should have as little agency as possible in the appointment of the members of the others. Were this principle rigorously adhered to, it would require that all the appointments for the supreme executive, legislative and judiciary magistracies should be drawn from the same fountain of authority, the people . . .[123]

Madison made it clear that he did not want a British-style House of Lords, a political aristocracy, nor a king. Like turning the proverbial chessboard upside down, the people would be the ultimate source of authority, not a king or a queen, not a titled lord in a castle, not a bishop, nor a Christian knight. The "pawn" — representing the people — would be the source of power.

Madison placed more faith in the American people than he did in individual politicians. He explained the main reason for separating the three branches of government was to protect the people from abuses by any one governmental body. Government officials would have to be kept in check by the power of the people:

> But what is government itself, but the greatest of all reflections on human nature? If men were angels, no government would be necessary. If angels were to govern men, neither external nor internal controls on government would be necessary.[124]

Madison's common-sense approach attracted broad popular support. Who would challenge him and proclaim that government officials were angels? The Constitution offered popular protections by separating the branches of government and separating authority within the branches. This concept of dividing authority to insure protection of the peoples' rights is further reflected in Madison's advocacy of the separation of Church and State.

Madison's interpretation of the Constitution explained how the people also would be protected from factions:

> It is of great importance in a republic not only to guard the society against the oppression of its rulers, but to guard one part of society against the injustice of the other part.[125]

He personalized his point that every American citizen may be in the majority or in the minority, depending on the issue. How would majority rule in a democracy not trample the rights of the minority? There were two ways, Madison explained. The first was to create an overpowering will within society for the stronger group to restrain itself from oppressing the minority. This level of consciousness was most difficult to attain. The second way was to encourage great diversity within society, so that no single group could gain a majority position over all others. This is why Madison was a great advocate of immigration. He viewed cultural diversity as something good for America. He never linked "mono-culture" and "English Only" concepts with patriotism. In contrast, he stood ahead of his time in supporting what is called today "multicultural education."

Madison championed the rights of the common citizen to enjoy liberty through our religious and civil rights. Both spiritual and temporal spheres needed to be balanced in the form of equal rights and equal responsibilities:

> In a free government the security for civil rights must be the same as that for religious rights. It consists in the one case in the multiplicity of interests, and in the other in the multiplicity of sects [religious denominations]. The degree of security in both cases will depend on the number of interests and sects; and this may be presumed to depend on the extent of country and number of people comprehended under the same government.[126]

While some people tried to suppress diversity, Madison espoused it as a healthy component of the well-being of society. He encouraged diversity in cultures, political viewpoints, religions, languages, education, and in society as a whole. "In the extended republic of the United States," he wrote, "and among the great variety of interests, parties, and sects which it embraces, a coalition of a majority of the whole society could seldom take place on any other principles than those of justice and the general good."[127] Madison concluded in his defense of the Constitution that the "larger the society," the more capable society would be to achieve "self-government." The Constitution provided the greatest opportunity to achieve "justice for all."

MADISON'S SPEECH AT THE 1788 VIRGINIA CONVENTION TO RATIFY THE U.S. CONSTITUTION

On June 2, 1788, Madison arrived at the State House in Richmond, Virginia, prepared to advocate the ratification of the U.S. Constitution. So large was the crowd, over 170 delegates and a huge public gallery, that the meeting had to be moved to a larger building on the campus of a local college called the New Academy.

Patrick Henry led the attack against the Constitution. On the third day of the debates, Madison rose to make his case supporting it. He addressed Henry's objections, setting them up like straw men, then gracefully knocking them over one-by-one. Madison spoke so softly that everyone had to be quiet to hear his powerful ideas. His humble voice barely rose above a whisper:

> I shall not attempt to make impressions by any ardent professions of zeal for the public welfare; we know the principles of every man will and ought to be judged, not by his professions and declarations, but by his conduct; by that criterion I mean in common with every other member to be judged; and should it prove unfavorable to my reputation; yet, it is a criterion, from which I will by no means depart.[128]

In essence, Madison was saying "actions speak louder than words." Courage was required to take a stand in such a politically charged environment. He bravely announced to his peers that he was willing to lay his reputation on the line to support the new Constitution.

In response to Henry's characterization of the opponents and proponents of the Constitution, Madison sought to re-unite the two factions to strengthen the United States:

> Comparisons have been made between the friends of this constitution, and those who oppose it: although I disapprove of such comparisons, I trust that, in points of truth, honor, candor, and rectitude of motives, the friends of this system, here, and in other states, are not inferior to its opponents. But, professions of attachment to the public good, and comparisons of parties, ought not to govern or influence us now.[129]

Madison refused to engage in a political mudslinging contest. After publicly acknowledging their integrity, he asked his opponents to listen to his frank viewpoints, unclouded by political partisanship:

> We ought, sir, to examine the constitution on its own merits solely: we are

to enquire whether it will promote the public happiness: its aptitude to produce this desirable object, ought to be the exclusive subject of our present researches.[130]

Would the Constitution promote public happiness? Madison focused the delegates on this central question. He recommended a "calm and rational investigation" to "prove and demonstrate" the facts of the matter.

Madison then addressed Henry's first objection:

> [Mr. Henry] told us, that this constitution ought to be rejected, because it endangered the public liberty, in his opinion, in many instances. Give me leave to make one answer to that observation: let the dangers which this system is supposed to be replete with, be clearly pointed out; if any dangerous and unnecessary powers be given to the general legislature, let them be plainly demonstrated, and let us not rest satisfied with general assertions of dangers, without examination.[131]

Madison challenged Henry to prove his case. If the Constitution would "endanger the public liberty," as Henry asserted, he would have to prove it.

Madison challenged Henry's scare tactics. After Henry speculated that future rulers would engage in tyranny and violence, sacrificing the people's liberty, Madison responded:

> Since the general civilization of mankind, I believe there are more instances of the abridgment of the freedom of the people, by gradual and silent encroachments of those in power, than by violent and sudden usurpations: but, on a candid examination of history, we shall find that turbulence, violence, and abuse of power, by the majority trampling on the rights of the minority have produced factions and commotions, which, in republics, have more frequently than any other cause, produced despotism.[132]

When Henry's speech sought to divide the delegates into two main factions, Madison pointed out that factionalism was at the root of the problem. That is one of the reasons why the Constitution was needed, he explained, to reduce factionalism and unite the states for the good of the people.

Madison showed why it was so important to protect the rights of the minority. Abuses of power by the majority led to attacks against people's religious and civil rights. This resulted in factionalism that was the greatest underlying threat to society:

> If we go over the whole history of ancient and modern republics, we shall find their destruction to have generally resulted from those causes. If we consider the peculiar situation of the United States, and what are the sources of that diversity of sentiment which pervades its inhabitants, we shall find great danger to fear, that the same causes may terminate here, in the same fatal effects, which they produced in those republics. This danger ought to be wisely guarded against.[133]

The Constitution, he suggested, offered their best safeguard. The Constitutional system of checks and balances would help to protect them against factionalism.

All was not well in America. People had just cause for concern. The depth of their concern, Madison pointed out, was demonstrated by the fact that the present meeting was filled to the rafters. The time had come for them to face America's real problems together, and the Constitution offered them a "remedy" to heal the ills of the country. The Constitution would help defend the rights of every citizen. As Madison explained, "A federal government is formed for the protection of its individual members."

Henry disliked that it would require "the consent of at least three-fourths of the states to introduce amendments." He stated that a bare majority would be sufficient. Madison pointed out that it also required three-fourths of the states to ratify the Constitution. This gave Madison another opportunity to reinforce his point that a simple majority should not be allowed to oppress a "trifling minority." In the opposite extreme, a tiny minority should not dictate to the vast majority.

Madison next addressed Henry's objection to the creation of some neutral ground [the District of Columbia], as a location for the nation's capital. Madison countered that this was more reasonable than placing the capital in one particular state, because that individual state would have state jurisdiction over that place. "If any state had the power of legislation over the place where Congress should fix the general government, this would impair the dignity, and hazard the safety of Congress."

Madison moved on to address Henry's next objection to a provision in the Constitution under Article 8, "To provide for calling forth the Militia to execute the Laws of the Union, suppress Insurrections and repel invasions." Madison defended the militia:

> . . . concerning the militia: this, I conceive, to be an additional security to our liberty, without diminishing the power of the states . . . the authority of training the militia, and appointing the officers, is reserved to the states. Congress ought to have the power of establishing an uniform discipline throughout the states; and to provide for the execution of the laws, suppress insurrections and repel invasions.[134]

The former state militias evolved into our present National Guard. The Constitution would help protect the security of the nation.

Madison speculated what might happen if they didn't have defenses in place:

> Without uniformity of discipline, military bodies would be incapable of action: without a general controlling power to call forth the strength of the union, to repel invasions, the country might be over-run, and conquered by foreign enemies. Without such a power to suppress insurrections, our liberties might be destroyed by domestic faction, and domestic tyranny be established.[135]

Under these auspices, the National Guard has been called out during times of civil and social unrest.

Henry also complained that the states would be required to relinquish some of their powers to the federal government. Madison pointed out that seven states had already done so by ratifying the Constitution. He reminded Henry that the power ultimately rested with the people:

> But, Sir, by this government, powers are not given to any particular set of men, they are in the hands of the people; delegated to their representatives chosen for short terms; to representatives responsible to the people, and whose situation is perfectly similar to our own; as long as this is the case we have no danger to apprehend.[136]

Henry had claimed that if the states gave up some of their powers, the result would be a loss of liberty that could lead to tyranny.

Madison countered that their liberties were in much greater threat from the dangers of factionalism:

> . . . the loss of liberty very often resulted from factions and divisions; from local considerations, which eternally lead to quarrels, he would have found internal dissentions to have more frequently demolished civil liberty, than a tenacious disposition in rulers, to retain any stipulated powers.[137]

Madison enumerated the various means through which nations had lost their liberties. The Constitution would protect them from the most dangerous threat — factionalism.

Henry further complained about the power of the Congress under Section 8 "to raise and support Armies." Madison warned what might happen without a standing army:

> But, suppose a foreign nation to declare war against the United States, must not the general legislature have the power of defending the United States? Ought it to be known to foreign nations, that the general government of the United States of America has no power to raise and support an army, even in the utmost danger, when attacked by external enemies? Would not their knowledge of such a circumstance stimulate them to fall upon us?[138]

Madison elaborated on his position, pointing out how vulnerable the United States was to foreign attack. Many of those in attendance, being veterans of the Revolutionary War, knew he was telling the truth.

While Madison advocated one federal republic, he further advanced his case in support of diversity regarding religions:

> I confess to you, sir, were uniformity of religion to be introduced by this system, it would, in my opinion, be ineligible; but I have no reason to conclude, that uniformity of government will produce that of religion. This subject is, for the honor of America, perfectly free and unshackled. The government has no jurisdiction over it — the least reflection will convince us, there is no danger to be feared on this ground.[139]

Madison made it clear that the United States federal government would have "no jurisdiction" over religions. This was a powerful statement in support of the separation of Church and State. Americans were not to fear the chilling prospect of federal agents intruding on their private religious practices. Religious freedom was to be enjoyed by all U.S. citizens.

The Virginia Convention was moved by Madison's reasonable oration. On June 25, 1788, Virginia passed a resolution in favor of ratification. A month later, on July 28, the Continental Congress formally ratified the U.S. Constitution. Madison and the Federalists succeeded in this major reform of the United States of America.

THE FIRST AMENDMENT AND THE BILL OF RIGHTS

The U.S. Constitution was not intended to be a document "cast in granite." To the contrary, the Constitution was designed to permit changes and additions in the form of amendments. Article 5 states in part, "The Congress, whenever two thirds of both Houses shall deem it necessary, shall propose Amendments to this Constitution . . . "

One of the most important features left out of the original Constitution was a declaration of religious and civil rights. In the winter of 1788, Madison set out to write a "Bill of Rights," the first ten amendments to the Constitution. On December 8, he wrote a letter to the Reverend George Eve, pastor of the Blue Run Church in Orange, Virginia. Madison stated in part, " . . . amendments, if pursued with a proper moderation and in a proper mode, will be not only safe, but may serve the double purpose of satisfying the minds of well-meaning opponents and of providing additional guards in favor of liberty."[140]

Madison spent that Christmas with George and Martha Washington at Mount Vernon. He then departed on horseback, arriving at his family home in time to usher in the new year. During the next month, Madison campaigned for re-election to Congress. He and his friend, James Monroe, visited many churches and courthouses in the region. In the poll of February 2, Madison won 57% of the popular vote. Although he lost a bid for the Senate by 5 votes, Madison won election to the House of Representatives. If he had lost, the "Bill of Rights," as we know it, might never have come into being.

Near the end of February, Madison headed for Mount Vernon. George Washington was the popular favorite to become the first President. Madison stayed with him for a week and worked on Washington's inaugural address. Washington trusted Madison and consulted with him closely on constitutional issues and matters of the presidency. Washington told him his viewpoints, then entrusted Madison to draft many of his most important documents.

On April 1, 1789, Madison began a new session in the House of Representatives, then meeting in New York City. He balanced the next month between the business of Congress and his service to Washington. On April 30, he attended Washington's inauguration. President Washington's first official act was to offer:

> . . . my most fervent supplications to that Almighty Being who rules over the universe, who presides in the councils of nations, and whose providential aids can supply every human defect, that His benediction may consecrate to the liberties and happiness of the people of the United States a Government instituted by themselves for these essential purposes.[141]

It is important to note that Madison and Washington did not view the acknowledgment of God as an infringement of the separation of Church and State. This viewpoint is reflected in the banner, "In God We Trust," found printed on U.S. currency. Madison did not find it inappropriate for President Washington to ask for God's blessings to make sacred the "liberties and happiness of the people."

President Washington called God the "Great Author of every public and private good." He recognized that the United States was "bound to acknowledge and adore the Invisible Hand which conducts the affairs of men . . ." The very creation of the United States was viewed by President Washington to be "distinguished by some token of providential agency." For God's divine assistance, Washington offered "pious gratitude, along with an humble anticipation of future blessings . . . "

President Washington then expressed his strong support for the U.S. Constitution. He promised:

> . . . that the foundation of our national policy will be laid in the pure and immutable principles of private morality, and the preeminence of free government be exemplified by all the attributes which can win the affections of its citizens and command the respect of the world.[142]

The first President pledged that the national policy of the United States would be based on "private morality," a deep personal understanding to do the right things in support of the nation. He implied that the "smiles of Heaven" could only be attained by regarding "the eternal rules of order and right which Heaven itself has ordained."

President Washington further acknowledged that the "sacred fire of liberty" and the "destiny of the republican model of government" were in the "hands of the American people." He asked people to " . . . decide how far an exercise of the occasional power delegated by the fifth article of the Constitution is rendered." The fifth article defines the power of the people to amend the Constitution.

Madison worked through the month of May collecting his ideas and materials for amending the Constitution. One side of him was hesitant to change the original document because once one begins, where does it end? However, there existed a pressing need to establish a Bill of Rights. His exhaustive work on the amendments carried past his original deadline of May 25.

Madison dated his "Amendments to the Constitution" June 8, 1789. This seminal document allows us to compare Madison's original ideas with the final form found in the first amendments, including the Bill of Rights. This is important because it illuminates, in many cases, Madison's original intent.

The First Amendment, in its final form, reads in part:

> Art. I. Congress shall make no law respecting the establishment of reli-
> gion, or prohibiting the free exercise thereof; or abridging the freedom of
> speech, or of the press or the right of the people peaceably to assemble,
> and to petition the government for a redress of grievances.[143]

The protection of religious freedom was on the top of Madison's list. He had
protested strongly over the years against religious "establishments," meaning
State-recognized religions, on the basis of separation of Church and State. Now
he laid the matter to rest.

The "free exercise" of religion clause has been the subject of much debate.
The phrase "free exercise" implies religious practices beyond mere freedom of
thought. People were not only free to pray, they also were free to practice their
religion without government interference. If "no law" could be made regarding
the "free exercise" of religion, then the federal government could have no legal
jurisdiction over the many ways people might "exercise" their religions.

In his original proposal for "Amendments to the Constitution," dated June
8, 1789, Madison recorded his original ideas on religious freedom:

> The civil rights of none shall be abridged on account of religious belief or
> worship, nor shall any national religion be established, nor shall the full
> and equal rights of conscience be in any manner, or on any pretext,
> infringed.[144]

Madison clarified that no one's rights should be lessened or curtailed regarding
either religious beliefs or religious worship. These protections extended to
"rights of conscience." As to the meaning of "establishment of religion," he
made it clear that this referred to prohibiting the establishment of a "national
religion."

Regarding the remainder of Article I, Madison's original text in the June 8th
document read:

> The people shall not be deprived or abridged of their right to speak, to
> write, or to publish their sentiments; and the freedom of the press, as one
> of the great bulwarks of liberty, shall be inviolable.
> The people shall not be restrained from peaceably assembling and consult-
> ing for their common good; nor from applying to the Legislature by peti-
> tions, or remonstrances, for redress of their grievances.[145]

The final version was made less wordy, yet conveyed much of the same meaning.
It is interesting that Madison viewed protesting against the government to be a
constitutional right. He probably would have been surprised that some
Americans today consider protesting against the government to be unpatriotic.
Madison would have considered it not only our right, but also our responsibility
in a free society.

Madison noted that Great Britain was not his model when it came to the
Bill of Rights. Much has been written crediting Great Britain and France as the
principal sources of ideas for the Constitution and the Bill of Rights. However,
Madison stated directly:

... their Magna Carta does not contain any one provision for the security of those rights, respecting which the people of America are most alarmed. The freedom of the press and rights of conscience, those choicest privileges of the people, are unguarded in the British Constitution.[146]

Madison viewed the protection of religious freedom and civil rights to be an American phenomenon. He did not look across the ocean in search of freedom. Europe was the place from which many of their ancestors had fled due to religious and civil persecutions. He found the roots of many of his ideas for freedom in America.

Madison wrote the original draft for the Bill of Rights when he was only 38-years-old. His proposed "Amendments to the Constitution" were referred on July 26, 1789 to a congressional select committee. It was not until mid-August that the House of Representatives addressed the proposed amendments. The Bill of Rights, representing the first amendment, was approved by Congress on September 25, 1789, but did not become the supreme law of the land until after ratification by the states two years later on December 15, 1791.

Madison continued to serve in the House of Representatives for eight years. The seat of the government changed from New York to Philadelphia during his term. He helped President Washington organize the Executive Branch, and he assisted Congress in forming a system for federal taxation. Furthermore, he joined forces with Thomas Jefferson in founding the Democratic-Republican Party.

In 1794, Madison fell in love with a twenty-six year old beauty named Dolly Payne Todd. Aaron Burr, an old classmate of Madison's at Princeton, introduced them. The fact that she was a widow with a child posed no problem for Madison. However, Dolly was a Quaker, and her religious leaders forbade her to marry outside of their church. When she married Madison, her religious leaders expelled her from the Quaker Church.

Undaunted by the public rebuke, Dolly Madison became the toast of Philadelphia social circles and was said to have a bubbly personality. She changed her mode of clothing from plain Quaker dress to the height of fashion for the late 18th century. She was praised as a warm and gracious hostess. When Thomas Jefferson became widowed, Dolly agreed to serve as the first honorary hostess of the White House. She is credited with initiating the traditions of the Inaugural Ball and the White House Easter egg roll.

In 1796, John Adams became President and Thomas Jefferson served as Vice President. Madison declined a presidential offer to serve as ambassador to France. The following year when his term was up in the House, Madison, Dolly, and her young son retired to the family estate of Montpelier in Virginia.

Madison did not get to relax long. In 1797, the political pendulum in Congress swung to the far right. Madison and his circles became outraged when Congress proposed the Alien and Sedition Acts. Under the guise of patriotism, the laws were intended to give sweeping powers to the federal government to investigate and to arrest people deemed a threat to the United States. Foreign males, age 14 or older, could be arrested and deported, their property and papers confiscated. Anyone — who wrote, published or even said something considered "false, scandalous and malicious . . . against the United States" or the President — could be arrested, fined up to $2,000 and imprisoned for up to two years. Madison viewed these acts to be outrageous and unconstitutional.

So urgent was the need to challenge the "Alien and Sedition Acts," the Virginia General Assembly stayed to address the issue on Christmas Eve of 1798. Madison had a hand in drafting the Resolution in which the Virginia State Legislature condemned these federal laws for turning the Presidency of John Adams into a "mixed monarchy":

> That the General Assembly doth particularly protest against the palpable and alarming infractions of the Constitution, in the two late cases of the "Alien and Sedition Acts" passed at the last session of Congress . . . [which] subverts the general principles of free government . . . [and grants] a power not delegated by the Constitution . . . a power, which more than any other, ought to produce universal alarm.[147]

Madison and his fellow Virginians took a strong stand against the actions of President Adams and a majority of Congress. Their protest against the federal government was not unpatriotic. To the contrary, they saw it to be a most patriotic act based on their strong defense of the U.S. Constitution. Madison and his supporters succeeded in winning a victory for civil rights. The "Alien and Sedition Acts" eventually were defeated. He later described their victory as "proper measures" to insure the "ordinary control of the people and Legislatures of the States over the Government of the United States."[148]

For the next two years, 1799 to 1801, Madison returned as the Orange County representative of the Virginia House of Delegates. He advocated a balance between state's rights and federal rights. In 1801, President Thomas Jefferson chose Madison to be Secretary of State. It was a time of turmoil on the high seas. Madison was thrust into international politics. He protested loudly against British and French seizures of American ships. In 1807, Congress passed an unpopular Embargo Act that only succeeded in chocking off trade, sending the economy reeling toward a depression. The act was soon repealed.

In 1808, Madison was elected the fourth President of the United States. He would serve two four-year terms. On March 4, 1809, he delivered his first inaugural address wherein he outlined his purposes in part:

- to support the Constitution, which is the cement of the Union, as well as in its limitations as in its authorities;
- to respect the rights and authorities reserved to the States and to the people as equally incorporated with and essential to the success of the general system;
- to avoid the slightest interference with the right of conscience or the functions of religion, so wisely exempted from civil jurisdiction . . .[149]

From the beginning of his Presidency, Madison made it clear where he drew the line regarding the "free exercise of religion." Federal government officials were directed to "avoid the slightest interference" with the "functions of religion."

Furthermore, he declared that the "free exercise of religion" was "wisely exempted from civil jurisdiction." This meant that neither federal nor state officials were to meddle in the peoples' religious affairs.

International affairs dominated Madison's attention. During the first year of his presidency, trade with Great Britain and France was prohibited. A year later, the ban was lifted. U.S. policy advocated neutral rights. When Napoleon pretended to support the U.S. position in 1810, Madison consented to proclaim "non-intercourse" with Great Britain. Americans were bristling over British incursions from the Atlantic Ocean to the American frontier. Great Britain maintained a series of trading posts within Indian territories west of the Appalachian Mountains and north into Canada. The U.S. Treasury was financially hurting, and American politicians began to realize the potential wealth that could come from the development of the West.

Under pressure from the "war hawks" in Congress, President Madison asked Congress on June 1, 1812 to declare war against Great Britain. The principal impetus of the War of 1812 was British seizures of American sea men and their cargoes. Madison's diplomatic attempts to resolve the conflicts peacefully had failed. The British Army invaded America and entered Washington, D.C., determined to burn the White House and take control of the city.

President Madison made an agreement with his wife, Dolly, before going out to consult with his generals. Dolly agreed to be ready to flee if British forces drew too close. However, with the sound of cannons ringing in the air, she remained on the top floor of the White House, glued to her spyglass in anticipation of her husband's return. She paused only to write an ongoing letter to her sister, relating events as they unfolded. In the twelfth hour, Dolly became determined to save a life-size portrait of George Washington by Gilbert Stuart. They struggled to get the screws out of the wall and finally succeeded in rescuing the painting. Dolly loaded up trunks of her husband's important papers, jumped into her waiting horse-drawn carriage, and galloped off to safety. Soon after, British soldiers arrived in force, and the White House was in flames.

In the wake of war, President Madison was re-elected to a second term. On March 4, 1813, he delivered his "Second Inaugural Address." The nation then was in the middle of the War of 1812 against Great Britain. Madison defended U.S. involvement as being "stamped with that justice which invites the smiles of Heaven on the means of conducting it to a successful termination."[150] General Andrew Jackson's victory at New Orleans helped bring the war to a conclusion.

War had made life very difficult for President Madison and the country as a whole. He bemoaned the hardships, the loss of life and that "cruel sufferings of that portion of the American people have found their way to every bosom not dead to the sympathies of the human race."

MADISON'S AUTUMN YEARS: STANDING STRONG FOR CIVIL RIGHTS & RELIGIOUS FREEDOM

From 1817 to 1836, Madison remained an active and outspoken patriot. He lived at Montpelier, but traveled widely, observing firsthand what was happening in the heartland of America. He frequently put pen to paper to protest against injustices he viewed in society. He especially was involved in the issue of States vs. Federal rights, a conflict that threatened to tear the Union apart.

Madison remained a strong advocate for civil rights and religious freedom for all Americans. On May 15, 1818, he wrote a letter to Judge M. M. Noah of New York:

> I have received your letter of the 6th, with the eloquent discourse delivered at the consecration of the Jewish Synagogue. Having ever regarded freedom of religious opinions and worship as equally belonging to every sect, and the secure enjoyment of it as the best human provision for bringing all either into the same way of thinking, or into that mutual charity which is the only substitute, I observe with pleasure the view you give of the spirit in which your sect partake of the blessings offered by our Government and laws.[151]

Judge Noah is best remembered as the founder of Hebrew College in Poughkeepsie, NY. Perhaps inspired by Madison's encouraging letter, the judge later prepared a plan for Hebrew College that welcomed students of all denominations.

Judge Noah publicly proclaimed his vision for the educational future of the growing Jewish community in America:

> The great increase of the Jewish population in our country, and the facilities and advantages which our free institutions hold forth to our co-religionaries throughout the world, the success they have already met with, and their general spirit of enterprise, warrant the belief, that in a few years the Jews will constitute a large portion of the freemen of this Union. It becomes therefore necessary to consider, what steps are required to improve their condition, and enable them to assume and maintain a proper rank among their fellow-citizens, and consequently, to secure for themselves and their posterity that consideration and respect, which a sound education and a high moral bearing cannot fail to achieve.[152]

Judge Noah established Hebrew College to help the coming generations of Jewish Americans, "to elevate their character as a separate and distinct people, and place them on the road to honour and preferment, in common with their fellow-citizens of other religious denominations." The college was bilingual and multicultural, providing a well-rounded, classical education, while offering classes in the Hebrew language, culture, and religious studies, as well as U.S. Federal law. He expressed the hopes of Jewish American parents who yearned "to see their children grow up with enlarged views and tolerant feelings towards other sects: still they wish them to be Jews, to understand their religion, to be able to explain its principles and defend its divine origin."

In August of 1820, Madison shared his thoughts on equal rights for religious groups in a letter written to Dr. Jacob De La Motta, the noted Jewish physician:

> Among the features peculiar to the political system of the United States, is the perfect equality of rights which it secures to every religious sect . . . Equal laws, protecting equal rights, are as best calculated to cherish that mutual respect and good will among citizens of every religious denomination which are necessary to social harmony, and most favorable to the advancement of truth.[153]

Dr. De La Motta lived in Philadelphia in his early days. He later moved to Charleston, North Carolina, where he helped build a synagogue. Madison encouraged him by confirming that Jewish people should enjoy equal rights and religious freedom in America.

The key to achieving religious freedom, Madison continued to assert, was the careful maintenance of a clear separation of Church and State. On July 10, 1822, he wrote a letter to Edward Livingston, the former mayor of New York City:

> I have no doubt that every new example will succeed, as every past one has done, in [showing] that religion and the government will both exist in greater purity the less they are mixed.[154]

Madison and Livingston were fellow alumni of the College of New Jersey. Livingston later resettled in Louisiana and became a congressman representing the state.

Throughout his life Madison remained dedicated to public service and education. In his autumn years he held a position as rector for the University of Virginia. In 1829, at the age of eighty, he was called back to serve as a delegate to the Virginia Constitutional Convention. When he rose to address the assembly, members reportedly "rushed from their seats and crowded around him":

> It is sufficiently obvious, that persons and property are the two great subjects on which Governments are to act, and that the rights of persons, and the rights of property, are the objects, for the protection of which Government was instituted. These rights cannot well be separated . . . The essence of Government is power; and power, lodged in human hands, will ever be liable to abuse.[155]

Madison launched into his main theme that the purpose of government was to protect the rights of the people. In revising the Virginia State Constitution, the elder statesman advised his listeners that they had designed the government in such a way as to protect the minority against the authority of the majority.

Madison then explained some fundamental differences between monarchies vs. aristocracies vs. republics:

> In Monarchies, the interests and happiness of all may be sacrificed to the caprice and passion of a despot. In Aristocracies, the rights and welfare of

the many may be sacrificed to the pride and cupidity of the few. In Republics, the great danger is, that the majority may not sufficiently respect the rights of the minority . . . honesty is the best policy.[156]

Madison confided that the key to framing a Constitution is a "spirit of compromise." Leaders of other nations were "surprised" by their ability to create the Constitution. "In the eyes of the world," Madison declared, the United States was a "wonder." The American government was nothing less than a "miracle." He concluded, "I have now more than a hope — a consoling confidence that we shall at last find that our [labors] have not been in vain."

By 1831, Madison acknowledged that he was the "only living signer of the Constitution of the United States:"

I happen, also, to be the sole survivor of those who were members of the Revolutionary [Continental] Congress . . . Having outlived so many of my contemporaries, I ought not to forget that I may be thought to have outlived myself.[157]

On morning of June 28, 1836, his niece, Mrs. Willis, reported that he was served his breakfast but could not swallow. She asked him, "What is the matter, Uncle James?"

Madison replied, "Nothing more than a change of mind, my dear." His head then dropped and his breathing ceased "as quietly as the snuff of a candle goes out."

James Madison passed away at the age of eighty-five. In his last letter, opened after his death, Madison wrote: "The advice nearest to my heart and deepest in my convictions is that the Union of the States be cherished and perpetuated."[158]

Conclusion

IN THE LIGHT OF HISTORY

The opinions of Franklin, Jefferson and Madison offer powerful insights into the original ideas upon which the United States was founded. Their writings illuminate the framers' original intent for the U.S. Constitution, Bill of Rights and other founding documents. Interpretations of Constitutional questions by the Supreme Court define our Constitutional rights as citizens of the United States. The justices consider original intent when defining the law. Ignorance of the law is not an acceptable defense. Therefore, "We the People of the United States of America . . ." possess not only a right, but also a responsibility to understand the law of the land. In the interest of upholding our civic duties we humbly offer this book, the first volume of "The U.S. Constitution & Bill of Rights Series."

Franklin, Jefferson and Madison were in agreement on at least six key issues related to Religion & the State.

1. Freedom of Religion is a fundamental right.
2. No one, especially government officials, should interfere with the free exercise of religion.
3. There should not be one official religion of the United States.
4. Federal tax dollars should not be allocated to favored churches or religious groups.
5. Different religions from around the world should be respected.
6. The separation of Church and State should be maintained.

They felt passionately about these principles as part of the founders' early vision for the United States. Their knowledge of history taught them well the tragedies of religious persecution and religious wars. They sought to protect Americans by firmly establishing our religious freedoms and civil liberties.

Volume Two in "The U.S. Constitution & Bill of Rights Series" will focus on civil liberties. The research is revealing how the founders defined our civil rights. This study will explain why they considered American civil liberties so important. By tracing the sources of original ideas on these issues we hope to clarify topics of debate, private discussions and personal feelings. Our initial findings reveal how passionately the founders felt about protecting American freedoms and liberties. This was why they fought the Revolutionary War. They took it very personally because they lost friends and family members in the war. They did not want their fellow patriots to have died in vain. Thus, the protection of our civil liberties was paramount.

Civil liberties were to be cherished and defended. Many of the founders considered it their patriotic duty to protest against anyone or any group that threatened to take away or limit the liberties and freedoms of American citizens. In fact, few issues ignited their emotions and patriotic fervor more strongly.

More than two centuries have passed since the establishment of the U.S.

Constitution and Bill of Rights. These documents remain as important today as they did then. We believe that Constitutional issues related to American civil liberties will continue to be an important topic in national and international affairs. In the past few years within the network of global media, thousands of articles and news programs have been devoted to the topic. We hope our contributions will help illuminate these issues in the light of history.

As a college professor, I used to give my students extra credit for writing essays on the U.S. Constitution and Bill of Rights. I wish that I could give some reward to almost 300 million Americans to accept the same challenge. Researching American history and learning about the U.S. Constitution can be a most challenging and rewarding experience. When we better understand our Constitutional rights, I believe that we can better assume our responsibilities as citizens of the United States of America. Moreover, the people of the world may be the ultimate beneficiaries as nations are inspired to guarantee their citizens freedom of religion and protection of fundamental human rights. If that lofty goal can ever be achieved, the history of the world will change forever.

Endnotes

INTRODUCTION

1. Associated Press, "Important Revolutionary Era Documents Found," *New York Times, Los Angeles Times, London Times* (November 1976); Louis Thompson, "Historian Gregory Schaaf Finds a Mother Lode of History among Neighbor's Keepsakes." *People Magazine* (January 24, 1977); Harvey Arden, Steve Wall, "Living Iroquois Confederacy," *National Geographic Magazine* (September 1987), p. 370.

2. Gregory Schaaf, *Wampum Belts & Peace Trees: George Morgan, Native Americans and Revolutionary Diplomacy* (Golden, CO: Fulcrum Publishing, 1990).

3. Thanks to Assistant Secretary General Robert Muller for inviting me to speak at the United nations. He and his wife, Margarita kindly hosted me in their home. Thanks to Onondaga Faithkeeper Oren Lyons and Senator Daniel Inouye for inviting me to testify before a Senate committee on Iroquois influences on the U.S. Constitution. See Select Committee of Indian Affairs, *Iroquois Confederacy of Nations,* 100th Cong. 1st sess., 1987, S. Hearing 100-610, pp. 7-33.

4. Gregory Schaaf, "American Indian Art Series": Vol. 1 - *Hopi-Tewa Pottery: 500 Artist Biographies* (1999); Vol. 2 - *Pueblo Indian Pottery: 750 Artist Biographies* (2000); Vol. 3 - *American Indian Textiles: 2,000 Artist Biographies* (2001); Vol. 4 - *Southern Pueblo Pottery: 2,000 Artist Biographies* (2002); Vol. 5 - *American Indian Jewelry I: 1,200 Artist Biographies* (2003); Vol. 6 - *American Indian Baskets: 2,000 Artist Biographies* (2004). Twenty volumes in total are planned for "The American Indian Art Series" see www.indianartbooks.com.

5. Robert B. Matchette, et. al., compilers, *Guide to Federal Records in the National Archives of the United States* (Washington, D.C.: National Archives and Records Administration, 2nd edition, 1998), 3 vols.; James H. Hutson, Chief, Manuscript Division, Library of Congress Manuscripts: An Illustrated Guide (Washington, D.C.: Library of Congress, 1993); James H. Hutson, *Religion and the New Republic: Faith in the Founding of America* (Lanham, MD: Rowman & Littlefield Publishers Inc., 1999); www.archives.gov; www.loc.gov

6. *The Papers of Benjamin Franklin* (New Haven, CT: Yale University Library, 1706-1782), 36 vols.; www.yale.edu/franklinpapers/indexintro.html; *The Thomas Jefferson Papers at the Library of Congress* (Washington, D.C., Library of Congress); http://memory.loc.gov/ammem/mtjhtml/mtjhome.html; Julian P., Boyd et. al, eds., *The Papers of Thomas Jefferson* (Princeton, NJ: Princeton University Press, 1950); Merrill Peterson, ed., *Thomas Jefferson. Writings* (New York: The Library of America, 1984). Alderman Memorial Library, *A Calendar of the Jefferson Papers at the University of Virginia* (Charlottesville, VA: University Press of Virginia); http://etext.lib.virginia.edu/jefferson/; www.yale.edu/lawweb/avalon/presiden/jeffpap.htm; *Papers of James Madison* at the University of Virginia,, published as follows: *Papers of James Madison: Congressional Series* (Chicago, University of Chicago Press, 1962-77; University Press of Virginia, 1977-91); *Papers of James Madison: Secretary of State Series,* University Press of Virginia, 1986-2000; *Papers of James Madison, Presidential Series* (1984-1999); (Charlottesville, VA; University Press of Virginia, 1984-1999); www.virginia.edu/pjm/; www.yale.edu/lawweb/avalon/presiden/madispap.htm.

7. Thomas Jefferson, "Declaration of Independence' (Philadelphia, PA, 1776).

8. Biographies of Franklin include: Walter Isaacson, *Benjamin Franklin: An American Life* (New York, Simon & Schuster, 2003); Edmund S. Morgan, *Benjamin Franklin* (New Haven, CT: Yale University Press, 2002); Louis P. Masur, ed., Benjamin Franklin, *Autobiography* (Buccaneer Books, 1996); H. W. Brands, *The First American: The Life and Times of Benjamin Franklin* (New York: Doubleday, 2000); Carl C. Van Doren, *Benjamin Franklin* (Reprint Services Corp., 1993); Lemay, J. A. Leo, ed., *Benjamin Franklin* (New York: Library of America, 1987). For a comprehensive bibliography on Franklin see www.loc.gov

9. Thomas Jefferson to George Washington (January 4, 1786); see www.cooperativeindividualism.org/jefferson_l_02.html

10. Virginia Constitution (June 29, 1776), in *The Federal and State Constitutions Colonial Charters, and Other Organic Laws of the States, Territories, and Colonies Now or Heretofore Forming the United States of America*, compiled and edited under the Act of Congress of June 30, 1906 by Francis Newton Thorpe (Washington, DC: Government Printing Office, 1909).

11. Thomas Jefferson to Edward Dowse (April 19, 1803).

12. Thomas Jefferson, "Doctrines of Jesus." Biographies of Jefferson include: Huge Howard, *Thomas Jefferson, Architect: The Built Legacy of Our Third President* (New York, Rizzoli, 2003); R.B. Bernstein, *Jefferson* (Oxford, UK: Oxford University Press, 2003); Michael Knox Beran, *Jefferson's Demons: Portrait of a Restless Mind* (Free Press, 2003); Daniel L. Dreisbach, *Thomas Jefferson and the Wall of Separation Between Church and State* (New York: New York University Press, 2003); Joseph J. Ellis, *The American Sphinx: The Contradictions of Thomas Jefferson* (New York: Alfred A. Knopf, 1997). For a comprehensive bibliography on Madison see www.loc.gov .

13. James Madison, "Memorial and Remonstrance against Religious Assessments" (June 20, 1785); Rutland v. 8, pp. 295-306. (hereafter cited Madison's Memorial of 1785)

14. Biographies of Madison include: Irving Brant, *Life of James Madison* (Indianapolis: The Bobbs-Merrill Company, 1941-61), 6 vols; Lance Banning, *The Sacred Fire of Liberty: James Madison and the Founding of the Federal Republic* (Ithaca, NY: Cornell University Press, 1995); Ralph Ketcham, *James Madison: A Biography* (New York, 1971; Charlottesville, Va.: University Press of Virginia, 1990 reprint). Robert A. Rutland, *James Madison: The Founding Father* (New York: Athenium, 1987); Jack Rakove, *James Madison and the Creation of the American Republic* (Glenview, Ill.: Longman Publishing Group, 1990). For a comprehensive bibliography on Madison see www.loc.gov

CHAPTER ONE

1. Commercial Directory of Northamptonshire (Pigot & Company, 1830); www.uk-genealogy.org.uk/england/Northamptonshire/

2. Benjamin Franklin, *Autobiography*, www.ushistory.org/franklin/autobiography/page02.htm

3. Ibid.

4. Ibid.; www.britannia.com/history/monarchs/mon44.html

5. Ibid.; www.britannia.com/history/h6f.html

6. Reverend John Williams, The Redeemed Captive Returning to Zion (1707); www.americastory.gov/jb/colonial/jb_colonial_deerfld_1.html

7. Samuel Eliot Morison, The Oxford History of the American People (New York: Oxford University Press, 1965), pp. 61-62; www.oldsouth.org/History/history.html

8. Benjamin Franklin, *Autobiography* (ca, 1773, 1786); see http://history.hanover.edu/courses/excerpts/111frank.htm

9. As part of my graduate training, Dr. Wilbur Jacobs taught me Ben Franklin's method for historical investigation. The technique was used throughout this book in honor of Franklin's literary style.

10. Benjamin Franklin, *Autobiography* (ca, 1773, 1786); see http://history.hanover.edu/courses/excerpts/111frank.htm

11. Benjamin Franklin, "Corruptio optimi est pessima," Silence Dogwood letter #9, *The New-England Courant* (July 23, 1722); www.historycarper.com/resources/twobfl/sd9.htm

12. Benjamin Franklin, Silence Dogwood letter #9, *The New-England Courant* (July 23, 1722); www.historycarper.com/resources/twobfl/sd9.htm

13. Ibid.

14. Ibid.

15. Ibid.

16. Ibid.

17. Ibid.

18. Ibid.

19. Ibid.

20. William Wollaston, The Religion of Nature Delineated (London: B. Lintot, 1722), 219 pp.

21. www.wikipedia.org/wiki/William_Wollaston

22. Benjamin Franklin, "A Dissertation on Liberty and Necessity, Pleasure and Pain" (London, 1725). See http://personal.pitnet.net/primarysources/franklindiss.html

23. Ibid.

24. Ibid.

25. *Britannica World Language Dictionary* (New York, 1954), vol. 2, p. 1352.

26. Benjamin Franklin, "A Dissertation on Liberty and Necessity, Pleasure and Pain" (London, 1725).

27. Ibid.

28. Ibid.

29. Benjamin Franklin, *Autobiography* (ca, 1773, 1786); see http://history.hanover.edu/courses/excerpts/111frank.htm

30. Ibid.; see www.pbs.org/benfranklin/l3_wit_self.html

31. Ibid.; see http://history.hanover.edu/courses/excerpts/111frank.htm

32. The exact date of the origin of Junto is not known. That portion of the records, which has been preserved, begins September 22d, 1758; but it had an earlier origin. It was a society for the mutual improvement of the members.

33. www.english.udel.edu/lemay/franklin/1728.html

34. Ibid.

35. Benjamin Franklin, "Articles of Belief and Acts of Religion" (1728); published in *The Writings of Benjamin Franklin: Philadelphia,1726 - 1757* (Philadelphia, PA), v. II; see www.historycarper.com/resources/twobf2/articles.htm

36. Ibid.

37. Ibid.

38. Ibid.

39. Ibid.

40. Ibid.

41. Ibid.

42. Benjamin Franklin, "On the Providence of God in the Government of the World" (1730), published in *The Writings of Benjamin Franklin: Philadelphia,1726 - 1757* (Philadelphia, PA), v. II; see www.historycarper.com/resources/twobf2/articles.htm

43. Ibid.

44. Ibid.

45. Ibid.

46. Ibid.

47. Ibid.

48. Ibid.

49. Benjamin Franklin, *Autobiography* (ca, 1773, 1786); see http://history.hanover.edu/courses/excerpts/111frank.htm

50. Ibid.

51. Ibid.

52. www.english.udel.edu/lemay/franklin/1731.html

53. www.pagrandlodge.org/giving/franklin2.html; www.grandlodgeofvirginia.org/whomason.htm#who; www.themasonichall.org/masonic_hall/masons.html

54. Benjamin Franklin, "Doctrine to be Preached" (1731); published in *The Writings of*

Benjamin Franklin: Philadelphia, 1726 - 1757 (Philadelphia, PA), v. II; see www.historycarper.com/resources/twobf2/articles.htm

55. Benjamin Franklin, "Compassion and Regard for the Sick," *Pennsylvania Gazette* (March 25, 1731); see www.historycarper.com/resources/twobf2/contents.htm

56. Ibid.

57. www.english.udel.edu/lemay/franklin/1732.html

58. Ibid.

59. Benjamin Franklin, *Poor Richard's Almanack* (1732-58); www.sage-advice.com/Benjamin_Franklin.htm

60. Benjamin Franklin, "Dialogue Between Two Presbyterians," *The Pennsylvania Gazette* (April 10, 1735); see www.historycarper.com/resources/twobf2/pg1735.htm

61. Benjamin Franklin, *Autobiography*; see also Bryan LeBeau, "Franklin and the Presbyterians: Freedom of Conscience Versus The Need for Order" (Creighton University, 2003); Carl Van Doren, *Benjamin Franklin* (Westport, CT: Greenwood Press, 1973), 131-132; Nichols, "Colonial Presbyterianism Adopts Its Standards," 61; Franklin, "Dialogue between Two Presbyterians," 27; Christensen, "Franklin on the Hemphill Trials," 424; Buxbaum, *Benjamin Franklin*, 82; http://earlyamerica.com/review/summer/franklin/index.html; www.onlineathens.com/stories/070303/fea_20030703020.shtml

62. Benjamin Franklin to father (ca. 1738).

63. Whitefield, Journals 341; www.english.udel.edu/lemay/franklin/1739.html

64. George Whitefield, "The Observation of the Birth of Christ, the Duty of all Christians; or the True Way of Keeping Christmas," sermon 16; www.reformed.org/documents/Whitefield/WITF_016.html

65. Benjamin Franklin, "Religious Mood in Philadelphia," *The Pennsylvania Gazette* (June 12, 1740).

66. Benjamin Franklin (Theophilus), "Relating to the Divine Presence," *General Magazine* (1741).

67. Sparks, Chapter 5; www.english.udel.edu/lemay/franklin/1743.html

68. Benjamin Franklin to Jane Mecom (July 28. 1743); see www.historycarper.com/resources/twobf2/letter4.htm

69. Jonathan Edwards, *Some Thoughts Concerning the Present Revival of Religion in New England, and the Way in Which It Ought to be Acknowledged and Promoted*; in *The Works of Jonathan Edwards* (Edinburgh: Banner of Truth, 1974), v. 1, part I, pp. 366-380.

70. Boston Newsletter, (January 17, 1745); www.english.udel.edu/lemay/franklin/1745.html

71. Benjamin Franklin, "Appreciation of George Whitefield," *The Pennsylvania Gazette* (July 31, 1746); see www.historycarper.com/resources/twobf2/pg41-47.htm

72. Benjamin Franklin to [Thomas Hopkinson?], "Refutation of Andrew Baxter's "Enquiry into the Nature of the Human Soul" (October 16, 1746).

73. Letter to Benjamin Franklin, "The Necessity of Self-Defense," *The Pennsylvania Gazette* (December 29, 1747), supplement; see www.historycarper.com/resources/twobf2/pg41-47.htm

74. Benjamin Franklin, "Proposal for a Day on Fasting in Pennsylvania" (1748), quoted by Van Doren in *Benjamin Franklin* (New York: Viking Press, 1938), p. 188.

75. Ibid.

76. Benjamin Franklin to George Whitefield (July 6, 1749); see www.historycarper.com/resources/twobf2/letter10.htm

77. Benjamin Franklin, *Proposals Relating To The Education Of Youth In Pennsylvania* (1749); www.christianparents.com/ffathers.htm; www.geocities.com/CapitolHill/Lobby/2101/proverbs.html

78. Benjamin Franklin to James Parker (March 20, 1750); see www.historycarper.com/resources/twobf2/letter12.htm

79. Francis Jennings, *The Invasion of America: Indians, Colonialism and the Cant of*

Conquest (Chapel Hill: University of North Carolina Press, 1975).

80. Wilbur Jacobs, *Dispossessing the American Indians: Indians and Whites on the Colonial Frontier* (New York: Charles Scribner's Sons, 1972); Wilcomb Washburn, *History of Indian-White Relations* (Washington, D. C.: Smithsonian Institution, 1988), in Handbook of North American Indians, v. 4.

81. John Fliegel, compiler, *Index to the Records of the Moravian Mission among the Indians of North America* (New Haven, CT: Research Publications, 1970); Edmund De Schweinitz, *The Life and Times of David Zeisberger* (Philadelphia: J. B. Lippincott, 1870); Paul A. W. Wallace, *Thirty Thousand Miles with John Heckewelder* (Pittsburg Press, 1958); Gregory Schaaf, *Wampum Belts & Peace Trees: George Morgan, Native Americans and Revolutionary Diplomacy* (Golden, CO: Fulcrum Publishing, 1990). http://catchlife.org/Zinzendorf.htm; www.huntington.edu/library/ubhc.html; www.huntington.edu/library/ubhc.html

82. Francis Jennings, *The Ambiguous Iroquois Empire: The Covenant Chain of Confederation of Indian Tribes with English Colonies from Its Beginnings to the Lancaster Treaty of 1744* (New York: W. W. Norton & Company, 1984); Francis Jennings, *The Invasion of America: Indians, Colonialism and the Cant of Conquest* (Chapel Hill: University of North Carolina Press, 1975); C.A. Weslager, *The Delaware Indians: A History* (New Brunswick, NJ: Rutgers University Press, 1972).

83. Benjamin Franklin to Dr. Samuel Johnson (August 23, 1750).

84. Benjamin Franklin, "Observations Concerning the Increase of Mankind" (Philadelphia, PA, 1751); http://bc.barnard.columbia.edu/~lgordis/earlyAC/documents/observations.html

85. Dr. Cadwallader Colden, "An Explication of the First Causes of Action in Matter" (New York, 1745); in Paul Russell Anderson and Max Harold Fisch, eds., *Philosophy in America* (New York: D. Appleton-Century Company, 1939). See also Benjamin Franklin to James Bowdoin (May 14, 1752), transcript in the Massachusetts Historical Society.

86. Benjamin Franklin to Joseph Huey (June 6, 1753), Letters, v. 4, pp. 504-6; see www.historycarper.com/resources/twobf2/letter19.htm

87. Ibid.

88. Ibid.

89. "Treaty held with the Ohio Indians at Carlisle, in October, 1753" (1753), 16p; printed in Carl Van Doren, ed., *Indian Treaties Printed by Benjamin Franklin* (Philadelphia, 1938), p. 123; Bruce E. Johansen, *Forgotten Founders: Benjamin Franklin, the Iroquois and the Rationale for the American Revolution.*

90. Benjamin Franklin to James Parker (1751); quoted in Van Doren, p. 209.

91. Cadwallader Colden, *History of the Five Indian Nations Depending on the Province of New York in America* (first published in 1727, was issued during 1747); in *The Letters and Papers of Cadwallader Colden*, vol. 9, 1937 and in Collections of the New York Historical Society for the year, 1935, pp. 359-434.

92. www.iroquoisdemocracy.pdx.edu/html/iroquoisleader.htm

93. Paul Wallace, The White Roots of Peace (Philadelphia, PA, 1946, 1986); Chief Jake Swamp and Gregory Schaaf, *The Great Law of Peace and the Constitution of the United States of America* (Tree of Peace Society, 1987); "Iroquois Confederacy of Nations: Hearing before the Select Committee on Indian Affairs," S. Con. Res. 76 (Washington, D. C., December 2, 1987).

94. Benjamin Franklin, "Albany Plan of Union," (Albany, NY, July 10, 1754), Queen's State Paper Office, British Museum, London, "New York Papers," Bundle Kk, No. 20, edited by E. B. O'Callaghan (Albany, NY, 1855), v. 6, pp. 853-92. Benjamin Franklin to James Alexander and Cadwallader Colden, "Short Hints towards a Scheme for Uniting the Northern Colonies" (1754), copy in New York Historical Society; also transcript in Library of Congress.

Proponents of the Indian Influence Thesis include Bruce E. Johansen, *Forgotten Founders: How the American Indian Helped Shape Democracy* (Boston, 1982), and Donald A. Grinde, Jr. and Bruce E. Johansen, "Sauce for the Goose: Demand and Definitions for 'Proof' regarding the Iroquois and Democracy," *William and Mary Quarterly* (1996), 3rd ser., v. 53, pp. 621-36.

Critics of the Indian Influence Thesis include Timothy J. Shannon, *Indians and Colonists at the Crossroads of Empire: The Albany Congress of 1754* (London and Ithaca, NY: Cornell University Press, 2000), 269 pp.

95. Benjamin Franklin, "Information to Those Who Would Remove to America" (1754); www.poormojo.org/cgi-bin/gennie.pl?Rant+135

96. Benjamin Franklin, *Poor Richard's Almanack* (1754).

97. www.christianheritagemins.org/articles/Benjamin%20Franklin.htm

98. Benjamin Franklin, "A Parable Against Persecution" (1755); published in *The Writings of Benjamin Franklin: Philadelphia,1726 - 1757* (Philadelphia, PA), v. II; see www.historycarper.com/resources/twobf2/articles.htm

99. *The Federal Almanack* (1795).

100. Benjamin Franklin to Elizabeth Hubbart (February 22, 1756); www.historycarper.com/resources/twobf2/letter24.htm; www.foothilltech.org/rgeib/amex/colonial/primary_sources/benjamim_franklin_to_elizabeth.htm

101. "Minutes of Indian conferences held at Easton in 11th month (called November), 1756" (Easton, PA, 1756), 45 pp., manuscript in the American Philosophical Society, Philadelphia, PA, doc. #123; www.amphilsoc.org/library/guides/indians/info/colls2.htm; http://webarchives.net/december_1999/teedyuscung.htm; Charles Miner, *History of Wyoming* (Philadelphia, 1845).

102. Shingas to Charles Stuart (November 1756), Charles Stuart, "Captivity," in *Mississippi Valley Historical Review* (1926), v. 13, p. 64. See also Randolph Downes, *Council Fires on the Upper Ohio* (Pittsburg, PA: University of Pittsburg Press, 1940), pp. 83-84.

103. *Pennsylvania Colonial Records*, v. 8, pp. 144-147.

104. www.stacks.com/catalog/AJan/bw1511.html

105. Benjamin Franklin, "The Way to Wealth," *Poor Richard's Almanack* (1758); *The Works of Benjamin Franklin*, edited by Jared Sparks (Boston, 1836), v. 2, pp. 92-103.

106. Benjamin Franklin, "Reasons Against Satirizing Religion," (December 13, 1757); see www.historycarper.com/resources/twobf3/letter1.htm

107. Benjamin Franklin, "A Letter from Father Abraham, to His Beloved Son," *The New-England Magazine* (August, 1758); see www.historycarper.com/resources/twobf3/abraham.htm

108. http://famousamericans.net/thomasbray/

109. www.glassarmonica.com/armonica/franklin/index.html

110. Crofton and Fraser, *A Dictionary of Musical Quotations* (Schirmer Books, 1985), p.70

111. www.users.qwest.net/~lopresti/bf.htm

112. www.gmu.edu/departments/economics/wew/articles/98/founders.htm

113. Benjamin Franklin, "A Narrative of the Late Massacres, in Lancaster County, of a Number of Indians, Friends of this Province, by Persons Unknown With Some Observations on the Same" (Philadelphia 1764); www.historycarper.com/resources/twobf3/massacre.htm

114. Ibid.

115. Ibid.

116. Benjamin Franklin to Rev. George Whitefield (1764); see www.fbaptistc.org/benjaminfranklin.html

117. Benjamin Franklin to Sarah Franklin, "Go Constantly to Church Whoever Preaches" (November 8, 1764); in Jared Sparks, *Life of Benjamin Franklin*, chapter 3; see www.ushistory.org/franklin/biography/chap03.htm

118. Ibid.

119. Ibid.; www.historycarper.com/resources/twobf3/letter4.htm

120. Jared Sparks, *Life of Benjamin Franklin*, chapter 3.

121. Franklin to Lord Kames (ca. 1767); in Sparks, Chapter 4; see *Life of Lord Kames*. Vol. IL 2nd ed., p. 112.

122. Benjamin Franklin, "Causes of the American Discontents Before 1768," (January 7, 1768); reprinted in *The London Chronicle* (August 30 and September 1, 1774); see

www.historycarper.com/resources/twobf3/disconte.htm

123. Benjamin Franklin, "A New Version of the Lord's Prayer" (ca. 1768); see www.historycarper.com/resources/twobf3/prayer.htm

124. Benjamin Franklin to Lord James (January 1, 1769); www.fbaptistc.org/benjaminfranklin.html

125. Benjamin Franklin, "Positions To Be Examined," (April 4. 1769); see www.historycarper.com/resources/twobf3/position.htm

126. www.digitalhistory.uh.edu/documents/documents_p2.cfm?doc=293

127. Benjamin Franklin, *Autobiography* (ca, 1773, 1786); see http://history.hanover.edu/courses/excerpts/111frank.htm; www.hants.gov.uk/localpages/central/winchester/twyford/

128. Benjamin Franklin, *Letter to the London Packet* (June 3, 1772); Benjamin Franklin Papers, v. 19, pp. 163-68; http://press-pubs.uchicago.edu/founders/documents/amendI_religions14.html

129. Ibid.

130. Ibid.

131. Ibid.

132. Ibid.

133. Benjamin Franklin to William Marshall, "The Increase of Religious as Well as Civil Liberty" (February 14, 1773); see www.historycarper.com/resources/twobf3/letter12.htm

134. Benjamin Franklin to Rev. Samuel Mather (July 7, 1773);see www.historycarper.com/resources/twobf3/letter12.htm

135. Patrick Henry, "Give Me Liberty or Give Me Death" (Richmond, VA, March 3, 1775).

136. Benjamin Franklin, "Proposed Articles of Confederation" (Philadelphia, July 21, 1775); see www.historycarper.com/resources/twobf3/articles.htm

137. "Declaration of the Causes and Necessity of Taking Up Arms" (July 6, 1775); www.save-a-patriot.org/files/view/precon2.html

138. Continental Congress, "The Olive Branch Petition" (July 5, 1775); www.geocities.com/Heartland/Ranch/9198/revbio/olivebra.htm

139. Thomas Paine, "Common Sense" (January 10, 1776); http://odur.let.rug.nl/~usa/D/1776-1800/paine/CM/sense01.htm

140. www.greatseal.com/committees/firstcomm/

141. Richard S. Patterson and Richardson Dougall, *The Eagle and the Shield* (Washington, D.C., 1976; James H. Hutson, *Religion and the Founding of the American Republic* (Washington, D.C.: Library of Congress, 1998), p. 51.

142. Hodder, Michael J., "The Continental Currency Coinage of 1776, a Trial Die and Metallic Emission Sequence" (Colorado Springs, CO: The American Numismatic Association Centennial Anthology, 1991); www.oldcoinshop.com/coinhistory/01-1776.htm

143. Continental Congress, "Fast Day Proclamation" (March 16, 1776); www.loc.gov/exhibits/religion/rel04.html

144. Carl L. Becker, *The Declaration of Independence* (New York: Alfred A. Knopf, 1922, 1942), pp. 154-71; For Julian Boyd's discovery of a Jefferson document illuminating revisions in the Declaration of Independence, see www.loc.gov/loc/lcib/9907/jeffdec.html

145. James H. Hutson, *Religion and the Founding of the American Republic* (Washington, D.C.: Library of Congress, 1998), p. 51.

146. George Washington, "General Orders" (July 9, 1776); John C. Fitzpatrick, ed., *The Writings of George Washington from the Original Manuscript Sources, 1745-1799*; http://memory.loc.gov

147. Ibid.

148. Thomas Paine, *The Crisis* (December 1776).

149. Benjamin Franklin to Charles Gavier, Comte de Vergennes; see Walter Isaacson, "Citizen Ben's 7 Great Virtues," *Time* (July 7, 2003);

www.time.com/time/2003/franklin/bffranklin5.html

150. www.loc.gov/exhibits/religion/rel04.html

151. Continental Congress, "Thanksgiving Day Proclamation" (December 18, 1777); www.loc.gov/exhibits/religion/rel04.html; James H. Hutson, *Religion and the Founding of the American Republic* (Washington, D.C.: Library of Congress, 1998).

152. "Treaty of Alliance Between The United States and France" (February 6, 1778); Hunter Miller, ed. *Treaties and Other International Acts of the United States of America* (Washington D.C.: Government Printing Office, 1931), v. 2, Documents 1-40 : 1776-1818; www.yale.edu/lawweb/avalon/diplomacy/france/fr1788-2.htm

153. Benjamin Franklin to Ministry of France (March 1778); www.leaderu.com/orgs/cdf/onug/franklin.html; www.worldviewweekend.com/book/chapter10.html

154. www.belcherfoundation.org/trilateral_center.htm

155. Benjamin Franklin to Richard Price (October 9, 1780); *Writings of Benjamin Franklin*, v. 8, pp. 153-54.

156. "U.S. Articles of Confederation" (ratified March 1, 1781); Charles C. Tansill, ed., *Documents Illustrative of the Formation of the Union of the American States* (Washington, D.C., Government Printing Office, 1927), House Document No. 398; www.yale.edu/lawweb/avalon/artconf.htm

157. Dr. James Thatcher, "Account of the Surrender at Yorktown" (October 19, 1781); "The British Surrender at Yorktown, 1781," EyeWitness to History, www.eyewitnesstohistory.com (2002).

158. Pierre-Andre Gargaz, *A Project of Universal and Perpetual Peace* (France, 1782; reprinted New York: George Simpson Eddy, 1922); www.belcherfoundation.org/trilateral_center.htm; www.globalpolicy.org/resource/unhist/jinx1.htm

159. John de Crevecoeur, *Letters from an American Farmer* (1782, Oxford University Press, 1999).

160. Benjamin Franklin to daughter, Sarah Bache (January 26, 1784); Albert Henry Smyth, ed., *The Writings of Benjamin Franklin* (New York: The Macmillan Company, 1905-7), v. 10.

161. Ibid.

162. Ibid.

163. Ibid.

164. Benjamin Franklin, "Remarks Concerning the Savages of North America" (1784); www2.latech.edu/~bmagee/202/franklin/Savages2.htm

165. Ibid.

166. Ibid.

167. www.amphilsoc.org/library/exhibits/treasures/louis.htm

168. www.english.udel.edu/lemay/franklin/1785.html

169. Benjamin Franklin, "Dangers of a Salaried Bureaucracy" (Philadelphia, June 2, 1787); "Debates in the Federal Convention of 1787 as reported by James Madison" contained within "Documents Illustrative of the Formation of the Union of the American States", pp. 138, selected, arranged, and indexed by Charles C. Tansill, published 1927 Government Printing Office as a result of House Concurrent Resolution No. 23; www.columbia-center.org/bllingg/bll/docs/constcnv.html

170. Benjamin Franklin, "Dangers of a Salaried Bureaucracy" (Philadelphia, June 2, 1787).

171. Ibid.

172. Ibid.

173. Ibid.

174. Ibid.

175. Ibid.

176. Ibid.

177. Ibid.

178. U. S. Constitution, Article II, Section 1, Clause 7;
www.house.gov/Constitution/Constitution.html

179. www.mountvernon.org/books/career.asp

180. Benjamin Franklin, "Speech to the Constitutional Convention" (1787), original text written in Dr. Franklin's hand added by James Madison to the "Journal."

181. Reuben G. Thwaites, The Jesuit Relations and Allied Documents: Travel and Explorations of the Jesuit Missionaries in New France, 1610-1791 (Cleveland, OH: Burrows Brothers, reprinted New York: Pageant, 1959).

182. Benjamin Franklin to James Madison, "Regarding Prayer at Constitutional Convention" (June 28 1787); James Madison, The Records of the Federal Convention of 1787, Max Farrand, editor (New Haven: Yale University Press, 1911), Vol. I, pp. 450-452

183. Ibid.

184. Ibid.

185. Ibid.

186. www.wallbuilders.com/resources/search/detail.php?ResourceID=19

187. Morris, pp.253-254; members.aol.com/EndTheWall/Franklin-prayer.htm

188. Benjamin Franklin, "Final Speech to the Constitutional Convention (September 17, 1787); www.claremont.org/weblog/000647.html

189. Morris, pp.253-254; www.members.aol.com/EndTheWall/Franklin-prayer.htm

190. Ibid.

191. Ibid.

192. www.members.tripod.com/globalnewsmagazine/electoral_college.htm

193. "Northwest Ordinance" (July 13, 1787);
www.yale.edu/lawweb/avalon/nworder.htm

194. Benjamin Franklin, Autobiography, section five;
www.worldwideschool.org/library/books/hst/biography/TheAutobiographyofBenjaminFranklin/chap33.html

195. Henrietta Elizabeth Marshall, This Country of Ours; The Story of the United States (New York: George H. Doran Company, 1917), chapter 64;
http://digital.library.upenn.edu/women/marshall/country/country-VII-64.html

196. George Washington, "First Inaugural Address" (April 30, 1789);
www.freedomshrine.com/documents/wash1st.html

197. Benjamin Franklin to Jean-Baptiste Leroy (Nov. 13, 1789); "Declaration of the Rights of Man and of the Citizen"(August 26, 1789);
www.usconstitution.com/DeclarationoftheRightsofMan.htm

198. Benjamin Franklin, "An Address to the Public Concerning Slavery" (November 9, 1789); www.usconstitution.com/AddresstoPublicConcerningSlaveryBenFranklin.htm

199. Ibid.

200. Ibid.

201. Ibid.

202. "The Constitution of the Pennsylvania Society for Promoting the Abolition of Slavery and the Relief of Free Negroes unlawfully held in Bondage" (1787);
http://tomscourses.tripod.com/abolit1.htm

203. Benjamin Franklin to Ezra Stiles (March 9, 1790); John Bigelow, ed., The Works of Benjamin Franklin (New York: Putnam's, 1904);
www.worldpolicy.org/globalrights/religion/franklin-religion.html

204. Ibid.

205. Ibid.

206. Ibid.

207. Thomas Jefferson, "On Benjamin Franklin" (February 19, 1791).

208. Ibid.

209. Ibid.

CHAPTER TWO

1. Frank Shuffelton, ed., Thomas Jefferson: A Comprehensive, Annotated Bibliography of writings about him, 1826-1997 (Charlottesville, VA: University of Virginia, 2001); see ttp://etext.lib.virginia.edu/jefferson/bibliog/

2. For Thomas Jefferson's patrilineal ancestry see www.poetsvisions.com/genealogy/jefferson.htm; and http://users.legacyfamilytree.com/USPresidents/8405.htm

3. For Thomas Jefferson's matrilineal ancestry see http://users.legacyfamilytree.com/USPresidents/7038.htm

4. www.sparknotes.com/biography/jefferson/section1.html

5. www.jefferson-hemings.org/randy.htm

6. http://homepages.rootsweb.com/~lpproots/Fountaine/mfm-01.htm

7. www.sparknotes.com/biography/jefferson/section1.html

8. www.ishipress.com/pafg34.htm

9. www.sparknotes.com/biography/jefferson/section1.html

10. www.americanparknetwork.com/parkinfo/cw/history/

11. www.sparknotes.com/biography/jefferson/section2.rhtml

12. www.sparknotes.com/biography/jefferson/section3.rhtml

13. Thomas Jefferson, "Virginia Constitution," draft 1, in Julian Boyd, *The Writings of Thomas Jefferson* v. 1, pp. 329-365; see also W. C. Ford, "Jefferson's Constitution for Virginia," *Nation*, LI (1890), v. 1,p. 107; Ford, v. 2, pp. 7-9; D. R. Anderson, "Jefferson and the Virginia Constitution," *American Historical Review* (1915-16), v. 21, pp. 750-4; Malone, *Jefferson*, v. 1, pp. 235-40.

14. Jefferson, "Virginia Constitution," draft 2, in Boyd, v. 1, pp. 329-365.

15. Jefferson, "Virginia Constitution," draft 3, in Boyd v. 1, pp. 329-365.

16. Jefferson to Thomas Nelson (May 16, 1776); in Boyd, v. 1, pp. 329-65. For biographical information on Thomas Nelson see www.ushistory.org/declaration/signers/nelson.htm

17. Virginia Constitution (June 29, 1776), in *The Federal and State Constitutions Colonial Charters, and Other Organic Laws of the States, Territories, and Colonies Now or Heretofore Forming the United States of America*, compiled and edited under the Act of Congress of June 30, 1906 by Francis Newton Thorpe (Washington, DC: Government Printing Office, 1909).

18. Jefferson, "Declaration of Independence" (adopted July 4, 1776). Transcription at www.archives.gov/exhibit_hall/charters_of_freedom/declaration/declaration_transcription.html

19. Ibid.

20. Ibid.

21. Ibid.

22. Ibid.

23. Ibid.

24. John Hancock (June 1776), Journals of the Continental Congress.

25. Jefferson to Edmund Pendleton (August 13, 1776); see www.yale.edu/lawweb/avalon/jefflett/let8.htm

26. Jefferson, "Rough Draft of Jefferson's Resolutions for Disestablishing the Church of England and for Repealing Laws Interfering with Freedom of Worship" (Before November 19, 1776); in Boyd, v. 1, pp. 530-559.

27. Ibid.

28. Continental Congress, "Resolution Regarding Religion" (November 19, 1776); in Boyd, v. 1, pp. 530-559.

29. Bernard Bailyn, *The Ideological Origins of the American Revolution* (Cambridge, MA: Belknap Press of Harvard University Press, 1967), pp. 261-72.

30. Jefferson, "Preamble to Resolutions on Religion," in Boyd, v. 1, pp. 530-559.

31. Jefferson, "On Separation of Church and State", in Boyd, v. 1, pp. 530-559.

32. Jefferson, "Bill for Exempting Dissenters from Contributing to the Support of the Church." (November 30, 1776).

33. Ibid.

34. Ibid.

35. Jefferson, "III. Jefferson's Outline of Argument in Support of his Resolutions". (November 1776).

36. www.geocities.com/tira_and_moon/meditate1.html

37. www.galileo.harvard.edu/

38. www.newton.cam.ac.uk/newton.html

39. Jefferson, "List of Acts of Parliament and of Virginia Assembly, 1661-1759, concerning Religion." (1776).

40. William Rastell, *A Collection of Statutes Now in Force*, numerous enlargements and abridgements from 1557 to 1706; Jefferson's edition was that of 1611 (L.C. Cat.; information from Miss E. M. Sowerby). Sir Mathew Hale, *Pleas of the Crown*, London, 1678, and later editions. Jefferson owned two editions. (L.C. Cat.; Library Catalogue, 1815, p. 76).

41. Jefferson, "Jefferson's Outline of Argument in Support of his Resolutions" (November 1776).

42. John Locke, "Letter of Toleration" (1689); Victor Nuovo, *John Locke: Writings on Religion* (Oxford University Press, 2000); www.rjgeib.com/thoughts/constitution/locke-bio.html

43. The notes on Shaftesbury are a paraphrase, with interpolations, of a passage in section 2 of "A Letter concerning Enthusiasm" (1708) in the 3d Earl of Shaftesbury's *Characteristicks of Men, Manners, Opinions, Times*, (London, 1711), v. I; see also Shaftesbury, *Complete Works, Selected Letters and Posthumous Writings*, in English with German Translation, ed. W. Benda, G. Hemmerich, W. Lottes, U. Schöldbauer, E. Wolff, et al. (Stuttgart: Fromman-Holzboog, 1981-) (in progress). Five series: I, "Æsthetics"; II, "Moral and Political Philosophy"; III, "Letters"; IV, "Commentaries"; "Documents and indexes". About 21 volumes are planned.

44. Jefferson, "Jefferson's Outline of Argument in Support of his Resolutions" (November 1776).

45. Rom.14.23.

46. Jefferson's Outline.

47. Ibid. .

48. Ibid.

49. Ibid.

50. Gregory Schaaf, *Wampum Belts & Peace Trees* (Golden, CO: Fulcrum Press, 1990).

51. Jefferson's Outline.

52. Jefferson, "Jefferson's Outline of Argument in Support of his Resolutions" (November 1776).

53. Ibid.

54. Ibid.

55. Ibid.

56. Ibid.

57. Ibid.

58. Ibid.

59. Dr. Martin Luther, "Disputation of Doctor Martin Luther on the Power and Efficacy of Indulgences" (1517); see http://www.iclnet.org/pub/resources/text/wittenberg/luther/web/ninetyfive.html

60. Jefferson, "Jefferson's Outline of Argument in Support of his Resolutions" (November 1776).

61. *The Bible*, James, Chapter 5, verse 14; quoted in Jefferson, "Jefferson's Outline of Argument in Support of his Resolutions" (November 1776).

62. Jefferson, "Jefferson's Outline of Argument in Support of his Resolutions" (November

1776).

63. "The Toleration Act" (England 1689); see
http://www.agh-attorneys.com/4_act_of_toleration_1689.htm

64. Jefferson, "Jefferson's Outline of Argument in Support of his Resolutions" (November 1776); John Milton: "The Reason of Church-Government Urg'd against Prelaty" and "Of the Reformation in England," in Milton's *Works* (Amsterdam, 1698), v. I; William Camden, *Britannia* (London, 1586).

65. Jefferson, "Jefferson's Outline of Argument in Support of his Resolutions" (November 1776).

66. Daniel Waterland, *Collected Works, with life by W. van Mildert*, 12 vols. (Oxford, 1823-8); *A Vindication of Christ's Divinity* (1719); *A Second Vindication*, (1723); *A Farther Vindication*, (1724); *A Critical History of the Athanasian Creed* (1723).

67. Jefferson, "Jefferson's Outline of Argument in Support of his Resolutions" (November 1776).

68. Ibid.

69. Ibid.

70. Ibid.

71. Ibid.

72. www.macedonia.com/english/origin.html

73. Jefferson researched many sources including the writings of Daniel Waterland (1683-1740), William Chillingworth (1602-1644), Eusebius (260-340), Conyers Middlleton (1683-1750), Joannes Zonaras (12th century), Louis Cousin (1678), and Thomas Broughton (1742).

74. The foregoing is a single-page MS, mutilated, in DLC: *Thomas Jefferson Papers*, 234: 41879 recto.

75. "Bill for the Revision of the Laws," (adopted October 24, 1776; Jefferson was joined by Edmund Pendleton, George Wythe, George Mason, and Thomas Ludwell Lee, Esquires, see JHD, Oct. 1776, 1828 edition, p. 41.

76. JHD, (Oct. 1776, 1828 edition), pp. 12, 14, 51

77. Jefferson, "Miscellaneous Notes on Religion" (Fall, 1776).

78. "Declaration of the Virginia Association of Baptists" (December 25, 1776) in Boyd, v. 1, pp. 660-63.

79. "Declaration of the Virginia Association of Baptists" (December 25, 1776) in Boyd, v. 1, pp. 660-63; see also W. T. Thom, "The Struggle for Religious Freedom in Virginia: the Baptists," *Johns Hopkins Univ. Studies in History and Political Science*, series XVIII (1900), pp. 48-9.

80. "The Revisal of Laws" (1776-1786); in Boyd, v. 2, pp. 305-24.

81. Jefferson, *Autobiography* in Ford, v. 1, p. 68.

82. Ibid.

83. Ibid. pp. 68-69.

84. Ford, v. 1, p. 58.

85. Hening, v. 9, p. 177.

86. Ford, v. 1, p. 58.

87. Report of *the Committee of Revisors Appointed by the General Assembly of Virginia in MDCCLXXVI* (1776-1779, published in 1784).

88. Ford, v. 1, p. 48.

89. Samuel Stanhope Smith to Jefferson (March 1779); in Boyd v. 2, pp. 246-49.

90. E.S. Gaustad, *Faith of Our Fathers: Religion and the New Nation* (Harper & Row: New York NY, 1987), pp. 141-149.

91. Jefferson, "A Bill for Establishing Religious Freedom" (1777, passed 1786); in Boyd, v. 2, pp. 545-556. See also Hening, v. 12, pp. 84-6; *Acts passed at a General Assembly of the Commonwealth of Virginia* (Richmond: Dunlap and Hayes 1786), p. 26-7. For legal statute see Code of Virginia, §57-1.The earliest draft of the bill is found in the Boston Public Library: "A

BILL for establishing RELIGIOUS FREEDOM, printed for the consideration of the PEOPLE," [Williamsburg, 1779]. Broadside, Boston Public Library, Evans 19350, Swem, "Va. Bibliog.," 7476, and Sabin 100041.

92. Jefferson, "A Bill for Establishing Religious Freedom" (1777, passed 1786); in Boyd, v. 2, pp. 545-556.

93. Ford, v. 1, p. 62.

94. Ibid., pp. 545-556.

95. Ibid., pp. 545-556.

96. Ibid., pp. 545-556.

97. Ibid., pp. 545-556.

98. Ibid., pp. 545-556.

99. Ibid., pp. 545-556.

100. The Bible, John, 8:32.

101. Ibid., pp. 545-556.

102. Ibid., pp. 545-556.

103. Jefferson to George Washington (January 4, 1786); see www.cooperativeindividualism.org/jefferson_l_02.html

104. James Madison to Jefferson (Jan. 22, 1786; Boyd, v. 9, pp. 194-209; JHD (Oct. 1785, 1828 edn.), pp. 12-15, 93-96, 115, 117, 134-135, 138-139, 143-4, 148.

105. *Acte de la République de Virginie, I qui établit la liberté de Religion* (Paris, 1786), four-page pamphlet, probably printed by Philippe-Denys Pierres; see Ford, v. II, p. 237; *An Act for establishing Religious Freedom, passed in the assembly of Virginia in the beginning of the year 1786* (Paris, 1786); eight-page pamphlet found by Dr. Rice, in the Bibliothéque de l'Institut de France, Paris, Sabin l00344.

106. Jefferson to George Wythe (August 13, 1786) in Boyd, v. 10, pp. 243-245; see also http://etest.lib.virginia.edu/jefferson/biog/1j12.htm; *Encyclopédie Méthodique*, (Paris, ca. 1786); reviews by Brissot, Claviére and Mazzei.

107. Ibid.

108. Ibid.

109. Jefferson to James Madison (Dec. 16, 1786) in Boyd, v. 10, pp. 602-606.

110. Ibid.

111. Jefferson to Peter Carr (August 10, 1787) in Boyd, v. 12, pp. 14-19.

112. Ibid.

113. Ibid. Jefferson cited his source, "See this law in the Digest Lib. 48. tit. 19 § 28. 3. and Lipsius Lib. 2. de cruce. cap. 2."

114. Ibid.

115. Ibid.

116. Ibid.

117. Jefferson to James Madison (December 20, 1787) in Boyd, v. 12, pp. 438-43.

118. Ibid.

119. Ibid.

120. Ibid.

121. Ibid.

122. Ibid.

123. Ibid.

124. "The Thomas Jefferson Hour"(PBS) presented an interpretation of Jefferson as an elitist in an explanation for the establishment of the electoral college system in presidential elections.

125. Jefferson to Edward Dowse (April 19, 1803).

126. Ibid.

127. Jefferson to Dr. Benjamin Rush (April 21, 1803).

128. Jefferson, "A Syllabus of an Estimate of the Merit of the Doctrines of Jesus, Compared to Those of Others" (April 23, 1803). [hereafter cited Jefferson's Doctrines of

Jesus]. This document has been the subject of much controversy. The full document contains critical statements regarding religion and warrants a larger analysis. For more extensive discussions, see the following: www.secularhumanism.org/library/fi/alley_18_4.html; www.angelfire.com/co/JeffersonBible/jeffbsyl.html; http://courses.drew.edu/FA2002/logon-900a-001/Jefferson/ThomasJefferson.html

In his own defense of his Syllabus, Jefferson explained himself further in an April 13, 1820 letter to his adoptive son, William Short:

> "DEAR SIR,
>
> Your favor of March the 27th is received, and as you request, a copy of the syllabus is now enclosed. It was originally written to Dr. Rush. On his death, fearing that the inquisition of the public might get hold of it, I asked the return of it from the family, which they kindly complied with. At the request of another friend, I had given him a copy. He lent it to his friend to read, who copied it, and in a few months it appeared in the Theological Magazine of London. Happily that repository is scarcely known in this country, and the syllabus, therefore, is still a secret, and in your hands I am sure it will continue so.
>
> But while this syllabus is meant to place the character of Jesus in its true and high light, as no impostor Himself, but a great Reformer of the Hebrew code of religion, it is not to be understood that I am with Him in all His doctrines. I am a Materialist; he takes the side of Spiritualism; he preaches the efficacy of repentance towards forgiveness of sin; I require counterpoise of good works to redeem it, etc., etc. It is the innocence of His character, the purity and sublimity of His moral precepts, the eloquence of His inculcations, the beauty of the apologues in which He conveys them, that I so much admire; sometimes, indeed, needing indulgence to eastern hyperbolism. My eulogies, too, may be founded on a postulate which all may not be ready to grant. Among the sayings and discourses imputed to Him by His biographers, I find many passages of fine imagination, correct morality, and of the most lovely benevolence; and others, again, of so much ignorance, so much absurdity, so much untruth, charlatanism and imposture, as to pronounce it impossible that such contradictions should have proceeded from the same Being. I separate, therefore, the gold from the dross; restore to Him the former, and leave the latter to the stupidity of some, and roguery of others of His disciples. Of this band of dupes and impostors, Paul was the great Coryphaeus, and first corruptor of the doctrines of Jesus. These palpable interpolations and falsifications of His doctrines, led me to try to sift them apart. I found the work obvious and easy, and that His past composed the most beautiful morsel of morality which has been given to us by man. The syllabus is therefore of His doctrines, not all of mine. I read them as I do those of other ancient and modern moralists, with a mixture of approbation and dissent . . . "

See also a subsequent letter, Jefferson to William Short, from Monticello, (August 4, 1820) in Merrill D. Peterson, ed., *Thomas Jefferson: Writings* (New York: Library of America, 1994), pp. 1435-1440.

129. Jefferson to Dr. Benjamin Rush (April 21, 1803).

130. Ibid.

131. A search of the Internet on Jefferson and Jews reveals that Jefferson's concern over being misinterpreted was not unfounded.

132 Jefferson's Doctrines of Jesus.

133. Ibid.

134. Ibid.

135. Ibid.

136. Ibid.

137. Ibid.

138. Jefferson to Pierre Samuel du Pont (April 1802).

139. Captain John Lewis, "Journal" (November 7, 1804).

140. Jefferson to Chief Wolf and People of the Mandan Nation (Washington, December 30, 1806); see www.yale.edu/lawweb/avalon/jeffind5.htm

141. Ibid.

142. Jefferson to Rev. Samuel Miller (January 23, 1808); see www.webwhiteandblue.com/jefferson/religion/religion_letters_pg2.html#Letter161

143. Jefferson to Thaddeus Kosciusko (February 26, 1810); see www.cooperativeindividualism.org/jefferson_p_03.html

144. Jefferson to William Canby (September 18, 1813); see www.cooperativeindividualism.org/jefferson_m_02.html

145. Ibid.

146. Jefferson to John Adams (October 12, 1813).

147. The Jefferson Bible (1904); see www.uua.org/uuhs/duub/articles/thomasjefferson.html

148. Jefferson to Charles Thomson (January 9, 1816); see www.cooperativeindividualism.org/jefferson_m_03.html

149. Joseph Priestley, *Letters to a Philosophical Unbeliever, History of the Corruptions of Christianity, History of the Early Opinions Concerning Jesus Christ*; William Enfield, *History of Philosophy from The Earliest Times, a translation of Johann Jakob Brucker's Historia Critica Philosophiae* (first published in six volumes in 1742—67).

150. Jefferson to Dr. Joseph Priestley (January 29, 1804): see www.webwhiteandblue.com/jefferson/religion/religion_letters_pg2.html#Letter161

151. www.uua.org/uuhs/duub/articles/thomasjefferson.html

152. Jefferson to N. G. Dufief (April 19, 1814); see www.cooperativeindividualism.org/jefferson_k_01.html

153. Ibid.

154. Ibid.

155. Jefferson to Miles King (September 26, 1814); memory.loc.gov/ammem/mtjhtml/mtjquote.html; www.cooperativeindividualism.org/jefferson_m_02.html

156. Jefferson to Charles Clay (January 29, 1815); see O.I.A. Roche, ed. *The Jeffersonian Bible* (1964) p. 328; www.cooperativeindividualism.org/jefferson_m_02.html

157. Ibid.

158. Ibid.

159. Jefferson to John Adams (May 5, 1817); see www.cooperativeindividualism.org/jefferson_m_02.html

160. Jefferson to Vine Utley (March 21, 1819); see www.cooperativeindividualism.org/jefferson_p_01.html

161. Jefferson to Benjamin Waterhouse (June 26, 1822); see http://odur.let.rug.nl/~usa/P/tj3/writings/brf/jefl268.htm

162. Ibid.

163. Jefferson to Dr. Thomas Cooper (November 2, 1822); see http://odur.let.rug.nl/~usa/P/tj3/writings/brf/jefl270.htm

164. Jefferson to James Madison (February 17, 1826); http://www.loc.gov/exhibits/jefferson/215.html

165. Jefferson to Roger C. Weightman (June 24, 1826); ME, v. 16, p. 181; see

http://etext.lib.virginia.edu/jefferson/biog/lj39.htm
166. Ibid.
167. Ibid.
168. http://etext.lib.virginia.edu/jefferson/biog/lj39.htm
169. Ibid.
170. *Holy Bible*, King James Version, Luke, 2:29-32.
171. http://etext.lib.virginia.edu/jefferson/biog/lj39.htm
172. Jefferson, "Epitaph" (1826); http://memory.loc.gov/ammem/mtjhtml/epitaph.html

CHAPTER THREE

1. Tecumseh, Shawnee Chief (1768, Ohio - October 5, 1813, Thames River, Ontario, Canada. See Frederick W. Hodge, ed., *Handbook of American Indians North of Mexico* (Washington, D.C., Bureau of American Ethnology, 1912), 2:714.

2. The James Madison Family Tree is published by the James Madison Center at James Madison University. Their website address is www.jmu.edu/madison/family/index.htm. A carefully crafted overview of Madison's biography has been compiled by James Madison's Montpelier Foundation that manages the historic estate. Their website address is www.montpelier.org. Highlights of the research of biographers Irving Brant and Ralph Ketcham appear at www.dcs.hull.ac.uk/public/genealogy/presidents.

In the study of American Indian history, my mentor was the late Dr. Wilbur Jacobs, past president of the Pacific Coast Branch of the American Historical Association. He was the author of many important books specializing in Colonial American Indian studies.

3. In the study of the European influences on America, I am greatly indebted to Dr. Abraham Friesen, my European history graduate school professor at the University of California, Santa Barbara. He focused my readings on the origins of different Protestant denominations. Madison's ideological development is the subject of a scholarly study by Lance Banning, *The Sacred Fire of Liberty & the Founding of the Federal Republic* (Ithaca, NY: Cornell University Press, 1995). (hereafter cited Banning)

4. In the study of American intellectual history, I am greatly indebted to Dr. Alexander DeConde, my American history graduate school professor at the University of California, Santa Barbara. He introduced me to important historical writings, including Bernard Bailyn, *The Ideological Origins of the American Revolution* (Cambridge, MA: Belknap Press & Harvard University Press). (hereafter cited Bailyn). See also James Madison to Rev. Thomas Martin (August 10, 1769), Papers of James Madison, v. 1, pp. 42-43; (hereafter cited PJM); Boston Sons of Liberty to Wilkes (June 6, 1768), MHS Procs., 47 (1913-14), p. 191.

5. James Madison to William Bradford, Jr. (November 1772), PJM, v. 1.

6. Samuel Eliot Morison, *The Oxford History of the American People* (New York: Oxford University Press, 1965), pp. 204-12. (hereafter cited Morison). It is surprising to many historians to learn that on December 2, 1987, the U.S. Congress passed a resolution officially recognizing, "the confederation of the original Thirteen Colonies into one republic was explicitly modeled upon the Iroquois Confederacy as were many of the democratic principles which were incorporated into the Constitution itself; and . . . on the occasion of the two hundredth anniversary of the signing of the United States Constitution, acknowledges the historical debt which this Republic of the United States of America owes to the Iroquois Confederacy and other Indian nations for their demonstration of enlightened, democratic principles of Government." See S. Con. Res 76, "Iroquois Confederacy of Nations," Hearing before the Select Committee on Indian Affairs, United States Senate (Washington, D.C., December 2, 1987), S. Hrg. 100-610. The resolution passed in the Senate 100-0, passed the House overwhelmingly and was signed by President George Bush, Sr. The author's testimony appears in this Senate Hearing report.

7. Gaillard Hunt, ed., *Writings of James Madison* (New York: G. P. Putnam's Sons, 1900-10),

v. 1, pp. 18-21. (hereafter cited WJM) "Even at Philadelphia, which had been so long celebrated, for the excellency of its police and government, and the temperate manners of its inhabitants, printed papers were dispersed, warning the pilots on the river Delaware, not to conduct any of these tea ships into their harbour, which were only sent out for the purpose of enslaving and poisoning all the Americans; at the same time, giving them plainly to understand it was expected, that they would apply their knowledge of the river, under the colour of their profession, in such a manner, as would effectually secure their country from so imminent a danger." — *Annual Register*, xvii., 49.

8. Ibid.

9. Ibid.

10. Ibid.

11. Ibid.

12. Ibid.

13. Hunt, WJM, v. 1, pp. 22-25.

14. Ibid.

15. Ibid.

16. William Wirt Henry, ed., *Patrick Henry: Life, Correspondence and Speeches* (New York: Scharles Scribner's Sons, 1891).

17. Hezekiah Niles, *Principles and Acts of the Revolution in America* (Baltimore: W. O. Niles, 1822).

18. Thomas Paine, *Common Sense* (Philadelphia, 1776); Moncure Conway, ed., *The Writings of Thomas Paine* (New York: G. P. Putnam's Sons, 1894-96), v. 1.

19. James Madison, *Autobiography*, pp. 198-99.

20. "Virginia State Constitution" (1776); Hunt, WJM, v. 1, pp. 32-41.

21. Ibid.

22. Banning, pp. 85-87. Banning evaluated the importance of Madison's amendment to the Virginia Constitution, appraising him "among the most advanced reformers of his age."

23. PJM, v. 1, pp. 173-75. See also Thomas E. Buckley, *Church and State in Revolutionary Virginia, 1776-1787* (Charlottesville, VA, 1977); and Thomas J. Curry, *The First Freedoms: Church and State in America to the Passge of the First Amendment* (New York, 1986).

24. Hunt, WJM, v. 1, pp. 32-41.

25. Ibid.

26 .Thomas Jefferson, "Declaration of Indpendence" (July 1776).

27. Warwick County petition, *JHDV* (May 1784), p. 8

28. John B. Smith to James Madison (June 21, 1784); Hunt, WJM, v. 1, p. 62.

29. James Madison to Thomas Jefferson (July 3, 1784); Hunt, WJM, v. 1, pp. 56-62; Rutland 8:195-199, see "Editorial Note."

30. Rives, v. 1, p. 560.

31. Hunt, WJM, v. 1, pp. 88-89; Rutland 8:195-199.

32. Rives, v. 1, p. 604. Madison wrote a praphrase of this speech "in a microscopic hand on the back of a letter."

33. Beverly Randolph to Monroe, 26 Nov. 1784 [DLC: Monroe Papers].

34. Rives, v. 1, p. 599. Only one petitition appeared against the measure.

35. James Madison to James Monroe (November 14, 1784); Hunt, WJM, v. 8, pp. 89-90.

36. Meade, *Patrick Henry*, v. 2, pp. 275-78.

37. James Madison to James Monroe (November 27, 1784); Hunt, WJM, v. 8, pp. 91-94.

38. James Madison to James Madison, Sr. (January 6, 1785), PJM, v. 8, p. 217; Banning, p. 90, fn. 54; Buckley, *Church and State*, pp. 106-07.

39. James Madison to James Monroe (December 24, 1784); Hunt, WJM, v. 8, pp. 98-99.

40. James Madison to Thomas Jefferson (January 9, 1785); Hunt, WJM, v. 8, pp. 102-19.

41. Ibid.

42. Ibid.

43. Ibid.

44. James Madison to James Monroe (April 12, 1785); Hunt, WJM, v. 8, pp. 140-41.

45. James Madison to James Monroe (April 28, 1785); Hunt, WJM, v. 8, pp. 142-43.

46. James Madison to James Monroe (May 29, 1785); Hunt, WJM, v. 8, pp. 143-45.

47. Ibid.

48. Ibid.

49. Rutland v. 8, p. 295.

50. Banning p. 91, fn. 58; Donald L. Drakeman, "Religion and the Republic: James Madison and the First Amendment," *Journal of Church and State* (1983), v. 25, pp. 427-45.

51. James Madison, "Memorial and Remonstrance against Religious Assessments" (June 20, 1785); Rutland v. 8, pp. 295-306.

52. Ibid.

53. Ibid.

54. Ibid.

55. Ibid.

56. Ibid.; see also James Madison to Thomas Jefferson, October 17, 1788, Madison, *Writings* [Hunt ed.], v. 5, p. 272; James Madison, *Notes of Debates in the Federal Convention* (Athens, Ohio, 1966), p. 77; *Federalist No. 10,* Cooke, ed., *The Federalist,* pp. 60-61.

57. Madison's Memorial of 1785; see also James Madison, "Annual Message to Congress" (December 3, 1816) in James D. Richardson, ed., *A Compilation of the Messages and Papers of the Presidents,* 1789-1897 (Washington, D.C., 1898-99), p. 1, 580.

58. Madison's Memorial of 1785.

59. John Locke, *Epistolia de Tolerantia: A Letter on Toleration* (ca. 1685); in Raymond Klibansky and J. W. Gough, eds. (Oxford, 1968).

60. Madison's Memorial of 1785.

61. Ibid.

62. Ibid.

63. Thomas Jefferson "Declaration of the Causes and Necessity for Taking Up Arms" (1775); in Julian Boyd, ed., *Papers of Jefferson,* v. 1, p. 194.

64. Madison's Memorial of 1785.

65. Ibid.

66. Ibid.

67. Ibid.

68. Ibid.

69. Ibid.

70. Ibid.

71. Ibid.

72. John Locke, *Epistolia de Tolerantia: A Letter on Toleration* (ca. 1685); in Raymond Klibansky and J. W. Gough, eds. (Oxford, 1968).

73. Madison's Memorial of 1785.

74. Ibid.

75. Ibid.

76. Ibid.

77. Ibid.

78. Ibid.

79. Ibid.

80. Ibid.

81. Ibid.

82. Ibid.

83. Ibid.

84. Ibid.

85. Ibid.

86. Ibid.

87. Ibid.

88. Ibid.

89. Ibid.

90. Ibid.; William Taylor Thom, *The Struggle for Religious Freedom in Virginia:The Baptists* (Baltimore, 1900), pp. 75-76.

91. Ibid.

92. Ibid.

93. Ibid. Madison cited the source of the quote as "Per Decl. Rights title."

94. Ibid.

95. Ibid.

96. Ibid.

97. James Madison to George Mason [of Green Spring] (July 14, 1826); see Rutland v. 8, p. 295.

98. James Madison to James Monroe (June 21, 1785) in Hunt vol. 8, pp. 146-148.

99. James Madison to General Lafayette (November 1826), in Madison (1865), v. 3, p. 543.

100. Ibid.

101. James Madison, "Protestant Episcopal Church Petition to the General Assembly of Virginia" (ca. July 1785); see Rutland v. 8, pp. 312-314; Hunt ed., v. 2, pp. 212-14. (hereafter cited Episcopal Church Petition of 1785.)

102. Episcopal Church Petition of 1785. The "law passed at the last Session" was approved by the House of Delegates on Dec. 16, 1784 and by the Senate on Dec. 28, 1784. See also Hening, *Statutes,* v. 11, pp. 532-37.

103. Episcopal Church Petition of 1785. See also James Madison to Thomas Jefferson, (Jan. 9, 1785); Bryd, *Virginia's Mother Church and . . . Political Conditions,* v. II, p. 353.

104. Episcopal Church Petition of 1785. See Rev. T. G. Dashiell, "History of the Church in Virginia from 1785 to the Death of Bishop Meade," *Addresses and Historical Papers . . . of the Protestant Episcopal Church in the Diocese of Virginia* (New York, 1885), p. 62.

105. Ibid.

106. Ibid.

107. Ibid.

108. James Madison to Thomas Jefferson (August 20, 1785); in Hunt, v. I, pp. 160-65.

109. Rutland v. 8, p. 389.

110. Thumas Jefferson, "An Act for Establishing Religious Freedom" (introduced October 31, 1785), bill #82; Rutland v. 8, pp. 389-394.

111. James Madison to Thomas Jefferson (January 22, 1786) in Rutland v. 8, pp. 472-482.

112. Ibid.

113. Ibid.

114. Rutland, v. 8, p. 394, fn. 5. See also Boyd, Papers of Jefferson, v. 2, pp. 545-46.

115. James Madison to Thomas Jefferson (January 22, 1786).

116. Ibid.

117. Continental Congress, "Resolution for a Constitutional Convention" (February 21, 1787); see James H. Charleston, et. al., *Framers of the Constitution* (Washington, D.C., & Danbury, CT, 1986), p. 22.

118. Morison 1965, p. 305.

119. Gouverneur Morris, "Speech at Constitutional Convention" (July 5, 1787), reported by James Madison, in Morison 1965, p. 308.

120. Preamble, U.S. Constitution (1787), originals at the United States National Archives, Washington, D.C.

121. Jacob E. Cooke, ed., *The Federalist,* (Cleveland World, 1961), no. 10, pp. 56-65.

122. Jacob E. Cooke, ed., *The Federalist,* (Cleveland World, 1961), no. 39, p. 250.

123. Jacob E. Cooke, ed., *The Federalist,* (Cleveland World, 1961), no. 51, p. 351.

124. Ibid.

125. Ibid.

126. Ibid.

127. Ibid.

128. James Madison, "Speeches in the Virginia Convention" (June 5, 1788); in Hunt, v. 5, pp. 123-37. (hereafter cited Madison's 1788 Speech). See also "Debates and other Proceedings of the Convention of Virginia . . . " (Petersburg, VA, 1788). "Journal of the Convention of Virginia" (1788); original in the Virginia State Library.

129. Madison's 1788 Speech.

130. Ibid.

131. Ibid.

132. Ibid.

133. Ibid.

134. Ibid.

135. Ibid.

136. Ibid.

137. Ibid.

138. Ibid.

139. Ibid.

140. James Madison to Rev. George Eve (December 8, 1788), PJM, v. 11, p. 416.

141. George Washington, "First Inaugural Address" (April 30, 1789); in *The Papers of George Washington* (hereafter cited PGW).

142. Ibid.

143. Bill of Rights, First Amendment, Article I (ratified December 15, 1791).

144. James Madison, "Amendments to the Constitution" (June 8, 1789); in Hunt, v. 5, pp. 370-89.

145. Ibid.

146. Ibid.

147. Virginia General Assembly, "Resolution" (December 24, 1798).

148. James Madison to Edward Everett (August, 1830), in Madison (1865), v. 2, p. 142.

149. James Madison, "First Inaugural Address" (March 4, 1809).

150. James Madison, "Second Inaugural Address" (March 4, 1913).

151. James Madison to M.M. Noah (May 15, 1818); in Madison (1865), v. 3, p. 97.

152. *The Occident and American Jewish Advocate* (September 1843), n. 6, Elul 5603.

153. James Madison to Dr. De La Motta (August 1820); in Madison (1865), v. 3, pp. 178-79.

154. James Madison to Edward Livingston (July 10, 1822); in Madison (1865), v. 3, p. 265.

155. James Madison, "Speech in the Virginia State Convention" (December 2, 1829).

156. Ibid.

157. James Madison to Jared Sparks (June 1, 1831), Madison (1865), v. 4, pp. 181-82.

158. James Madison," at the White House website: www.whitehouse.gov/history/presidents/jm4.html

Index